FOCUS: SCOTTISH TRADITIONAL MUSIC

Focus: Scottish Traditional Music engages methods from ethnomusicology, popular music studies, cultural studies and media studies to explain how complex Scottish identities and culture are constructed in the traditional music and culture of Scotland. This book outlines vocal traditions such as lullabies, mining songs, Scottish ballads, herding songs and protest songs as well as instrumental traditions such as fiddle music, country dances and informal evening pub sessions. Case studies explore the key ideas in understanding Scotland musically by exploring ethnicity, Britishness, belonging, politics, transmission and performance, positioning the cultural identity of Scotland within the United Kingdom. The companion website (www.routledge.com/cw/mckerrell) hosts select audio examples and web links for further research.

- Part I is an introduction to Scotland's musical history and its relationship to the sound and context of current performance practice.
- Part II examines Scottish music through ethnicity, Britishness, politics and performance.
- Part III focuses on the mediatisation of Scottish music and otherness in Scottish traditional song.
- The selected audio tracks present both traditional and contemporary sounds of Scottish music at home and abroad.

Simon McKerrell is Senior Lecturer in Music and Head of the International Centre for Music Studies at Newcastle University, UK.

The **Focus on World Music Series** is designed specifically for area courses in world music and ethnomusicology. Written by the top ethnomusicologists in their field, the Focus books balance sound pedagogy with exemplary scholarship. Each book provides a telescopic view of the musics and cultures addressed, giving the reader a general introduction to the music and culture of the area and then zooming in on different musical styles with in-depth case studies.

FOCUS ON WORLD MUSIC

Series Editor: Michael B. Bakan

FOCUS: SCOTTISH TRADITIONAL MUSIC

Simon McKerrell

Newcastle University, UK

Routledge
Taylor & Francis Group

NEW YORK AND LONDON

Acquisitions Editor: Constance Ditzel
Series Editor: Michael Bakan
Marketing Manager: Emily Littlehales
Copy Editor: Alex Woodcock

Cover Design: Jayne Varney
Production Manager: Sarah Hudson
Proofreader: Elizabeth Kent
Companion Website Designer: Lauren Nauheimer

First published 2016
by Routledge
711 Third Avenue, New York, NY 10017

and by Routledge
2 Park Square, Milton Park, Abingdon, Oxon, OX14 4RN

Routledge is an imprint of the Taylor & Francis Group, an informa business

© 2016 Taylor & Francis

Library of Congress Cataloging in Publication Data
A catalog record for this book has been requested

ISBN: 978-0-415-74192-7 (hbk)
ISBN: 978-0-415-74193-4 (pbk)
ISBN: 978-1-315-81499-5 (ebk)

Typeset in Minion
by Swales & Willis Ltd, Exeter, Devon, UK

Printed at CPI UK on sustainably sourced paper.

This book is for Stephanie, Niamh and Kinnon; unsurpassed joy.

Contents

Figures

Tracks

For audio tracks and further information please see the companion website: www.routledge.com/cw/mckerrell.

Series Foreword

The past decade has witnessed extraordinary growth in the areas of ethnomusicology and world music publishing. With the publication of both the ten-volume *Garland Encyclopedia of World Music* and the second edition of the *New Grove Dictionary of Music and Musicians* (2001), we now have access to general reference resources that ethnomusicologists and world music enthusiasts of even just a few years ago could only have dreamed of. University and other academic presses – Chicago, Oxford, Cambridge, Illinois, Temple, Wesleyan, Indiana, California, Routledge – have produced excellent ethnomusicological monographs, edited volumes, and smaller-scale reference works in ever-increasing numbers, many accompanied by CDs, DVDs, and other media that bring the musics described vividly to life. A host of new introductory-level textbooks for freshman/sophomore-level world music survey courses have come out too, along with new editions of long-established textbooks catering to that market. New instructional resources for teaching these same kinds of introductory survey courses have been created in addition, the Oxford Global Music Series perhaps most notable among them. And the internet has of course revolutionised everything, with thousands upon thousands of Web-based resources – from superb scholarly and educational resources such as Smithsonian Global Sound (www.smithsonianglobalsound.org) and *Grove Music Online* to the wild frontiers of YouTube and myriad commercial online music providers – all now available from your desktop at the click of a mouse.

Yet for all of this profuse and diverse publishing activity, there remains a conspicuous gap in the literature. We still lack a solid corpus of high quality textbooks designed specifically for area courses in world music, ethnomusicology, and interdisciplinary programs with a strong music component. The need for such texts is greatest where courses for upper-division undergraduate and entry-level graduate students are taught, but it extends to courses at the freshman and sophomore levels as well, especially those enrolling music majors and other students who are serious and motivated.

What has been needed for such courses are books that balance sound pedagogy with exemplary scholarship, and that are substantive in content yet readily accessible to specialist and non-specialist readers alike. These books would be written in a lively and engaging style by leading ethnomusicologists and educators, bringing wide interdisciplinary scope and relevance to the contemporary concerns of their readership. They would, moreover, provide a telescopic view of the musics and cultures they addressed, zooming in from broad-based surveys of expansive music-culture areas and topics toward compelling, in-depth case studies of specific musicultural traditions and their myriad transformations in the modern world.

This is precisely what Routledge's *Focus on World Music* series delivers, with books that are authoritative, accessible, pedagogically strong, richly illustrated and accompanied by a compelling compact disc of musical examples linked integrally to the text. I am delighted to be part of the team that has brought this exciting and important series to fruition. I hope you enjoy reading these books as much as I have!

Michael B. Bakan
The Florida State University
Series Editor

Preface

The principal aim of this book is to provide a much needed and up-to-date introduction to Scottish traditional music for all readers. When I first began performing and studying Scottish traditional music I quickly became aware that there was very little literature directly dealing with Scottish traditional music and also that much of it was historical or invoked an older conceptualisation of music and culture before globalisation and mass media became pervasive in everyday life. That is why in this book, the main emphasis is on people making traditional music today. So much of the scholarship of music has been written about objects (scores, recordings, people, instruments) and in recent years many scholars of culture have begun to focus anew on the social aspects of music; because as any ethnomusicologist will tell you, there is no music without people. Traditional and folk music (which are today increasingly distinct activities) often rely heavily on a sense of nationhood and have been repeatedly implicated in the construction of nationalisms throughout the world (as the other books in this series demonstrate). It is appropriate therefore that one of the best ways of gaining an understanding of a nation and its culture is to examine the social and cultural life of its traditional music. That is why in this book the overriding perspective is on how people construct a sense of belonging to Scotland and Scottishness through participating in traditional and folk music regardless of where they live in the world. I also showcase in the latter chapters of the book some new applications from ethnomusicology and discourse analysis that I hope enable the reader to see how contemporary analytical approaches can help us to better understand Scotland's traditional music in a newly commodified and mediatised culture.

Following the approach of other books in this series, the book is divided into three parts, organised thematically around key analytical perspectives:

1   Part I provides an introduction to the social organisation of Scottish traditional music today and sketches a few of the key historical figures and trends. The focus in Part I is on how traditional music has and does help people to find a sense of belonging to Scotland and Scottishness, and how this has been achieved throughout the modern period.

2   Part II provides three brief sketches of the politics, people and place of Scottish traditional music, drawing out key themes of egalitarianism, protest, communication, digitalisation and the mythological construction of the place of the Scottish Borders. This emphasises a relational understanding of Scottishness constructed in and through traditional music.

3   Part III focuses in more detail on the mediatisation of Scottish traditional music and the fundamental shift in communal conceptualisations of authenticity in traditional music. This part also brings multimodal discourse analysis to bear on folk song to examine the notion of Scotland as an alterior Other within the United Kingdom, and finally provides an overview of the history of analytical scholarship in Scottish traditional music and how this has changed in modernity.

I do hope in this volume to provide material of interest both to the uninitiated and to long-term aficionados of Scotland and Scottish traditional music. You will also find more information, music and teaching resources at the companion website (www.routledge.com/cw/mckerrell). The book however is not intended to be an encyclopaedic history or analytical contribution covering the entire nation. I have selected particular traditions, social contexts, people, songs and tunes because of their importance and relevance to the social life of Scottish traditional music. There are of course many aspects left aside, or covered admirably elsewhere. I have tried to signal this in the text, and particularly to synthesise much of the really stimulating scholarship that has been done in the recent past. However despite this inevitably partial account, it is my intention that any reader of this volume will be provided with an overview of the key developments in Scottish cultural life that have shaped traditional music, and that they might be offered some new and helpful analytical tools appropriate to the traditional arts in the twenty-first century. As usual, any flaws, factual or critical, are mine alone.

Simon McKerrell
March 2015

Acknowledgements

I would like to acknowledge the assistance of many individuals and some organisations in the writing of this book. My thanks go to Newcastle University and the Arts and Humanities Research Council UK for supporting this research with an Early Career Fellowship grant without which it would not have been possible (AHRC grant AH/L006502/1). Many thanks to Michael Bakan and Constance Ditzel and Routledge for taking the plunge and assisting throughout the process. I would like to make a special thank you to Peggy Duesenberry and Jo Miller who both in many ways set myself and others off on musical adventures that will echo down through the decades. Michael Bakan, Desi Wilkinson, Jo Miller, Gary West, Andy Hunter and Goffredo Plastino have all also directly contributed to improving this volume in various ways – thank you. To all my other colleagues and students at the International Centre for Music Studies at Newcastle University, a heartfelt thank you, both for your pragmatic support during my research leave, especially Sarah Greenhalgh and Agustín Fernandez, who have been unstintingly supportive throughout. To all those who play, sing, dance or listen to Scottish traditional music in any of its myriad forms, 'here's tae us, whae's like us, nae many, and their aa deid!' Without Stephanie, Niamh and the rest of the Allan clan, none of this would have happened, and it would not have been such fun; thank you all.

PART I

The Social Life of Scottish Traditional Music

CHAPTER 1

Introduction

This book is about Scottish traditional music. That phrase carries with it a great deal of cultural meaning constructed over many years about what is 'traditional', 'Scottish' and even what can be termed 'music'. In this book, the key approach to understanding music is to understand music as a form of *belonging*: typically, a sense of belonging to a shared culture, belonging to an ethnic, political, mythological, gendered or geographically bounded nation or community where we share music, dance, stories, ideas, practices and experiences. In the modern period traditional music more than any other type of music, overtly constructs a sense of belonging. That is because most people's conception of what folk or traditional music is, is deeply grounded in a shared sense of *authenticity* that has historically been tied to nationalism and ethnic identities. Authenticity in traditional music is at the very heart of understanding our relationship to the music and to each other, and in Scotland, as elsewhere in the late modern West, authenticity is increasingly becoming defined by practice rather than by more established ideas about oldness, ethnicity, geography or politics. Through the practice of performing, listening, dancing and debating together, those involved in Scottish traditional music construct a sense of belonging that speaks to us most strongly when we are actively engaged in the music. But today, the oldness of a tune or a song, or whether it was composed or written down in Scotland, or by a Scot, are no longer guarantees of authentic Scottish traditional music. There has emerged in Scotland over the past sixty years a complete transformation in what we consider to be Scottish traditional music. The sense in which we define Scottish traditional music has radically shifted our attention onto the sound and context for performance rather than the musical texts and narrative histories that used to mark the boundaries of what could be considered Scottish traditional music.

This transformation began in 1951 with the People's Céilidh in Edinburgh, forerunner to the Edinburgh Fringe, and has continued in the subsequent revival and afterwards, to alter the social life of Scotland, Scots (at home and abroad), and the notes themselves. Consequently, the sense of belonging to and of a Scottish traditional musical community emerges in practice; how, when, where and what we perform, listen and discuss. This book sets out to deal with some of the new understandings of Scottish traditional music today in the twenty-first century and to present an overview that will provide the reader with a broad understanding of Scottish traditional music both historically, and how it is manifested today.

Most definitions of traditional music or folk music have tended to rely upon detailed descriptions of the characteristics of musical sound, often within a discourse that privileges the authenticity of the oral tradition to mark out traditional or folk music out as a form of music that has special audible and cultural characteristics that derive from the authentic oldness of musical practice in a particular ethnic or political, or geographic community. However, this conception only really emerged in the nineteenth century, whereas before the mid-nineteenth century the discourse surrounding Scottish traditional music, and other traditional musics were really identified and understood as 'national music'.

These types of definition relying mostly upon oldness as the central characteristic of authenticity are problematic for traditional music today. The problems stem both from the method of transmission, and from the nature of the communities that perform and listen to traditional music. Gelbart (2007) discusses the definition of 'folk music' as one part of a co-dependent binary opposition with 'art music'. He discusses their emergence as categories before about 1850 during the discourse of European enlightenment, and before the discourse surrounding 'popular music' begins. He isolates the traditional item (i.e. the song or tune) as at the heart of the problematic term 'folk'.

Today, a useful way of thinking about these types of music is to understand the social processes that have formed, and are forming, notions of tradition and authenticity. In this book, the particular community and music is defined through the understanding of Scottishness. Thus defining Scottish traditional music is for me, about defining the shared sense of belonging for members of that *community of practice*. Scottish traditional music undoubtedly exists and is flourishing with unprecedented numbers of performers, listeners and teachers, both in Scotland and its sizeable diaspora. Therefore, if we are to meaningfully understand what Scottish traditional music is, and how it acts in the world and shapes culture and identity, we have to understand something of the social world that supports Scottish traditional music, and to examine contemporary performance in the context of a late modern Western nation-state.

Authenticity and Belonging

Traditional music in today's world is about belonging: belonging to a community of musicians, singers, a culture, a particular nationality or ethnicity. But belonging also implies that there are those who do not belong. The history of scholarship of Scottish traditional music has been in one sense a history of understanding how Scots music constructs belonging to Scotland and Scottishness but it has most often focused quite narrowly upon the objects of tradition; the songs, tunes, books, manuscripts and also the composers and collectors of traditional music. Less attention has been paid to the performers, the audiences, and the social world in which Scottish traditional music has lived. This is most obvious in the approaches to understanding the crucial concept of *authenticity* in folk and traditional music.

The term 'authenticity' has a long and complex history in music studies. The term itself has been variously defined, particularly in the early music movement where authentic historical performance is important to creating an understanding of the music and identity within that community of practice. If traditional music is about belonging then authenticity implies that there are true or sincere ways of belonging and that some performance practices, tunes and songs are more authentic than others. The key point in understanding authenticity today in traditional music is to understand that it is a social concept, used, defined and discussed by the communities that participate in traditional music and who use ideas about the authenticity of material and performance to establish the boundaries of ways of belonging to the community. When we talk, write and discuss traditional music, we are engaging in a social process of negotiation of belonging and for different people in their own community, what is authentic or not is key to this sense of negotiated belonging. In this sense, authenticity is a plural concept. What is authentic for one performer or listener may be on the very edge of acceptable practice for another, similarly, many of us in Scottish traditional music are part of more than one community. Ways of playing Scottish traditional dance music such as reels, jigs and hornpipes differ considerably between different constituencies within the Scottish traditional music community. What is unacceptable within a pub session, or pilloried as too slow, too conservative and too dot and cut may be very authentic performances for competitive performers or professional musicians. We all exist in layered musical worlds, where the deeper one understands, the more nuanced and thick our understanding of how to perform and listen to music.

One of the key ways in which traditional music has developed a social sense of belonging is in the negotiation of the canon of repertoire and the ideas about how we perform that canon. A canon of repertoire is essentially a socially defined set of tunes, songs and performance practices that are agreed upon as acceptable by those within the community of practice. Again, the importance of this resides in the negotiation between people to debate, establish and agree upon a shared set of tunes and songs that form the canon – i.e. canon formation is a social process. However, historically traditional musicians and scholars of music tended to focus on the origins of individual tunes and songs in order to establish their authenticity. That is why scholars of Scottish traditional music have largely concentrated their efforts on establishing the origins of tunes, composition and first publication of songs, etc., because finding a date or a first instance, seems to provide us with proof of the oldness and hence authenticity of traditional music. In fact, if one subscribes to authenticity as a social process, it is the discourse about music that constitutes the understanding of authenticity as a social process. Sometimes, exciting and innovative performers break the rules or compose new music that is subsequently accepted into the canon of authentic traditional music through discussion and repetition by consensus. So, through time, different canons of traditional music change and adapt by negotiation, making the authentic canon a changing set of socially defined tunes, songs and performance practices.

Scotland contains 5,295,000 people, which is 8.38 per cent of the total population of the United Kingdom.[1] After referenda on a Scottish Assembly in 1979 (no), Scottish political devolution in 1997 (yes) and Scottish independence in 2014 (no); Scotland remains part of the United Kingdom alongside England, Wales and Northern Ireland but has its own devolved parliament in Edinburgh with responsibilities for a range of legislative issues. However, within the political union of the United Kingdom, there are a number of broad differences between these nations that have resulted in distinct socio-cultural differences. Scotland has had a distinct national identity for centuries, and was an independent country until the Union of the Parliaments with England in 1707. In 1999 Scotland got her own parliament back again with devolution of power from London and, since then, there has been a growing cultural confidence and consequent growth in traditional music. In Scotland three languages are spoken today that are key to understanding traditional music, English, Gaelic and Scots. English and Scots are by far the most dominant, but for a long time Gaelic was spoken throughout Scotland. Today Gaelic speakers only account for about 1 per cent of the population but Gaelic has a much greater significance than this for Scottish culture because of the rich heritage of Scottish Gaelic tunes and songs. Scotland is still a religious country with a large Christian population of Protestants (32 per cent) and Roman Catholics (16 per cent). However, there are a large group of about 37 per cent who have no religion and some regard Scotland as moving towards secularism. Culturally however, Scotland is distinct from the other nations of the United Kingdom and has retained its own separate educational, religious and legal systems throughout the union which has continued to support a distinct ethnic and national identity. Today, 83 per cent of Scotland's residents feel Scottish. This result is the overall combination of 61 per cent of Scotland's residents who identify as being of 'White Scottish' ethnicity and feel Scottish is their only national identity, and a further 22 per cent who are from other ethnic groups and feel they have a Scottish national identity, or are 'White Scottish' whose Scottishness is combined with British or other national identities (Simpson and Smith 2014). Musically too, Scotland has developed a distinct traditional music that has its roots in Scots and Gaelic culture and over the last 250 years, much of this musical culture has emigrated along with Scots

Figure 1.1 Photograph of Willie MacPhee the traveller musician (by kind permission of Timothy Neat)

to other countries such as Canada, New Zealand, America, South Africa and Australia, where it has flourished and found new forms (see Chapter 7).

Part I of this book is intended to give the reader a broad introduction to the basic forms and social contexts for Scottish traditional music today, and to introduce the reader to certain key aspects of Scotland's cultural history. In Part II we take a closer look at some of these political differences and how they have been performed in song (Chapter 4) and in Chapter 5 we examine what sort of people are actively involved in Scottish traditional music today. In Chapter 6 we consider how important the concept of place, the mythological construction of landscape, has been to Scottish traditional music, and particularly to the Scottish Borders. In Part III we focus in more narrowly upon some of the ways in which Scottish traditional music has been mediated and how globalisation and the digitalisation of contemporary culture are changing Scottish traditional music (Chapter 7). In Chapter 8 we take a detailed look at and how text, music and image combine multimodally to create a sense of Scotland as an Other within the United Kingdom. In the final chapter of this book we take a brief look at how the notes of Scottish traditional music have been understood and analysed by scholars in ethnomusicology and folklore and how these approaches have changed our understanding of the musical structures and authenticity of Scottish traditional music.

The Sound of Scottish Music

Today, it is quite widely accepted in ethnomusicology that a nation's traditional music, or a regional musical culture cannot simply be defined by its sonic characteristics. There are too many different musical styles and constituencies within any one nation to be reduced to a few simple musical characteristics (see Chapter 9). That however, does not mean that music cannot still *sound* Scottish, Irish, Breton or Brazilian to different people. There are some very generic sonic characteristics which one could suggest are often heard in a particular musical culture. In fact, most ethnomusicological, and increasingly in other approaches to traditional music from disciplines such as cultural sociology, ethnology, musicology, cultural studies and folklore, have shifted gradually over the last century towards identifying and defining traditional musics by their socio-cultural characteristics rather than their sonic characteristics. In Scotland, the definitions of the sound of Scottish music have often focused upon its modal scales, instrumentation and the prevalence of the double cut and dot rhythmic duplet, that is commonly known as the 'Scotch snap'.[2] Asking the question, 'what does Scottish traditional music sound like?' is a bit like asking, 'what does Scottish soup taste like?'. Scottish soups come in a tremendous variety of flavours, colours, consistencies, and at different temperatures and in various parts of a meal. However, it would probably be uncontroversial to claim that soup is mostly liquid, often hot and often made with vegetables. Scottish traditional music is also incredibly various; however, it is usually performed by solo or small groups of musicians and singers, often using acoustic instruments and often employing relatively dot and cut rhythms. This description of course, is so generalised as to be almost useless, so perhaps the question needs to change from 'what does Scottish traditional music sound like?', to 'when is Scottish traditional music?'. This is a *relational* and more socially useful construction of musical understanding. And really it is this question that can lead us into a more rewarding understanding of Scotland, Scottishness and Scottish traditional music and is the focus of the first part of this book.

In addition to the Scots-, Gaelic- and English-language Scottish traditional song, some people have talked about the 'big five' instruments in Scottish music which are bagpipes, fiddle, clarsach, accordion and whistle (Francis 1999: 29). And there is an important distinction that underlies the social practice surrounding these instrumental traditions which is their relationship as musical instruments to other forms of music. I make a distinction between the indigenous instruments of Scotland and the non-indigenous instruments which is significant when it comes to placing and judging the authenticity of their respective traditions. Because Highland bagpipes are indigenous to Scotland (although played throughout the world) they are deeply embedded in national culture and inextricably conjoined with Scotland and Scottishness. This is not of course the case with other instruments such as the fiddle, the accordion and the piano where many different styles of music are possible and played. Thus the public reception of bagpipe music, or clarsach music has the advantage of a more direct authenticity linking them to Scottishness, whereas other non-indigenous instruments have to establish authentic practice and reception through other means.

These other means of authenticity mainly lie in the performance of particular repertoire which is acknowledged (or established) as *old*. Performers routinely construct oldness as a means to authenticity through methods such as on stage stories, vernacular folklore, CD liner notes, previous recording histories, tune titles, teaching lineages, source singers/musicians or other reportorial sources, etc. However, interestingly in a multimodal sense, it is not only the textual or verbal evidence that can establish the authenticity of particular repertoire, but performers of traditional music learn a semiotic language of authenticity that is constructed in other aesthetic modes of communication. The principal mode of aesthetic communication is performance practice. But in addition there are other important communicative strategies such as sartorial style, accent (particularly in diasporic and mass-mediated contexts), teaching lineages, somatic performance practice (in contrast to the audible) and more indirect methods such as album cover artwork, website design and construction and the performance contexts themselves (hearing a piper outdoors at a Highland games in Scotland would necessarily lend a sense of aesthetic authenticity to the listener).

Notes

1 Figures drawn from 2011 UK census data from National Records of Scotland, © Crown copyright, 2014: www.scotlandscensus.gov.uk.

2 The Scotch snap was recognised abroad even by the mid-eighteenth century as a distinctive characteristic of Scottish music (Gelbart 2007: 47).

CHAPTER 2

The Social Life of Scottish Traditional Music

If Scottish traditional music is primarily about belonging, then it is clear that we can belong to different groups both at the same time, and through time, moving between different communities during our lifetime. Scottish traditional music has been performed in many social contexts and venues ranging widely from the most formal competition platform to the informal performance for pleasure in the family home. In this section I will introduce some of the key performance contexts to try and answer the 'when' of Scottish traditional music, and to explain the social contexts that often still mark out important ritual, musical, or just fun spaces in people's lives.

Today, one can hear live performances of Scottish traditional music in situations ranging from pub sessions, to concert halls to weddings to festivals and across the radio and television, both within Scotland and elsewhere. What is distinctive today in the twenty-first century for Scottish traditional music is its widespread popularity as a grassroots musical community of practice. Traditional music in Scotland has never been so widely heard on public broadcasts or so strongly supported in state sponsored tourism initiatives and Scottish traditional music enjoys a national media profile that has emerged since Scottish devolution at the turn of the twenty-first century. Part of this cultural shift in Scottish public life can be explained by the changing political life and partly by the success of the Scottish folk revival in the 1950s, '60s and '70s. Unlike in Ireland, Scotland has never pursued a public policy of strongly linking traditional music to Gaelic medium education for all Scots, and the massive cultural strength that grew out of Irish nationalism after the 1922 independence was not mirrored in Scotland. Thus Scottish traditional music is not tied to the indigenous Gaelic language in the way that Irish traditional music is. Scottish traditional music is the preserve of many classes of people in Scotland but, since the 1960s, has predominantly been most actively pursued by well-educated, middle-class urban Scots (see Chapter 5). Scottish traditional music has also managed to transcend socio-economic class through its continued professionalisation and commercialisation as a genre, yet the left-leaning tendencies of the post-war generations still remain in spirit if not in social practice. Scottish traditional music has not only been tied to the Highlands and Islands, or *Gaelteachd* of Scotland, because of the strength and vibrancy of lowland traditions such as the civilian pipe bands of the Central Belt, the traditional music of the Borders, or the accordion and fiddle clubs spread right across Scotland and particularly in the concentrated diasporic regions such as Nova Scotia, New Zealand and Ontario.[1] It has not been confined to one or two generations, but the sense of a belonging to Scottish traditional music is now spread across classes, and ages from cradle to grave. Taking account of the baby boomers of the immediate post-war generation who were involved in the folk revival of the 1950s and '60s, their children and grandchildren, Scottish traditional music is now more widespread than ever before. The massively exciting instrumental revival and exploration of the 1970s and '80s led many new young musicians to begin exploring their musical heritage (including this author) and, today, there are classes up and down the country as well as a burgeoning Fèisean (lit. 'Festivals') movement providing tuition and access to Scottish traditional music for the very youngest members of society. The pioneering work of Jo Miller and Dr Peggy Duesenberry at the Royal Conservatoire of Scotland (then titled the Royal Scottish Academy of Music and Drama) in the 1990s led directly to a new degree in Scottish traditional music that launched in 1996. This built upon the legacy of the collecting work of the School of Scottish Studies, and brought together leading performers of Scottish traditional music to create a unique tertiary education experience at the only Scottish conservatoire. Today there are a number of tertiary courses for traditional music in Scotland, across various institutions such as the Universities of Edinburgh and the Highlands and Islands, and educators in Scottish traditional music are at the forefront of developments in distance learning and online tuition to provide greater understanding and access to traditional Scottish culture. Scottish traditional music is also taught alongside other traditional musics in institutions such as my own at Newcastle University, and at universities in Ireland, Canada and the United States. There has been an astonishing explosion in the digitalisation of Scottish traditional music in social media since the turn of the twenty-first century. Fans, audiences and performers have a disproportionately large presence on Twitter, Facebook and numerous other online fora. This has done much to raise the public profile of Scottish traditional music, and furthermore to bring those interested together in a digital community of interest, sharing tunes, songs and stories. This fairly rapid digitalisation and institutionalisation of Scottish traditional music has had a profound effect on both the public perception of the music, and on performance practices. There are numerous new jobs that support traditional music in education departments, local government, in the music, tourism, policy and heritage industries. Today, it is now possible to continue the study of Scottish traditional music both informally and formally as much as one wishes from birth to death.

I have chosen to look at belonging in the social context of Scottish traditional music because that is, in my view, often the primary meaning that motivates people to perform, listen and work in ways that support Scottish traditional music. In this section we will examine Scottish traditional music in a variety of contexts moving from intimate to organised, from the family to mass-mediated performance. The mixture between organisation, intimacy, communication and mediation all act to create a sense of the *publicness* of musical performance (Hesmondhalgh 2013). Some performances of Scottish traditional music are heard only in the family home and are never recorded or distributed; these could be described as intimate and private family performances. Many are recorded, distributed via radio or television and repeatedly broadcast to millions of people; these would quite rightly have a high degree of publicness and would be described as mass mediated.

I have deliberately chosen not to use the terms formal to informal, both because of the implied sense of a linear continuum between the two, and also because of the implied sense in which there is always a gravitation towards the formal from the informal. In this sense I want to encourage a view of Scottish traditional music that radiates outwards from the intimate social contexts towards more organised performance contexts. In Scotland, North America, Australasia, South Africa and in many other places where Scottish traditional music is most popular, there are often strong intergenerational connections between families who perform Scottish music such as fiddle tunes, for Scottish dancing, bagpiping, or Gaelic song. Yet, today, Scottish traditional music has become *deterritorialised*, which means that it can be played anywhere, by anyone, and the older notions of a music tied to the geographical limits of Scotland have by and large disappeared. In this way, Scottish traditional music is part of a larger trend for many traditional musics throughout the world, where the communities that perform and support the music are now spread across the world. This has been facilitated by globalisation and the emergence of the internet to support communities of practice that create a sense of belonging to, and participation in, Scottish traditional music (see Chapter 5, on the people of Scottish music). The fiddler living in Seattle can now be just as good

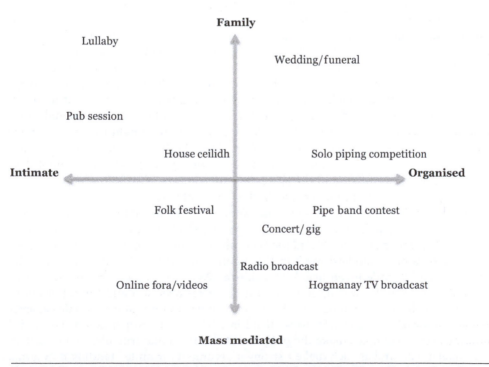

Figure 2.1 Hesmondhalgh's Model of Publicness adapted for *Scottish Traditional Music* by the author

performer of Scottish traditional music as the fiddler living in Edin-
now have access to many recordings of authentic Scottish traditional
will potentially have access to the highest quality teachers of Scottish
c, so long as they can afford to pay for it. And this has given rise to a
litional music studies which is the emergence of the capitalisation and
n of traditional music, discussed in more detail in Part III of this book.

One of the most interesting aspects of studying music today is that a musical style, instrument, performer, society or culture, never has one history. There are therefore many stories, tunes and songs to be told, understood and performed. This is one of the reasons why scholars of traditional music have often grappled with authenticity, which for a long time was the scholarly attempt to find an original or true history of music rooted in the past. Many traditional musics, particularly in regions of high tourism, have commercialised and commodified their customs, stories and musical practices. Scotland has been doing this for quite a long time, since perhaps the turn of the nineteenth century, or even earlier. Inventing different stories, changing and re-arranging songs and tunes, inventing or re-imagining the contexts for performance and the instruments upon which musicians perform has been a central facet of Scottish traditional music in the modern period. The British Army transformed the manner and music of piping, collectors, arrangers and high Scottish society bowdlerised, popularised and transformed many Scottish traditional songs. Music hall performers such as Harry Lauder took old tunes and fashioned new words for them, constructing a kitsch and massively popular new genre that reflected early-twentieth-century society and values. Many revivalist organisations were formed in the closing decades of the nineteenth and first few decades of the twentieth centuries. One of the largest, An Comunn Gàidhealach (the Gaelic Association) was founded in 1891 and instituted musical harp competitions the following year. The subsequent re-imagining and revival of the instrument led to the foundation of The Clarsach Society in 1931, whose principal aim was to preserve and reinstate the 'ancient Celtic harp' in Scotland. An instrument once very male, exclusive to Gaelic court culture and very high status, and that had completely disappeared from everyday practice, was transformed, becoming very female and popular throughout Scotland. Many of the eighteenth- and nineteenth-century collections of Scottish traditional music borrow from each other, re-fashioning styles, settings and sentiment to construct their own version of a musical Scottishness. Robert Burns both composed, borrowed and re-invented many traditional songs from those he heard and collected to be published in the *Scots Musical Museum* in the late eighteenth century. Two of the most popular collections of Scottish traditional music in the nineteenth century were both published in 1816; Alexander Campbell's *Albyn's Anthology*, which included much Gaelic Jacobite material, and Captain Simon Fraser's ever popular collection, *Airs and Melodies Peculiar to the Highlands of Scotland and the Isles*, which included 'more than two hundred tunes and became a standard work in the popular instrumental tradition during the nineteenth and twentieth centuries' (Donaldson 1988: 93). The kilt, made popular in the nineteenth century, was itself an invention (or re-invention and formalisation of earlier vernacular sartorial practices) designed to impress a romantic nationalist agenda upon the first visit of George IV to Scotland in 1822 (Trevor-Roper 2008). These and numerous other examples make the point that there is no one true history of Scottish traditional music, and as such make a stronger argument for understanding it in terms of belonging and social practice. The search for origins or the *urtexts* of Scottish traditional music is therefore complex and often politically motivated. That is why when thinking about what is really 'Scottish' or 'true' it is helpful to think about authenticity in Scottish traditional music as a social process; to understand the reasons why, when and how people have mobilised Scottish traditional music for their own accounts of Scottishness. When we understand who plays and sings and why, and in what contexts, we can today perhaps understand Scotland musically in a more plural manner.

So, by beginning from the family and examining Scottish traditional music in its most intimate contexts and then moving towards more organised contexts, we should not assume that is the inevitable direction of travel for anyone learning to perform or understand this music. Most human beings involved in music making do so in multiple different social settings throughout our lives, and learn to adapt our performing and social practices according to the ways in which others teach us as we learn how to belong. And it is this sense of belonging which exists in the types of repertoire we play, how we play it, how we dress, speak and behave which contribute to our total understanding of our sense of who we are, and how music helps us to construct ourselves. This, for many begins in the home.

Scottish Traditional Music and the Family

Scottish traditional music has been an intimate part of family life in Scotland since before it was even given a name. Lullabies, love songs, reels, jigs, airs, work songs such as threshing, spinning and weaving songs, quern songs for milling flour, have all been at various times part of everyday family life. Much of what we call Scottish traditional song has its roots in the everyday chores and lives of ordinary Scots and although some of these tasks have changed, many of the songs remain part of Scottish culture. For example, very few people in modern society have a need to manually shrink tweed cloth, yet waulking songs remain a central part of the Gaelic traditional repertoire. Similarly, milking a cow and spinning and weaving by hand have largely disappeared, but the work songs that accompanied and aided these tasks still form a part of the traditional repertoire. There are of course other songs, such as lullabies, comic songs, children's rhymes and songs, love (sometimes called 'lyric') songs, and much traditional instrumental music, which still retains a function in family life today, and are still sung and played by families in the home. Both Gaelic and Scots songs retain a large canon of central repertoire drawn from the social lives of families and localities that reflect centuries of change, yet allow local communities and families to recall and perform their culture anew for each other. Gaelic, Scots and English language communities have constructed social categories or genres of songs that are subject to change across time and place, so that:

> Genre is a fluid category . . . the boundaries of category are always being redrawn, and songs considered to belong in a given category are often diverse in structure, style and provenance . . . [and] individual meaning is constructed . . . through the very social processes of transmission and performance.
>
> (Conn 2012)

This must be borne in mind when considering categories and genres of traditional music and song, for the people that sing and play them, categorisation is only useful in that it reflects back social practices and values; the people making music is what really matters. Stephanie Conn goes on to describe the power of home and family musical experience in Canadian Scottish Gaelic communities:

> While public performance of songs is valued by Gaelic communities and is an important way to draw in young people and learners (it is, after all, the door I came in myself), it is through the practice of song in more private settings that singers in Gaelic communities acquire a core repertoire through various methods of transmission, negotiate a relationship with written and oral sources, and develop a personal style. Home is the place where many singers collect an array of objects to evoke the sense of previous performances and singers – not only books and tapes but also photograph albums, clippings and tapes, and it is largely at home that memory is cultivated as a powerful tool in the transmission of repertoire and style, providing meaning and context of the songs on a personal, community, and cultural level.
>
> (Conn 2012)

For Conn's informants these Gaelic songs were crucial to constructing their sense of identity within the family and local contexts in Atlantic Canada. This is a widespread phenomenon in diasporic families around the globe. Dougal also demonstrates how Scottish songs were a key aspect of personalising a diasporic Scottishness amongst families in Australia and New Zealand helping them to perform their identities 'with a sense of place, home and family' (Dougal 2011).

Lullabies

In Scottish traditional music there are many lullabies and dandling songs. Dandling songs are sung whilst gently bouncing a baby on your knee to sooth or entertain (the baby and the adult); lullabies are sung throughout the world to send a child to sleep. In the Gaelic tradition there are two main types of lullabies, those that employ a narrow range of notes very repetitively, often only three or four and those with a wider range of notes that borrow from non-Gaelic popular musics (Campbell et al. 2014). The soft melodies and repetitive phrases in lullabies help them to achieve their purpose. Some of the best known lullabies in Scottish traditional music include 'Baloo Baleerie', 'Dream Angus' and the ancient Gaelic lullaby (Gaelic *luinneag*) 'Griogal Cridhe' (Beloved Gregor).

This lullaby is a good example of how oral tradition has enabled us to rediscover aspects of Scottish culture that for centuries, only survived because people sang, played, spoke or performed them. It also demonstrates the sheer complexity of traditional music and its porosity with other forms of art such as poetry, dancing and literature. This song was most probably composed as a poem of lament in 1570 and has flourished in oral tradition over the entire modern period, and is still popular today. It was first printed in 1813 by Patrick Turner, a collector of Gaelic poetry and song from Cowal, in his *Comhchruinneacha do dh'Orain Taghta, Ghaidhealach* (Blankenhorn 2014). Since then, it has been printed numerous times in the nineteenth and twentieth centuries in many forms, with verses added, changed and removed according to the wonderful creativity of the singers of this song, and like many other Gaelic songs, the 'improving' impulses of the educated elite Victorians. It is both a poem and a song, and many Gaelic poems were composed to be sung, so the distinction as normally thought of today is sometimes an Anglicised projection onto Gaelic and other cultures. The first time the poem was collected by Turner from oral tradition, it was long (around seventeen stanzas) and its subsequent adaptation in oral tradition shows a much shorter form, more easily memorised and sung (often about four verses with chorus). The song is a lament, usually sung slowly, which tells a simple story about the murder of Griogair Ruadh (lit. 'red-haired

Griogal Cridhe (Beloved Gregor)

[text and tune as per Tomie's published arrangement in JFSS 1911]

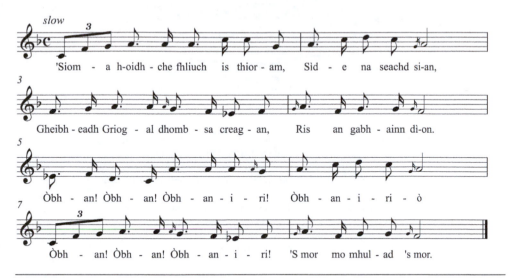

Figure 2.2 Transcription of Frances Tolmie's version of *Griogal Crìdhe* from JFSS 1911 (Tolmie et al. 1911: 196)

Gregor') who was the clan chief of the MacGregors and was beheaded in 1570. (For more on the linguistic and narrative aspects of Gaelic lullabies see Hillers 2006.) This song also demonstrates one of the key aspects of Gaelic and Scots traditional song which is the use of nonsense syllables, sometimes called 'non-lexical' syllables by scholars to show that they have no semantic meaning. The chorus of the song is often sung as follows:

Chorus with non-lexical vocables:

(Original Gaelic)
Obhan, obhan, obhan i ri,
Obhan i ri ò
Obhan, obhan, obhan i ri,
'S mór mo mhulad, 's mór!

(English translation)
Obhan, obhan, obhan i ri,
Obhan i ri ò
Obhan, obhan, obhan i ri,
Great is my sorrow, great!

The words here do not carry any particular meaning but they fit well the tune to which this song is often sung and also have a soothing effect, which has made this poem-song popular as a lullaby for soothing infants. 'Bh' in the word 'obhan' is lenited in Gaelic which means for an English speaker it is quite close to the phonetic sound of 'v'. You can hear some of them at the Tobar an Dulachais website maintained by the University

Dream Angus

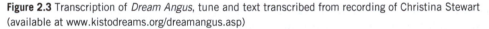

Can ye no hush yer weepin'	Dreams to sell, fine dreams to sell,
A' the wee bairns are sleepin'	Angus is here wi' dreams to sell o
Birdies are nestling, an' nestling' the gither	Hush my wee bairnie an' sleep wi' oot fear
But my bonnie bairn is waken yet	Dream Angus has brought you a dream my dear

Dreams to sell, fine dreams to sell,	Soon the lavrock sings his song
Angus is here wi' dreams to sell o	Welcoming the coming dawn
Hush my wee bairnie an' sleep wi' oot fear	Lambies coorie doon the gither
Dream Angus has brought you a dream my dear	Wi' the yowies in the heather

Hear the curlew cryin' o	Dreams to sell, fine dreams to sell,
An' the echoes dyin' o	Angus is here wi' dreams to sell o
Even the birdies are cuddled up sleepin	Hush my wee bairnie an' sleep wi' oot fear
But my bonnie bairn is weepin' greetin'	Dream Angus has brought you a dream my dear

Figure 2.3 Transcription of *Dream Angus*, tune and text transcribed from recording of Christina Stewart (available at www.kistodreams.org/dreamangus.asp)

of Edinburgh (www.tobarandualchais.com) and there is more information, recordings and lyrics available on the *Education Scotland* website.[2] Another traditional Scottish lullaby 'Dream Angus' demonstrates many of the characteristics of lullabies throughout the world and some particularly Scottish elements as well.

(Transcription note: Like many Scottish tunes, the original recording uses the notes of the diatonic major scale with a flattened seventh degree, in this case, the tune is in C major with a flattened seventh. Hence this is transcribed with an F major key signature. For more on why this should not be described as 'myxolidian' see Chapter 9. Tune and words from a prescriptive transcription from Christina Stewart's performance, see www.kistodreams.org/dreamangus.asp.)

Intimate Social Musical Life

After the family home, the two most widespread and intimate social contexts for traditional music in modern Scotland are the pub session and music for dancing. In the pub session (or, more commonly amongst musicians, just 'session') musicians and singers collect together in a pub at a regular time and place each week or month and have a drink and play traditional tunes and songs with each other. These are fairly intimate settings in that normally the performers all know one another and look forward to these sessions as the social highlight of their week or month. The performance of Scottish traditional music in the pub is a relatively new phenomenon emerging only during the course of Scottish folk revival in the 1950s and '60s, mirroring that of Irish traditional music. The format, where these sessions usually begin at 8 or 9 p.m. and involve constant music-making until last orders are called, has now been established as a mainstream musical practice in Scottish life. The social interaction, repertoire, venue and style of performance all contribute to a particular construction of social belonging. Often in Scotland, sessions have a particular musical identity which has been carefully curated by the leading musicians at the session, often over many years. For example, for decades now there has been an inclusive, very Scottish famous pub session in Edinburgh at Sandy Bell's pub opposite the National Museum of Scotland. Other bars such as the Royal Oak in Edinburgh have a reputation for supporting singers. Sessions are held regularly, particularly in the winter months throughout Scotland and abroad in places with high diasporic populations such as Cape Breton, Ontario, New Zealand and throughout the United States. There are many such sessions in Glasgow, including long-running ones held in pubs such as Babbity Bowsters, the Lismore and, until its demise in the late 2000s, the Victoria Bar session in Glasgow. This last took place in the town centre by the river Clyde and was known for over eighty years as a Scottish pub session with a particularly Irish flavour, where many Glaswegian-Irish Scots met together to play and enjoy each other's company. The musicians from this session have moved wholesale to another bar in the Southside of Glasgow called The Ivory, more sympathetic to their music. Today, there are many regular pub sessions taking place throughout Scotland and in the diaspora at which regulars exchange, learn, enjoy and perform traditional music and cultivate a sense of belonging to an informal community.[3]

In pub sessions, as in other more intimate social settings such as the family home, the performance of Scottish traditional music is acting both as an aesthetic art form and as an act of belonging; the very act of playing music together creates a bonding between the musicians and the other people present in the bar. Not only are they sharing their expertise and skills as traditional musicians, but perhaps more importantly, the playing style and rhythmical *entrainment* create a shared bodily excitement and sense of fun (for further information on this concept see Clayton 2013). This sense of coming together both aesthetically and in sharing embodied communication can create a powerful feeling of social connection to the other musicians and people in the bar. As social beings, this shared sense of fun mixed with a real embodied communication of traditional music can create a lasting experience of shared excitement and belonging. If, as is common, those people participate in the session over many months and years, it can create a very strong communal bond between not just the musicians themselves, but the regulars who attend the pub and live within the local community. This is partly why pub sessions are now so popular and found a permanent place in the practices of Scottish traditional music in the post-war period.

Traditional dancing in Scotland

Scottish traditional music has been performed for dancing for as long as people have felt the urge to sing or play a melody for others to dance. Many, if not most, forms of Scottish traditional instrumental music have their origins in music for dancing. In particular, reels and jigs are the most common forms of tune types for Scottish dancing. Popular too are strathspeys, a type of tune which, along with *piobaireachd* (see below), are forms of music uniquely indigenous to Scotland. *Puirt-a-beul* (lit. 'music from the mouth') is the name given to Gaelic vocal music either sung for dancing or just for entertainment. Before the ownership of musical instruments became a widespread phenomenon in Scotland many people sang for others to dance to.

Today, there are five main forms of dance in Scotland which are performed to the performance of traditional music: step-dancing; céilidh dancing; old-time dancing; Scottish country dancing and Highland dancing. This is not quite the same thing as stating that there are five forms of 'traditional dancing' in Scotland. There is an important difference to be understood as well as key distinctions in performance contexts which arise from the social context of dance in Scotland. Of these various forms, the first three are considered vernacular and more informal styles of dance and the latter two are recognised as more formal performance genres controlled by the Royal Scottish Country Dance Society (RSCDS),[4] formed in 1923, and the Scottish Official Board of Highland Dancing (SOBHD).[5] The Scottish Traditions of Dance Trust (STDT) has taken a role in the promotion of various forms of more informal dance since the mid-1990s. However, the proliferation of rules and standardisation of dances in the more formal country and Highland dancing communities is more evidence of the ongoing tendency of Anglo-American society towards standardising and formalising various cultural forms. Significantly though, all of the various forms of dancing in Scotland have seen a growth in the last two decades with many innovative new dances and motifs added in their various styles.

The strathspey tune type takes its name from Speyside, a region of central Scotland, where the river Spey runs, combining this with the Scottish word 'strath' meaning a large glen or valley. It is thought to have been established through the popularisation and development of the form by the famous fiddle players from Speyside, such as the Browns of Kincardine-on-Spey and the Cummings of Grantown-on-Spey, who developed the performance practices relating to the strathspey. However, it may have been more widespread than this in Gaelic Scotland and simply attributed to Speyside musicians because of their greater cross-cultural communication with English speakers in early modern Scotland (Lamb 2013). The first mention of the strathspey as a specific tune type or dance is in 1749 in the Menzies MS, and from that point on, the tune type begins to emerge in printed collections of music and MSS of the eighteenth and nineteenth centuries, although the evidence suggests that in the eighteenth century there

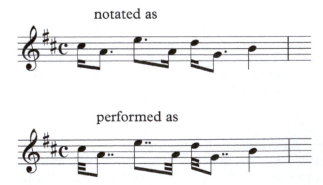

Figure 2.4 Example of strathspey rhythm

was no clear distinction between music for dancing and dancing itself (Lamb 2013). Will Lamb has also cited evidence to support the idea that in early modern Scotland there was little difference between the strathspey and the reel and both were thought of as forms of dance that developed from earlier Gaelic vocal dance music (2014, 2013). Today, however, strathspeys are understood as a particular tune type in 4|4 time, where the key characteristic is the highly polarised rhythms of semi-quavers (sixteenth notes) with dotted quavers (eighth notes), producing a jagged rhythmical feel performed fairly quickly between 100–120 beats per minute (bpm). The strathspey is a particularly Scottish tune type now played throughout the world which gives a highly bouncy feel and is used for several types of dancing.

Although strathspeys are usually notated on the page with single dot and cuts (3:1 rhythmical ratio) they are often played as though double dot and cut (7:1) to support the very bouncy rhythm of the strathspey genre:

The *incipit* in Figure 2.4 is taken from one of the quintessential and oldest Scottish strathspeys, *Tullochgorm*, first printed in the Duke of Perth MS in 1734 (Gibson 2013). The title of the tune is an anglicisation of the Gaelic for grey or blue hill, which is of course disputed, partly because of the social link between colours, the supernatural and small hills in Scottish folklore. However, the tune itself is one of the best known and oldest examples of a strathspey in Scotland, and has been played as a reel as well on many instruments.

There has been controversy surrounding step-dancing in Scotland. In the late 1980s the fiddler Alasdair Fraser and piper Hamish Moore discovered Cape Breton step-dancing and began promoting it in Scotland (Melin 2005: 28). They suggested that Cape Breton step-dancing, a relaxed, vernacular form of dance performed to traditional music in the eastern seaboard of Canada, perhaps represented an older form of Scottish dancing that travelled with emigration. And also therefore that it might represent a more authentic form of traditional dancing from Scotland that had survived untouched by nineteenth- and

Tullochgorm

(traditional arr. S. McKerrell)

Figure 2.5 The strathspey *Tullochgorm* (setting by the author)

twentieth-century formalisation and stylisation that has occurred in other types of traditional dance and music. The suggestion quickly took hold that this form of step-dancing from Cape Breton was truly an original form of Scottish dance that had existed prior to mass emigrations from the Highlands and Islands of Scotland from the late eighteenth and early nineteenth centuries in a cultural context where it was an 'inter-linked and interdependent whole within the supportive framework of language and culture' (Dickson 2009: 204). Moreover, the actual style of Cape Breton step-dancing seemed to many performers and dancers to embody a more informal and spontaneous somatic practice that was in keeping with ongoing revivalists' attempts to reconstruct authentic traditional music. This was controversial because it positioned step-dance as the 'truly' Scottish dance form in opposition to the more widespread and established dance styles of Scottish country dance and Highland dance. In Scotland, step-dancing had been eclipsed in the nineteenth century by the more formal (and organised) country dancing, and at weddings and other significant social occasions by céilidh dancing. However, step-dancing as an informal and percussive practice had not died out in Scotland. The very few individuals who could remember how to dance the steps have been reported in the literature as often embarrassed or reticent about step-dancing, viewing it as an archaic and socially distant form of performance (Bennett 1994; Melin 2005). The widespread popularisation of Scottish country dancing with its standardised steps, particularly for teachers in the early twentieth century has been cited as the key influence in popularising Scottish country dance (Bennett 1994). Naturally enough, those who perhaps did know the step-dances found that they had little or no social context in which to perform them, leading to an almost total decline. Furthermore, the group dances and growth of opportunities for Scottish country dance led to a great popularisation of Scottish country dance in the twentieth century that continues today.

Particularly interesting from a scholarly viewpoint was that this mini-revival and controversy rested upon the flow of ideas and practices from the diaspora back to the Scottish home, taking with it the possibility for opening up other genres of cultural performance that could potentially be found to have kept alive in Cape Breton and other concentrated diasporic communities. In the 1990s, certain traditional musicians and dancers began to advocate the view that much of our traditional music had been irrevocably changed and 'polluted' by the late-nineteenth- and early-twentieth-century fashions for collection, formalisation and publication in art music formats which had 'stultified' performance practices. At one point, certain musicians were passing individually to each other secret field recordings of dance music played in Cape Breton that supposedly represented the pure, authentic practice that Scotland had lost forever, and that now could be resurrected by a select group. The key issue was that Cape Breton step-dance offered a model for a revival of truly authentic Scottish percussive dancing that went back far enough in time before the widespread importation of continental European dance aesthetics into the Scottish dancing community; thereby offering a model of truly authentic indigenous Scottish dance.

Powerful performance of attractive music and dance made converts of many musicians and dancers, particularly within Gaelic communities. There has been a musical and danced richness that has evolved out of this debate in Scotland, and now informal, percussive step-dancing is very much part of Scottish traditional culture, imported from the diaspora back home. However, the suggestion that Cape Breton step-dance is essentially a purer, older form of Scottish dance, is now regarded as the revivalist's zeal for ethnic authenticity blinding them to social and historical realities:

If it had remained as popular in Scotland as in Cape Breton, step dancing would also have developed uniquely due to its social and cultural circumstances. In reality it did not so develop, as the social and cultural circumstances in Scotland prioritized and favoured other aesthetics rather than percussive step dancing.

(Melin 2005: 32)[6]

One of the key legacies from this debate in the 1990s and early 2000s has been the reha- bilitation of the intertwining aesthetics of music, dance, song and drama as holistic and interconnected social practices. This is evident today in the Fèisean movement[7] and in the successful Ceòlas summer festival that is one of the very positive developments insti- gated in 1996 by Hamish Moore in the Outer Hebrides.

One of the most popular forms of Scottish traditional music has always been the dance music of Scottish dance bands. Dance bands as they emerged in the twentieth century have had various instrumental line-ups, but central has been the use of the accordion. Today the piano-accordion is the most popular free reed instrument in Scot- land, but it has not always been so. The success of free reed instruments such as the melodeon, concertina, piano-accordion, diatonic button accordion and many others, has been both their relative affordability and audibility. Free reed instruments first arrived in Britain in the 1820s and '30s and the most popular of these instruments were the melodeon and diatonic accordions, diatonic implying that the accordion is designed in a push–pull mechanisation that allows the player to play within one key easily. These held sway until after the First World War, when larger, piano-accordions became more popular for dance bands. The dance bands of Scotland have been extremely popular and in many ways set the aesthetic standards in the mid-twentieth century for what Scottish traditional dance music should sound like, through regular broadcasting on the television and radio (Duesenberry 2000). Usually Scottish dance bands are formed around a lead instrumentalist who plays piano-accordion, and then has either a fiddle or second 'box' (accordion) and is accompanied by piano and drums. Other instruments have been popular including saxophone, double bass amongst others, but the pattern of two accordions, fiddle with piano and drums was set by the mid-twentieth century and became the most popular form of recorded Scottish traditional music.

Undoubtedly the most famous bandleader of the twentieth century was Sir Jimmy Shand (1908–2000) who has had a far-reaching influence on performance practice in Scot- land. He was born in Fife and quickly rose to prominence on the accordion, as a player, bandleader, composer and broadcaster. He invented his own accordion which was named the 'Shand Morino', with three rows of diatonic buttons, and this attracted a large follow- ing. Jimmy Shand is also responsible for the tonic chord at the end of each set which was popularised through his recordings.[8] His influence was huge both because of his musical talent and the massive sales of his recordings in the UK. Jimmy Shand signed to EMI in 1943 and, 'by 1949 each of their 78s were selling in excess of 50,000 copies'.[9] In 1955 his band recording of 'The Bluebell Polka' reached number 20 in the UK national charts and the band appeared on *Top of the Pops*, BBC television's flagship popular music programme. There is a statue of Sir Jimmy Shand in Auchtermuchty in Fife. Today, there are numerous Scottish dance bands carrying on the tradition of playing music for dancing throughout Scotland and across the world, and many of the leading composers and arrangers of Scot- tish traditional music such as Alasdair MacCuish, Robert Black, John Carmichael and Ian Muir continue to re-invent this musical tradition in the twenty-first century.

Figure 2.6 Portrait of Sir Jimmy Shand by George Bruce (1995) (by kind permission of National Galleries Scotland [Acc. No. PG 3009])

The travellers and their music

The 'travellers' is the name given to the nomadic people who for centuries have travelled around Scotland buying, selling ('hawking'), mending and tinsmithing, pearl-fishing and entertaining the settled population. Also known as the 'Summer Walkers' or in Gaelic *Ceardannan*, they are an established community within Scotland and they have made, and continue to make, a massive contribution to Scottish cultural life. 'Tinker' is a derogatory label that they do not welcome and has its genesis in the now archaic practice of tinsmithing and metalwork that travellers used to perform. 'Gypsies' (derived from the word 'Egyptians') on the other hand are a separate race of people that have also migrated to Scotland. Some intermingling has occurred between the two populations, however the travellers and gypsies regard themselves as distinct peoples. Most of the economic basis for travelling people to make a living on the road has disappeared and today many of them are settled but still carry on the traditions of the travellers, thus 'traveller' describes an ethnic population and not nomadism in Scotland. The importance of the traveller singers and musicians to Scottish traditional music is that they represent to many people in Scotland a link with indigenous Scottish traditional songs, tunes, stories and customs that have been lost by the majority settled population of Scotland. Thus they were promoted particularly during the revival in the 1950s and '60s as 'tradition bearers', or authentic performers of Scottish traditional music who through their separation from ordinary Scots, strong oral culture and nomadism had kept alive much of the oldest indigenous traditional music. The travellers as an authentic internal other, have in a sense restored some of Scotland's forgotten cultural memory and in this way have allowed fans of their music and particularly revivalists, to construct again a new and deeper sense of belonging to Scotland through the cultural memories of a once ostracised, yet authentic internal Other.

Famous traveller families in Scotland include Stewart, Alexander, MacDonald, Cameron, MacAlister, MacGregor, Williamson and MacMillan. This community have in general been ostracised by the settled population throughout history. This has been a common thread throughout Europe, with many communities not welcoming travellers to their communities. During the Scottish Reformation gypsies and tinkers were doubly penalised both for their nomadism (signifying a sense of otherness and danger for settled peoples) and because of their brilliance as pipers, fiddlers and singers which ran counter to the religious Reformation's rejection of aesthetic pleasures in favour of newly formed Protestant ethics. In the nineteenth century legal measures restricting the use of traditional camping grounds were increased. Their nomadism and itinerant occupations were seen as problematic but simultaneously as a source of pride by travellers. Historically however, these discriminatory attitudes were not so common in the Highlands, particularly in Sutherland and Caithness where large traveller populations were long established and valued for their skills. Today, governments are still legislating against these communities and yet amongst the Scottish traditional music community, they have, and are held up as icons of authenticity.

The music of the travellers reflects their lifestyle traditionally based around seasonal agricultural work such as fruit picking, harvesting, flax pulling (the 'berry-pickers of Blair' etc.) and many other casual tasks such as tinsmithing, scrap trading, harvesting, beating, and busking. This lifestyle was hard, particularly in winter, and almost all members of the family would work and thus they lived beyond the bureaucratic and socio-economic constraints of ordinary Scots, as summed up by the renowned traveller singer and storyteller Duncan Williamson thus:

> Ye wake up in the morning an' ye hear the birds singin' . . . ye've no worries, no one tells ye what to do . . . you have nothing but you have everything. It's so peaceful . . . you come and go as you like . . . no need to keep up with the boss. Ye don't *need* these things.
>
> (Williamson in Munro 1996: 141)

The travellers have always closely guarded their own culture but during the folk revival in Scotland, their music and particularly songs, came to the fore through musicians such as Stanley Robertson, Belle Stewart, her daughter Sheila and Jeannie Robertson. This brought a new value to their music which in turn brought them increased status and security. Their role in the folk revival in Scotland played an important part in improving public acceptance of the value of their culture. This has led inevitably to a commodification of their culture which has now changed the performance practice and dynamics of transmission amongst travellers. Kinship, lifestyle and travelling are important to the travellers and they rely on relatives and other travellers for support, which led to a fiercely protective and insular culture. Outsiders were excluded by use of the 'cant' or special travellers language. There is both Scots-English and Gaelic cant in Scotland.

Much of the travellers' music and stories were brought to prominence by Hamish Henderson who recognised that their culture was one of the great 'jewels' of Scotland. He set out with a tape recorder to document many thousands of songs, tunes and stories in the 1950s, now held in the School of Scottish Studies archives at the University of

Figure 2.7 Hamish Henderson (by kind permission of Timothy Neat)

Edinburgh. Their stories and songs preserved narratives that are sometimes centuries old in the oral tradition. Hamish and others were responsible for seeking out and popularising musicians such as Alec and Belle Stewart whose family, styled 'the Stewarts O Blair', and in particular one of their daughters, Sheila, is recognised as making a substantial contribution to the understanding of Scottish traditional music. Henderson also popularised the singing of Jeannie Robertson who had settled in Aberdeenshire and is regarded as one of Scotland's finest traditional singers in the modern period.

The travellers' tradition of music and stories has always been a family tradition, but luckily for those of us interested in Scottish culture, a tradition now shared with us through recordings and concerts both at home and abroad. In this sense, whether heard in a cottage in Perthshire (the home of the Stewarts) or in a concert hall in Pittsburgh, this is intimate social music that creates a shared bond. Much of the power of the travellers' music is to be heard both in the compelling narratives of their songs and ballads, as well as the distinctive performative style that is characteristic of traveller singers. This style subjugates the individual singer or storyteller as a vehicle for the tradition, allowing the narrative and emotion of the performance to take centre stage. You will find in listening to traveller singers that they characteristically employ elongated vowels, and use vocal timbre very fluidly and prioritisation of the narrative in the song all combine to create a powerfully affective performance. This total emotional engagement in performance is usually called the *conyach* by travellers. One of the key singers who most embodied this phenomenon in recent times was Sheila Stewart.

Figure 2.8 Jeannie Robertson (by kind permission of Timothy Neat)

Sheila Stewart (1937–2014) was one of five children born to Alec and Belle Stewart in Blairgowrie, Perthshire. She absorbed many songs directly from her mother and from her uncle Donald. Here she describes how her life and song were merged in her traveller childhood in her own words:

Figure 2.9 Sketch of Sheila Stewart by Timothy Neat (by kind permission of the artist)

Actually, I was severely brainwashed into the ballads, the songs, the stories and because I showed an interest – It became a function and a natural way of life to me. I never knew of anything else . . . .

We were devoted . . . to the songs and the ballads. Even the men on my mother's side of the family all sang. My grandfather – old Dan McGregor – folk would come [from] all over to the berry picking and camp beside him; they say he could sing the birds off the trees. He was a brilliant ballad singer . . . and it was just passed down. Well, you see it was my Uncle Donald that got it from his father; but I was brought up with my mother and father, my two grannies . . . and my Uncle Donald was the most important man in my life. And I was made to do it. Mind you, it paid off at times cause the rest of the kids would come in and say 'Can we go to the pictures tonight . . . Can we get some money for the pictures?' 'No, away you go!' and yet, if my uncle had a dram, 'Sheila, sing us a song,' and he would hand me ten shillings. Ten shillings then was a lot of money and I would get it . . . for singing an old ballad, making him distraught and the tears flowing oot of his e'en – sitting cuddling a cabbage, one time, I'll always remember! And he would give me money for singing the one song. So you can understand how unpopular I was with my cousins . . . When they had céilidhs I could do what I liked then . . . sitting round the campfire outside. Our folk coming into my mother's house having céilidhs. My mother's house was a great céilidh house, you know. She had three different rooms all facing the one way – facing the door. She had three céilidhs going on – a céilidh in every room. There was musicians, singers, pipers, storytellers and everything was going on in my mother's house. We used to go to Jeannie's [Robertson] – when she camped at the Brig o' Ribbon . . . Grandfather says 'Jeannie's here . . . Let's go for a drink with Jeannie.' And we hae a campfire and we'd sit and tell stories and have a joke. The men would go and play quoits or the pitch and toss. The women would sit craicing,[10] then all of a sudden the fire was big enough and we'd sit there and hae a céilidh. My granny – my father's mother . . . from the West coast was Agnes Campbell. Aye, she was a good singer – sang the same songs as us . . . Perthshire, you see. She got married and came into Perthshire. All the Travellers long ago . . . came to Blairgowrie to do the berry picking and that's where they all met up. Working holiday, you see – picking berries . . . The travellers came because it was great. The families made a lot of money.

(Stewart 2000)

Céilidh

From Gaelic, lit. 'to visit'. The term is widely used to describe either an evening of song, music and dance amongst friends or to describe a social dance evening where people gather to dance to Scottish traditional music. Céilidh bands usually use accordion, fiddle and drums to perform for informal social dances or, sometimes more formal, organised social dancing such following the conventions of the Royal Scottish Country Dance Association (RSCDS), now held throughout the world.

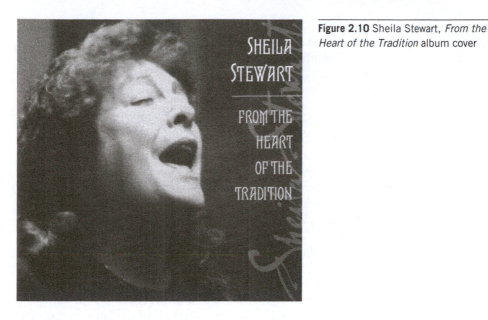

Figure 2.10 Sheila Stewart, *From the Heart of the Tradition* album cover

Listening to a ballad

On her album, *From the Heart of the Tradition* (Stewart 2000), we hear twenty captivating songs and ballads sung by Sheila Stewart. Listen to the Scottish ballad 'The Twa Brothers'.[11]

Track 1. Scottish ballad, 'The Twa Brothers', performed by Sheila Stewart (see companion website: www.routledge.com/cw/mckerrell).

In this ballad you will hear a tale about two 'pretty boys', William and John who fight after a wrestling match where John ends up dying after being stabbed by William. In the ballad there are a number of references to the supernatural through key motifs such as 'the merry green woods' and 'the grass is growing green'. Green is always associated with the supernatural in Scottish ballads, as in the same way the colour yellow very often symbolises marriage. Numbers also take on semiotic significance in ballads, where 3 signifies mystical significance, 7 is used as a measure of time or people, e.g. 'seven sons, daughters, brothers, sisters, knights . . .', and 9 usually is used for counting objects or men (Wimberly 1965: 330). Notice also how a conversational framing device of asking 'what will I tell to . . .' is used to introduce various verses of the ballad. This is a ballad device that helps the performer to remember the narrative and gives voice to the emotions of the characters in the narrative.

Farm culture and the bothy ballads

'Bothy ballad' is in many ways an odd title, due to the rarity of the 'bothy system' in Scottish agriculture. Essentially, however, a bothy ballad is a narrative song that deals with the subject of agricultural life, in a predominantly mid-nineteenth-century North East Scottish context; or in other words a song that tells a story about farm life. Bothy ballads were most popular in North East Scotland between 1840 and 1880, when they were part of the social life of farm labourers. The labourers worked on a 'feeing system' and were employed by a farmer for either six or twelve months, changing their employers at 'feeing fairs' each May and November.

There were two systems of bothy life: the bothy system and the chaumer system, the latter of which was more popular because workers had their meals served to them in the farm kitchen. In the bothy system, workers were housed with their families in 'bothies', simple farm buildings which often lacked running water or basic facilities such as toilets. A strict social hierarchy existed on the farms, which is reflected in the songs themselves. Usually the most senior person was the grieve, or farmer, who controlled the labour and hired the workers. Below the grieve was often a foreman or foremen, then came the ploughmen, the orramen (lit. 'other men') and then ordinary labourers and farm boys. Many of the songs deal with the reputation of the farmers and farms and were sung by the workers in celebration or castigation of their employers. There was also a secret society called the 'horseman's word', essentially a formalised bond between 'ploughmen, farrowers and blacksmiths centred on north-east Scotland' (Neat 2009: 4). This society involved the ritual passing on of advantageous knowledge of horses and included songs, poetry and oaths.

Songs also deal with harvesting and other agricultural practices on the farms. In Scots, 'hairst' is the word for harvest, and in the following text of the bothy ballad 'The Hairst O Rettie' we can see how much of the agricultural life of the workers is described in the song. We also hear about the first machines that came in to displace agricultural labourers and which, when combined with urbanisation, agricultural depression and the 1855 Stamp Act (making printing of other songs cheaper), brought about the end of this particular form of work in nineteenth-century Scotland. Bothy ballads have ceased to exist as functional song but are still sung today, particularly in festivals and in the North East of Scotland, where they remain a valuable genre of traditional Scots song.

'The Hairst o' Rettie'[12]

I hae seen the hairst o' Rettie noo, (*hairst* = harvest)
And twa-three aff the throne.
I've heard for sax and seven weeks (*sax* = six)
The hairsters girn and groan. (*hairsters* = harvesters; *girn* = whine)
Till a covie Willie Rae ('*covie*' is a NE traveller word for 'a guy')

Wi a monthie an' a day
Ca's a' the jolly hairster lads
Come blithely doon the brae.

O' a monthie an' a day, my lads,
The like was never seen;
It beats to sticks the fastest strips
O' Vickers' best machine. (*Vickers* = an agricultural brand name)

The Speedwell she taks up the rear,
The Victory clears the way;
And twenty acres daily yields,
Laid doon tae Willie Rae. (*Laid doon* = laid down [i.e. cleared])

He drives them roond and roond the field
At sic an awfu' rate: (*sic* = such)
Wiles them kindly oot and in   (*wiles* = coaxes)
At mony's a kittle gate.   (*kittle* = tricky)
And wiles them gently ow'r the steens   (*steens* = stones)
And mony a hidden hole,
And he'll come by nae mishanter   (*mishanter* = misfortune)
If ye leave him wi' a pole.

He sharps their teeth tae gar them bite;   (refers to a reaping binding machine)
He taps them on the jaws,
And if he sees them dowie-like,   (*dowie* = dreary)
He'll brawly ken the cause: (*brawly* = brilliant)
A boltie here, a pinnie there,   (*boltie* = bolt; *pinnie* = pin)
A little oot o' a tune;
He'll quickly stop their wild career,
And bring the clishack doon.

He whittles aff the corners,   (*whittles* = carve with a knife)
And makes crookit bitties straucht,   (*straucht* = straight)
Sees that man and beast
Are equal in a draucht,   (*draucht* = pulling a plow)
An' a' the corners neat an' square
And nae a shafe agley;   (*shafe agley* = sheaf out of line)
And he'll coont wi' ony dominie   (*dominie* = church minister)
Frae Deveron tae the Spey.

He's nae made up wi' mony words
Or kent tae puff and lee,
But just as keen a little chap
As ever you did see.
And if you're in search o hairvest work
Upon a market day,
Take my advice, be there in time
And look for Willie Rae.

Noo he hae got it in aboot,
An' a wer things be ticht,   (*ticht* = tight)
We'll gaither roond the festal board   (*festal* = festival)
Tae spend a jolly nicht;
Wi' Scottish sangs and mutton broth   (*broth* = soup)
Tae charm our cares away;
We'll drink success tae Rettie,
And my bandster Annie Maclean.

Come all ye jolly Rettie lads,
A ringin' cheer – Hurra!
A band o' better workin' chaps

A gaffer never saw.   (*gaffer* = boss)
Sae eager aye tae play their pairt,
And ready for the fray
Twas you that made the boatie row,
Was steer'd by Willie Rae.

Organised Solo Performance

Scotland, like related Celtic cultures in Ireland and Brittany, has a highly developed solo performance culture in contemporary traditional music. Usually solo performances in public form part of competitive contexts and without inferring any value judgement, are often the most conservative and elitist contexts for the performance of Scottish traditional music. Solo competition performance is also where some of the highest quality performances of Scottish traditional music take place. Sometimes, such as at festivals of traditional music and culture, solo performance is encouraged for singers and often for children performing in local competitions. It is not typical in the community, but it is fundamentally important, and for some performers it represents their normal performance practice. Solo performance is most widespread in traditional Scots and Gaelic song, competition fiddling, amongst singer-songwriters but is most widely practised amongst pipers.

Figure 2.11 Piper Greg Wilson competes in the solo piping at the Argyllshire Gathering in Oban (photo by the author)

Solo piping

Perhaps the best-known national musical instrument of any culture is the Scottish bagpipes. There are around fifty to sixty different types of bagpipes in Europe alone, and in Scotland there are three different types of which the Highland bagpipes are without doubt the best known and most widely played. The instrument in its current form is indigenous to Scotland and is very widely played throughout the world, both as a solo instrument and in pipe bands (see below). The bagpipes are constitutive of Scottish traditional music in myriad ways, but crucially they have provided much of the core repertoire of tunes that we can say with confidence are thought of as Scottish traditional music. Bagpipe tunes such as the jigs 'The Jig of Slurs' (comp. Pipe Major George S. MacLennan) and 'Rory MacLeod' (comp. Pipe Major Donald MacLeod), or the reel 'Alick C. MacGregor' (comp. George S. MacLennan) are known throughout the world as Scottish traditional tunes. Yet, piping and pipers have for complex reasons remained slightly apart from the rest of the Scottish traditional music community, as a separate strand of tradition. Whereas pipe tunes have passed easily over to other traditions, fiddle, harp, songs and accordion tunes for instance have not, for the main part, passed into piping repertoires. This has been recognised in policy where piping is seen as having 'shared roots' but its own institutions and traditions are quite separate from other musical traditions (Francis 2010: 7).

The bagpipes have also acquired over time a complex history of invented romantic and nationalistic public symbolism that is difficult to disentangle from their authentic and everyday histories, but which make them a powerful and far-reaching symbol of Scotland both in sound and image.

Piping today happens mainly in three distinct contexts: (1) Solo competition piping; (2) pipe bands; and (3) in folk bands (with other instruments). Of these, by far the most popular are pipe bands, now spread throughout the English-speaking world. Piping is also inextricably linked with drumming and dancing. Piping, pipe-band drumming and competitive Highland dancing are now global communities of practice where many competitors travel particularly between Scotland, Canada, America, Australia and New Zealand on an international competitive and summer school circuit. For some, the sheer popularity and reach of the instrument is surprising. For instance, there are over 1,000 pipe bands in the Tri-state area of the United States and piping has been popular in California since the 1900s. The pinnacle of every competing band's year is the World Pipe Band Championship, held in Glasgow since 1947, usually in mid-August. This event has grown over decades and today regularly hosts more than 220 competing pipe bands from around the world, with some 40,000 visitors and 8,000 pipers and drummers travelling annually to Glasgow.[13] Piping itself represents the largest community of musicians in Scottish traditional music not least because of the influence until the mid-twentieth century of British imperialism and Scottish emigration. Today there are pipers in many parts of the world, but the Anglophone world where most Scots emigrants settled contains the largest populations of bagpipers.

Organologically, the instrument itself reflects its imperial history, with ivory traditionally used for the projecting mounts, silver or gold sometimes used for ornamental mounts, African blackwood for the sounding drones and chanter, and a bag traditionally made of sheep or cow hide. These days many different materials are used, such as Gore-Tex, neoprene for the bags, carbon fibre, metals, plastic and compressed cardboard for the reeds and others besides. An important distinction between various forms of bagpipes is whether they use a conical or parallel bored chanter (which produces the melody). Scottish bagpipes use conical bored chanters, which along with a thick and short double reed provide volume and a very rich harmonic range, especially when heard with the drones.

The music of the Scottish bagpipes still falls strictly into two main types, light music (derived from the Gaelic, *cèol beag*) and piobaireachd (in Gaelic, *cèol mór*).

Bagpipe music

cèol beag (light music)	*cèol mór* (piobaireachd)
marches (2|4, 3|4 retreats, 6|8, etc.)	gatherings
strathspeys	laments
reels	salutes
hornpipes	short tunes
jigs	marches etc.
slow airs/marches	

In general the solo competitions for piping involve the performance of three categories: (1) piobaireachd; (2) march, strathspey and reel; (3) hornpipe and jig competitions. The *cèol beag*, or light music, are the everyday tunes that are often shared with other instruments and much of Scottish traditional music is made up of these types of tunes.

Piobaireachd, which literally means 'pipering', from Gaelic (sometimes anglicised to pibroch), is a unique form of theme and variations music developed in Gaelic culture in the late medieval and early modern period. Key to the history of piobaireachd is the MacCrimmon family who were hereditary pipers to the MacLeods of Dunvegan. They were a high status family of pipers that performed and composed piobaireachd for the MacLeods for several centuries from around the sixteenth to the nineteenth centuries. The dynasty continued strongly until around 1777 when Domhnall Ruadh MacCrimmon, the last hereditary piper-teacher emigrated for America. He joined the British Army and was killed at Long Island, New York. However, there were also a number of MacCrimmons who flourished in North Carolina and the hereditary piping dynasty continues today in a different economic and social context.

Piobaireachd fall into the five main types shown above and because they are a longer theme and variation form, and usually take between ten and twenty minutes to perform, although there are short piobaireachd such as 'A Flame of Wrath for Squinting Patrick' (Gaelic *Lasan Phadruig Chaogaich*) that can be performed in seven or eight minutes and the longest tunes such as 'The Lament for Donald Ban MacCrimmon' (Gaelic *Cumha Dhomhnuill Bhain Mhic Cruimein*) or 'Donald Gruamach's March' (Gaelic *Spaidsearachd Dhomhnuill Ghruamaich*) can take up to twenty-five minutes to perform. Piobaireachd today is almost exclusively performed in solo competitions and 'there are about 320 distinct pieces of music, recorded in about 600 independent versions' (Cannon 2000: 1). Competition as a performance context tends to produce quite tight canonical boundaries and to slow the pace of change, composition and repertorial innovation, and because of this solo competitive piping has tended to focus upon the pre-1850 repertoire of composed piobaireachd, which through age and tightly defined performance practices has meant that very few new piobaireachd have been composed, and even fewer publicly performed.

Listening to piobaireachd

Many people, including those who count themselves as knowledgeable about Scottish traditional music, often struggle to understand piobaireachd and how to experience it aurally. The light music and dance tunes of Scottish traditional music almost exclusively

Figure 2.12 Music for the piobaireachd, 'Farewell to the Laird of Islay'. Music reproduced here by kind permission of the Piobaireachd Society, www.piobaireachd.co.uk

use repetitive 2- or 4-bar phrases in a standard question and answer structure (see Chapter 9). However, piobaireachd is very different with a ground (Gaelic urlar) which sets out the melody followed by increasingly skeletonised variations with increasingly complex variations. In addition, every tune has a range of traditions associated with playing it, and very small differences in timing today have a substantial aesthetic impact on the educated listener. Understanding piobaireachd is of course an acquired skill and one that, like many other forms of complex music, takes some time to develop. There is, however, for many people a deep enjoyment and aesthetic response to piobaireachd, particularly once one understands what and how the musical and expressive structures work.

Key elements that make piobaireachd playing a musical and expressive structure lie very often with the subtle stressing of particular melody notes within the piece. One reason this is sometimes difficult for listeners is because the bagpipes do not have any dynamic control, i.e. they play at the same volume and with a constant sound throughout the performance. This means that any stressing a player wants to make in the expression of the tune requires the lengthening or shortening (sometimes called 'cutting') of individual notes, and very often how players do this depends upon the type of performing tradition that they have been trained in. Furthermore, as well as listening for the important stressed notes and articulation of phrases in piobaireachd, skilled players often emphasise particular patterns of phrase structure that are then reflected in the stresses in each subsequent variation, so that a tune will hold together coherently as a musical performance not just linearly through time but also structurally and vertically with correspondences between variations throughout the performance.

Track 2. Piobaireachd 'Farewell to the Laird of Islay', composed Angus MacKay, non-copyright 1840s, performed by Simon McKerrell, from the 2012 album, *Live at the King's Hall* (see companion website: www.routledge.com/cw/mckerrell).

Listen to the piobaireachd 'Farewell to the Laird of Islay' (comp. Angus MacKay) performed by the author, Simon McKerrell. In this tune you will notice that in general, each bar of the tune has an arch structure, rising and then falling. This is important as it helps to create the sense of a single phrase, within the longer line or variation. In the performance you might notice that the longest stresses are reserved for the opening and closing melody notes of each bar, and that the final notes of each line and variation receive slightly longer. This helps to show the sense of completion and finality, much the same way as cadences do in other forms of music. When listening to bagpipes, the drone is of course ever present and constantly interacting with the melodic movement. It is the sense of consonance and dissonance against the drones that is a generative musical force in bagpipe music, and many bagpipe tunes often resolve to A, which is the same fundamental to which each of the three drones is tuned.

When listening to the tune, ideally with the score, try to understand how each succeeding variation relates to the ground, or main melody played at the start. You will notice that the important melody notes of the ground are the notes which are taken and used to create the skeleton structure of the following variations. You should also notice that the tune is played mostly with a strong, weak, weak, strong phrase structure in each bar which helps to orient the listener and provide melodic interest. As the tune progresses you will notice that each succeeding variation employs increasingly complex ornamentation, until towards the end, in the *crunluath-a-mach variation* (lit. 'the crowning going out') there are complex ornaments performed on each of the main melody notes. The tune, like many other piobaireachd, follows this set of ornamental variations: ground or main melody; variation 1, skeleton melody; 2, *taorluath* singling variation; 3, *taorluath* doubling variation; 4, full *taorluath* variation; 5, *crunluath* variation; 6, *crunluath-a-mach* variation. Notice that many of the slightly elongated notes occur in the same places in each succeeding variation, giving life to a sort of structural coherence across the variations. Many piobaireachd follow a similar pattern employing an overall scheme of 1, a ground or *urlar* in Gaelic that lays out the melody of the tune; followed by 2, a reductive, skeleton variation of this melody in a dithis or *suibhal* variation. This is then often followed by 3, a *taorluath* variation that employs complex ornamentation set to the skeleton melodic structure; and finally 4, a *crunluath* (lit. 'crowning') variation which uses the most complex type of bagpipe ornamentation still in practice today. Each of these variations can have 'doublings' which involve repeating the variation and removing the cadential points and substituting them with simple ornamented melody notes. The tune is supposed to gather momentum as it progresses and finally at the end of the tune, the first line of the ground is played again to complete the performance.

Scottish solo piping continues to thrive almost exclusively through competition around the world. It is also a very male dominated activity and, through its association with Scottish services and the British military, is still a very white one. In the last fifty years there has emerged a professional class of pipers who are now performing, teaching and communicating on a global platform.[14] Piping is now moving more rapidly than any other form of Scottish traditional music into the digital era, with online lessons, downloadable tuition packs including audio and video files, online fora and communities and real-time video streaming of international competitions becoming popular amongst many pipers. As a form of solo performance, pipers today tend to play indoors and their audiences are mainly for other pipers making a very tight-knit community with little interaction with other types of traditional music or instruments. Recently however, with major festivals such as the Piping Live! festival in Glasgow,[15] and the ongoing integration of piping with other instruments, this tradition has opened up somewhat and since the 1980s has been exploring and arranging Irish and other Scottish musical traditions for the bagpipes.

Solo competition is also popular today amongst Gaelic singers, accordionists and fiddlers. Many of which take place at regional 'Provincial Mods' in the regions of Scotland and at the annual 'National Mod' held in a different town in Scotland every year. These are festivals of Gaelic music and culture that were initially modeled on the Welsh Eisteddfod and began in Scotland in 1892. Locally, these are opportunities for many young children to perform their own music for the first time, giving them a sense of belonging both to Gaelic culture and also to meet and share music with other young people in the region. Today the Mod acts as a focal point in the year for Gaelic speaking society and is often televised on Scotland's national Gaelic-medium broadcasting channel, BBC Alba (see 'Mass-Mediated Music' below). The competitions at the Mod range across different styles and instruments and include age-defined competitions for solo and group performance. The solo performances are all performed in Gaelic and include categories such as poetry recitation, solo singing, *Òran Mòr*, and set pieces for voice, fiddle, bagpipes, clarsach and choirs. They often feature 'prescribed pieces' as is the norm in solo piping competitions too, which act as a means of encouraging particular versions of songs, poems and tunes deemed authentic and suitable by various gatekeepers involved in An Commun Gaidhleach.[16]

In this way, and in common with other competitive traditions, the pace of musical change is slow in the competitive repertoire and in performance practice.

Organised Social Music

Scottish society has always organised itself into clubs, associations and societies. This will to institutionalise has been evident right throughout Scotland's modern period and stems both from the deep-seated notions of social class in Scotland and from longstanding literacy in Scottish life. Scotland was one of the most literate of European nations in the eighteenth century, 'it is likely that at least in the rural Lowlands and the smaller towns by c. 1760 reading literacy was very extensive' (Devine 1999: 97–8). The organisation of musical social life in Scotland can be traced all the way back to the pre-modern Gaelic court culture, through to the preservationist instincts of the Highland Societies of Scotland and London, to the romantic nationalism of the Celtic revivalists at the end of the nineteenth century, to the revivalist and radical impulses of the twentieth-century folk revivalists. It is difficult to imagine meeting any seriously devoted aficionado of Scottish traditional music who has not at one stage in their life been a member or office holder of a society or Scottish organisation promoting traditional culture.

Key institutions such as the Scottish Country Dance Society (established 1923, later, 'Royal' in 1951), An Commun Gaidhleach (established 1891, responsible for the national Mod), the Piobaireachd Society (1903), the Clarsach Society (1931), the Royal Scottish Pipe Band Association (1930, initially the Scottish Pipe Band Association, 'Royal' from 1980), the Competing Pipers Association, and in more recent history, the Lowland and Borders Pipers Society (1983), the National Association of Accordion and Fiddle Clubs (1971), Hand up for Trad (2002) and the Traditional Music and Song Association (1966) have all invested time and effort in promoting and recording Scottish traditional music over the last several decades. In addition to these institutions, other organisations regularly put on festivals, competitions, accordion and fiddle club meetings, pipe band competitions, Gaelic choral recitals and Gaelic-medium music competitions such as those in the national Mod.

One other context in which Scottish traditional music is performed very regularly is in teaching, or as sometimes discussed in traditional music, 'passing it on' (for a more detailed discussion of this area see Miller 2007). Scholars of traditional music throughout the late nineteenth and twentieth centuries have tended to make a distinction between oral and literate transmission of traditional music and culture. It is true of

Figure 2.13 The Spirit of Scotland Pipe Band going on to compete in the 2008 World Pipe Band Championships (photo by Derek Maxwell)

course to suggest that oral tradition has been at the heart of Scottish traditional music, and I sometimes prefer to discuss it in terms of 'aural' transmission of music, given that so much of it today is instrumental rather than sung. However, whether oral or aural transmission, it is fair to say that this is central to not just Scottish traditional music, but the music of many cultures throughout the world, and has had a profound effect not just on the mechanics of how traditional tunes and songs are transmitted, but also upon the very definition of what constitutes traditional music itself.

Scotland's relatively advanced early literacy, brought with it wholesale changes such as the invention and popularisation of the novel in nineteenth-century Britain and a comparatively long record of musical notation in relation to other traditional musics around the world. Increasing literacy also affected the teaching of traditional Scottish music, of which the overwhelming institutionalisation at the end of the nineteenth century and beginning of the twentieth was paramount. It is also important to remember that after the invention of the phonograph (1877) and the gramophone (1888), people were increasingly able to record and listen back to Scottish traditional music without others present, which has particularly changed the nature of musical transmission and education. Probably the most profound effect of musical recording has been the creation of traditional music as an 'object', irrevocably changing the ways in which we experience and learn traditional music forever and leading eventually to the commercialisation of traditional music (see 'Mass-Mediated Music' below).

Pipe bands

Pipe bands emerged from military musical practices in the nineteenth century. Today, pipe bands are probably the most popular form of participation in any form of Scottish traditional music at home or abroad. Military pipe bands developed in the latter half of the nineteenth century and the first civilian bands were formed in the 1880s and '90s, often by ex-servicemen who wished to form a pipe band in usually working-class towns and cities throughout Lowland Scotland. The pipe band community is a very organised and deeply social activity and they have consequently had a powerful effect within communities across the world. With the exception today of the global elite pipe bands, most bands are firmly based in their communities and perform regularly throughout the year for civic functions such as gala days, remembrance days, competitions and festivals. Pipe bands in Scotland are almost all competitive to differing degrees and many compete throughout the summer months in local, regional and national championships run by the Royal Scottish Pipe Band Association (RSPBA).[17]

Because they are usually highly local organisations, there are strong social ties between the members, and they also support strong intergenerational links with older players of the pipes and drums, often passing on their knowledge for free to younger players. Other institutions, notably the Boys Brigade, also play an important grassroots role in the formation and education of pipe bands in Scotland. Many of the leading pipers and drummers of the twentieth century were lucky to benefit from the free training and musical education in Boys Brigade and school pipe bands across the country.

Historically, pipe bands emerged within the British Army as part of an expansionist British imperialism in the nineteenth century and a disproportionate number of Scots served as soldiers all over the world. For decades during the eighteenth and early nineteenth centuries, the British Army had allowed individual Scottish officers to keep personal pipers, and music for the army had been provided by fifes and drums. However, in 1854 the British Army issued a War Office order that allowed each of the Highland regiments to pay for pipers and drummers and the military pipe band was born

(Cannon 1988: 152). The invention, by John McAdam, of the 'macadamisation' process for roads in the first decades of the nineteenth century meant that men could now more easily march in step with each other and coordinate their footfalls to military marching music. Pipers and drummers played duty tunes to mark the regular rituals of daily military life and also performed on the battlefields of the eighteenth and nineteenth centuries.

Much of the ritual and custom including the uniforms of kilts, brogues, black jackets and Glengarrys (military style headgear), as well as the marching, parading conventions and titles such as Pipe Major etc., were all imported into civil society direct from military life. The strong association and signification of military traditions alongside the iconic sound and image of pipe bands has made them very popular with quasi-military services such as the fire, police and prison services. The earliest non-military pipe bands include the Brechin Pipe Band (c. 1878), Kirriemuir Pipe Band (1979), the Burgh of Govan Pipe Band (1885), Accrington Pipe Band in England (1885) and the Wallacestone and District Pipe Band (1887).[18] Perhaps because of their strong influence on working-class and military and civilian services, pipe bands have become very popular throughout the Anglophone world. They were established in the United States and Canada in the very early years of the twentieth century and California, Ontario, British Columbia and the New York/New Jersey/Connecticut Tri-state areas have all had long histories of excellent Scottish traditional music.[19]

South Africa and New Zealand also have long diasporic histories of piping, drumming and Scottish traditional music. And like so many other aspects of Scottish traditional music, the entire pipe band world has organised itself into a distinct hierarchy with many organisations and associations throughout the world. It is fair to say that the community of musicians across the various Scottish traditional musical traditions has had a long-standing and deep-seated impulse for institutionalisation, structure and control, to a level not seen in any comparable traditional arts contexts elsewhere.

The music of pipe bands is also highly organised and as well as playing set pieces, as demanded by competition, also often features many new bagpipe and drumming compositions. Tunes for community bands often feature simple and compound time marches, often 4|4, 3|4 (sometimes called 'retreat' marches as a throwback to their military origins) and 6|8 marches. All of these tune types run over two or four parts (or 'measures'). Like dance music, each part is usually eight bars in length and repeated with a 2-bar question and answer structure. The structure of these tunes reflects both oral tradition where repetition is central to producing memorable tune structures, and their origins where 2-bar phrase structures emerged for dance. More elite bands will always play the march, strathspey and reel format, and often will play medleys of other tune types such as reels, airs, jigs and hornpipes. The march, strathspey and reel format is identifiably Scottish and is common across the piping, pipe bands, fiddle and accordion traditions.

Pipe band drumming developed originally from army drumming and has developed into a highly complex art. A pipe band usually has snare drummers, several tenor drummers and one bass drummer. Leading snare drummers of pipe bands have often been accomplished percussionists in other fields, and the drummer Alex Duthart (1925–86) brought many innovations to pipe-band snare drumming, introducing elements of Swiss and jazz style drumming. Elite pipe bands often have an international membership, have adopted many innovative musical practices, perform in major concert venues across the world and have become semi-professionalised in recent years. Leading pipe bands such as the Field Marshall Montgomery Pipe Band, the Simon Fraser University Pipe Band and Boghall and Bathgate Pipe Band practice throughout the year and can count some of the very best pipers and drummers amongst their membership.

Track 3. March, strathspey and reel performance by Field Marshal Montgomery Pipe Band, www.youtube.com/watch?v=_mwLnXCLFvk (see companion website: www. routledge.com/cw/mckerrell).

Listening guide: The pipe band begins with two drum rolls which allow the pipers to inflate their bags and coordinates the start of the march. In particular when listening try to listen to how the accents on the drums relate to the melody of the pipe tunes. Often drummers accentuate the key notes of the melody the pipers are playing, but similarly, they some-times play around with these emphatic stresses and bring more syncopation to the performance. The entire melody is performed in unison by the entire band. All the tunes are canonical pipe-band tunes and are considered traditional. Listen to the role the drones play against the melody of the bagpipe chanters. The drone provides melodic impetus for the melody of the pipes through a shifting aural relaxation and tension of the melody against the drone. All the pipers and drummers enter the strathspey and finally the reel very tightly in close unison. Because bagpipes do not have any dynamics, this role is taken on by the drummers who provide musical dynamics throughout the performance. Pipe bands are judged on how well they play together. In the video you can see the judges circling the pipe band taking notes. It is important to note that all the way through this march, strathspey and reel, there is a strong polarised rhythm between the long and short notes. This takes many months for the band to rehearse. What are the differences between the march, strathspey and reel? How do the drummers and pipers blend together?

Scottish traditional music and religion

Scottish traditional music as a social activity which people engage in for fun and ritual has had a fraught relationship with organised religion. Scots were ardent reformers, catching on quickly to the European Reformation in the sixteenth century, yet the Gaelic speaking areas of Scotland largely aligned with Roman Catholicism and went largely untouched by the Protestant Reformation. This was not simply an issue of language and literacy, but also cultural and it gave rise to one of the most distinctively Scottish musical traditions – Gaelic psalm singing. Very few Gaels, like Scots and English speakers in the sixteenth, seventeenth and eighteenth centuries could read their own language, although a far greater proportion of the population spoke Gaelic as their native, first language. The churches and clergy of Scotland therefore required a simple means of imparting God's word to their congregations. Out of this the tradition of precenting emerged. This is the tradition whereby the minister, priest or senior layperson in the congregation sings out a line of the Bible or other recognised religious text. The congregation then sing back the line in repetition together and in this way the churches sustained both the literate and oral traditions that were needed amongst populations where literacy was in a minority. In Scotland, this practice only survives amongst Gaelic speakers and is an incredibly beautiful sonic phenomenon recognised throughout the world as one of the great indigenously Scottish musical practices. The question of whether this is 'tradi-tional' music is perhaps not so important, but certainly it has been an oral tradition in Scotland passed down through communal and ritual practice in Gaelic communities for centuries. Today the practice survives mainly in the Western Isles, but there are many recordings of this music available online.[20]

One of the key aspects of this tradition is its astonishingly melismatic, ornamen-tal style, where the congregation sings back the text in a heterophonic manner, whilst maintaining a kind of overall unified performance of the contour of the melodic line.

Because Gaelic culture has also been a deeply musical culture, there have been many famous precentors in religious communities in the *Gaelteachd*, many with wonderful singing voices and particularised vocal styles. Listen to the way in which the contour is taken up by the singers and yet they approach the vocal line with great individual variance, arriving together through a shared conception of the melodic contour at the closing point of the line. Listen too for the highly ornamented vocal style characteristic of this type of Scottish vocal music.

Track 4. Scottish Gaelic psalm singing, www.youtube.com/watch?v=k3MzZgPBL3Q (see companion website: www.routledge.com/cw/mckerrell).

Mass-Mediated Music

> A lot of people who are interested in traditional music don't need to read about it in the papers or hear about it on the radio. Most traditional music in Scotland outside the folk revival has never had a voice in the media.
>
> (Freeland Barbour)

Recording, commerce and the mass media

Scottish traditional musicians were early leaders in this field, and the earliest recordings of Scottish traditional music were simultaneous with the commercialisation and emergence of the gramophone industry in the late nineteenth and early twentieth centuries. The earliest known recording of Scottish traditional music was the '28th May 1889 when the cornettist John Mittauer played "Within a mile of Edinboro Town"' (Dean-Myatt 2009). However, prior to this, Alexander Graham Bell, the famous inventor of the telephone, had been using the most famous Scottish song 'Auld Lang Syne', to demonstrate his new invention.[21] Companies such as Beltona, Parlophone and Columbia recorded many traditional musicians and music-hall performers in the first decades of the twentieth century. Undoubtedly the most famous amongst them was Sir Harry Lauder (Irving 1968).

Commercial companies in the early days of recordings for commercial release often held recording sessions in locations designed to capture sound to release to the market. The earliest known recording of a pipe band was done in this way in 1909 by the German Homophon Company, who recorded the Govan Police Pipe Band in Glasgow (Dean-Myatt 2009). In Chapter 7 we examine the mediation of Scottish traditional music and how this has brought about a deeper sense of mediatisation since the 1990s. Scottish traditional music has always been bookish and has had a very long tradition of publication and collection. However since the revival of the 1950s and '60s, Scottish traditional music has increasingly been broadcast on the radio and on television.

Revivalists, nationalisms and the creation of the past

Scottish traditional music is generally understood to have gone through a major revival in the 1950s and '60s. And the current popularity of Scottish traditional music around the world is largely due to the success of this revival. Yet, the revival in Scottish traditional music did not simply bring old tunes and songs to the attention of a new, younger and mostly urban audience; it also picked up where the romantic revivalists of the 1880s, 1890s and early twentieth century left off, leading eventually to the professionalisation and commodification of Scottish traditional music. The revival featured heavily the music of the travelling communities of Scotland and this provided a direct link for many to the performances of indigenous Scottish culture that many in the settled population had moved away from, lost or simply forgotten.

Scotland's folk revival was more heavily political than those in England and Ireland and the politics were very different to the earlier revivalists of the late nineteenth century and Edwardian period. From the nineteenth-century collectors the idea of gesunkenes Kulturgut was inherited by the Edwardian folk revivalists (Boyes 2010: 69). This is the idea, coined by the German Hans Naumann, that folk culture must have been originally composed by the upper classes or literate elite and gradually through time had been copied and 'descended' into the 'peasantry' where it became jumbled and unintelligible. These ideas and surrounding theories were later adopted by the Nazi party as partial justification for their extreme ideology (Green 1997: 420). They had followed the evolutionist ideas of the key thinkers in nineteenth-century England, such as Darwin and Tylor, and often transplanted biological concepts unaltered directly onto folk music. For instance, Tylor's doctrine of survivals:

> When a custom, an art or an opinion is fairly started in the world, disturbing influences may long affect it so slightly that it may keep its course from generation to generation, as a stream once settled in its bed will flow on for ages . . . an idea, the meaning of which has perished . . . may continue to exist, simply because it has existed.

These evolutionary ideas were central to the English first folk revival, and particularly to Cecil Sharp, who collected over 5,000 individual items of English and diasporic music and dance, making him still England's most significant (and much debated) collector. These ideas also motivated many collectors in England and Scotland to try and collect songs, tunes, dances and stories ideally from the older, rural and illiterate population. This ideology of revivalism meant that they felt they had the opportunity to collect music and dance from those people who were supposedly 'untarnished' by urbanisation and industrialisation, which had changed so much of both Scotland and England's way of life. These ideas might seem strange to us, and there is more than a casual elitism to them, although the late-Victorian and Edwardian revivalists who were collecting in Scotland and often in the home counties of England never mobilised their ideologies for overt racism in the way that happened in Germany. The racial or 'blood and soil' nationalism of the late nineteenth century is abhorrent to today's generation of scholars, and the First and Second World Wars radically shifted the scholarly position on race and ethnicity, introducing a strong strand of cultural relativism which became a foundational principle in the foundation of the scholarly discipline of ethnomusicology in the early 1950s. There has recently, however, been a rise again in the appropriation of traditional music by the far right in Britain, and subsequent fight-backs by the artistic communities[22] and nationalism in Scotland and within the twentieth-century folk revival moved irrevocably towards civic and social democratic forms of nationalism in the post-war period.

Scottish traditional music and the BBC

The principal provider of British public service radio broadcasting has been the BBC, and more specifically BBC Scotland. They began radio broadcasting in Scotland in

March 1923 with the then private British Broadcasting Company, which became a public corporation three years later (Harvie 1998: 128). Scottish television broadcasting by the BBC began in 1952, from the 'Kirk o Shotts' transmitter, to an estimated 41,000 television sets in Scotland. A useful proxy for the cultural impact of mass-mediated television broadcasting can be seen in the growth of television purchases, which grew in the following decade to 1,119,000. As Scotland's only public service broadcaster since the inception of radio, BBC Scotland has played a very significant and powerful role in the cultural transmission of traditional music and national culture. At times, this relationship has been enthusiastic, with the BBC acting as an important promoter of Scottish values and culture, however, BBC Scotland has also played a more authoritarian and paternalistic role in Scottish cultural life, both in terms of programming choices and as an active arbiter of musical aesthetics.

Scottish traditional music has found a home mostly on BBC Radio Scotland, which reaches around one million listeners a week[23] and which has provided dedicated programmes dealing with Scottish traditional music and arts more broadly since their inception. Most early broadcasts on BBC Radio Scotland were live, with an audience. In the first half of the twentieth century editing was elementary and very expensive, therefore most programmes required dedicated scripts for broadcast. For decades now, the BBC has produced Gaelic-language radio output via BBC Radio nan Gàidheal and its earlier incarnations, where Gaelic traditional music and culture take centre stage. With the exception of *Travelling Folk* and *Take the Floor*, Scottish traditional music only began to emerge more prominently in programming during the 1990s. This coincided with the emergence of traditional music in cultural policy in Scotland, particularly in the late 1990s and then with increasing visibility post-devolution in 1999.

In 2008 the BBC introduced BBC Alba, a television channel broadcasting in the evenings in partnership with the private firm MG Alba. Much of the output of this channel has featured professional traditional musicians and with the shift towards television has brought another layer of commodification for traditional music in Scotland: it has certainly attracted non-Gaelic speakers too.

BBC Radio Scotland has almost always provided one dedicated programme for the piping tradition, and one or two other radio programmes dedicated to Scottish traditional dance music in its wider contexts. Notable amongst these have been the long-running *Take the Floor*, with Robbie Shepherd, dedicated to the dance bands of Scottish music, and *Travelling Folk*, hosted by one of Scotland's greatest singers, Archie Fisher, from 1983–2010 and since then by the leading fiddler Bruce MacGregor. The latter has been the station's flagship 'folk' programme for decades. *Pipeline* and *Crunluath* serves pipers, drummers and pipe bands throughout the world.

There are other past and present commercial radio programmes produced in Scotland, focusing on traditional music, such as the long-running *The Thistle & Shamrock*,[24] hosted by Fiona Ritchie for the US National Public Radio but produced in Scotland, and the various Scottish traditional music programmes on Celtic Music Radio,[25] produced in Glasgow for both a local and international audience online. That there are not more independent or commercial radio stations dedicated to traditional music out of the approximate 650 radio stations in the United Kingdom is perhaps surprising, but as the listening audience moves towards greater choice in digitalisation, so the delivery and format of radio and television broadcasting is changing. In recent years, the World Pipe Band Championship has been broadcast on television and featured on their website. The BBC website featuring the programme and results in the weeks following the 2013 event 'had almost 200,000 page views, with around 70% from outside of the UK', which is one measure of the increasing digitalisation of traditional music (BBC 2013: 6).

The presentation of Scottish traditional music on radio and television has always been strictly controlled, with BBC producers acting effectively as cultural gatekeepers, setting the aesthetic standards for public consumption. In the twentieth century, and to some extent also now, the BBC has adopted a paternalist stance towards the listening and viewing public, not just in choosing and producing original creative content, but also acting as a patron of the arts (Duesenberry 2000: 23). However, broad comparison between the output of the BBC and the commercial or public broadcasters in other nations facing greater commercial competition can show that the BBC's virtual monopoly in British broadcasting has allowed them to produce programmes of very high quality. In the middle years of the twentieth century in particular, the BBC in Scotland actively acted as cultural arbiters of style and taste, and where traditional music was close enough to Western art music practices, the BBC felt warranted in imposing classical ideals of intonation, accuracy, and general musicianship.

The BBC has wielded, and continues to wield, great cultural authority through their aesthetic and programming choices in broadcasting Scottish traditional music. There is no physical difference between a 'fiddle' used for performing traditional music and a standard 'violin'; the differences lie in the performance practice and aesthetic approach. Fiddle music was therefore notionally familiar to BBC music producers who for most of the twentieth century were overwhelmingly classically-oriented, so they felt confident in actively making aesthetic choices in what and whom to broadcast. This influenced both the audience conception of what Scottish traditional music was and how it should be played. The BBC managed this through their choice of musicians, selection of material and went so far as to produce its own orchestral arrangements of fiddle tunes to be performed by its own in-house orchestra (Duesenberry 2000: 29). This was controversial and produced points of conflict between the BBC hierarchy and their audience of fiddlers in Scotland, particularly around the adoption of classical violin techniques for broadcasting traditional fiddlers and the ensemble arrangements of Scottish dance music. In the early decades of the radio broadcasts in Scotland, they favoured art music interpretations of traditional music: '"Refined" violinists were preferred to "rough" fiddlers, and the "rough" performers were accorded no status as representatives of a living tradition of musical folklore' (Duesenberry 2000: 44). Controversy was not limited to fiddling. As Neat notes, the BBC was a very reluctant broadcaster of Jeannie Robertson (and presumably other traveller singers):

> During the mid fifties recordings of her songs were broadcast as part of just two or three programmes . . . Hamish [Henderson] knew that 'taste' needs to be cultivated and he believed that the BBC was not doing its duty.
>
> (Neat 2009: 28)

> Indeed Henderson states in a letter to the Glasgow Herald newspaper that the broadcast he had made in June 1953 was, 'the first programme of Folksong sung by natural singers which the Scottish BBC has ever put on'.
>
> (Henderson in Neat 2009: 35)

Similarly, dance bands with fewer than four musicians, 'were rejected for a sound considered too thin' (Duesenberry 2000: 290). The BBC was particularly influential, via its own aesthetic ideals, derived from art music practice and its familiarity with big bands, in establishing unison melody playing, unified harmonic and rhythmic backing and rhythmic lift within Scottish dance band performance. Moreover, because piobaireachd and piping were distant from Western musical practices, performed on a different instrument with non-diatonic intonation and its own musical and aesthetic conventions unfamiliar to Western art musicians and producers; piping was treated as an Other, which allowed piping broadcasts to develop some editorial independence.

However, for a long time, and particularly since the millennium, the BBC has been a strong advocate of Gaelic traditional culture, positively producing and promoting Gaelic traditional song and Gaelic-medium broadcasting in Scotland and online. Also, as well as having a substantial influence on the publicly mediated understanding of Scottish music, the BBC has had a profound effect upon the fostering and promotion of talent in Scotland, both in terms of supporting and broadcasting new, young artists, as well as providing access to the leading performers of the day for various communities of musicians and audiences within Scotland and, increasingly, worldwide. In a progressively mass-mediated world, the BBC has been both the most significant patron and advocate for Scottish traditional music and its most powerful authority. Radio producers in particular have had virtually a free hand in influencing communal conceptions of musical taste through their choices about what, whose and which versions of traditional music should be broadcast.

During the 1940s and '50s the BBC began to audition beyond their regular broadcasters for fiddle players. Hector MacAndrew (1903–80), from Fyvie in Aberdeenshire, was one of the few traditional fiddle players to be regularly broadcast by the BBC after successfully moving through the Corporation's post-war audition process. He played a variety of music on the BBC, including performances in documentaries, recitals of solo fiddle music and performances on agricultural, drama and children's programmes (Duesenberry 2000: 146–7). He was a fiddler much respected by fiddlers themselves, and had the ability to play across traditional and classical music. His music is intense and expert and he himself suggested that the tune 'The Marquis of Huntly's Farewell' is the, 'finest strathspey in the Scottish idiom'.[26]

Figure 2.14 Portrait of North Eastern fiddler Hector MacAndrew, by kind permission of Ian Green of Greentrax Records (www.greentrax.com) and the MacAndrew family

Track 5. March, strathspey and reel 'John MacFadyen of Melfort / The Marquis of Huntly's Farewell / Marchioness of Tullibardine's Reel', as played by Hector MacAndrew from the album, *Legend Of The Scots Fiddle* (Greentrax CDTRAX335) (MacAndrew 2009). By kind permission of Ian Green of Greentrax Records (www. greentrax.com) (see companion website: www.routledge.com/cw/mckerrell).

Notes

1 In this book both Gaelic-, Scots- and English-derived Scottish traditional music is not compartmentalised by linguistic community (as previous writers have done). This supports this author's view of the permeability of those linguistic communities within Scotland and the diaspora in song and tune, and because scholarly representations of these linguistically-derived categories of song and society construct a false sense of social difference.

2 www.educationscotland.gov.uk/scotlandssongs/about/songs/lullabiesdandlings/index.asp. And at www.kistodreams.org.

3 Many of these are listed on https://thesession.org.

4 Royal Scottish Country Dance Society (RSCDS), www.rscds.org.

5 Scottish Official Board of Highland Dancing (SOBHD), www.sobhd.net.

6 See also Doherty (1996) on this point, and for further discussion of this debate and detailed research on Cape Breton music and the Scottish dimension see Conn (2012); Feintuch (2004); Sparling (2007, 2008, 2011).

7 www.feisean.org.

8 See musical examples at www.jimmyshand.com and www.youtube.com/watch?v=g3hAtxZXNrA.

9 www.jimmyshand.com [accessed 11 October 2014].

10 'Craicing' in this context refers essentially to informal socialising.

11 You can hear Sheila Stewart singing this ballad at the School of Scottish Studies archive online Tobar an Dulachais: www.tobarandualchais.co.uk/en/fullrecord/74637/8;jsessionid=B25922A0DF9888B8 B096937C6002BB5A.

12 You can hear a full version of this song being sung at: www.tobarandualchais.co.uk/en/full-record/16694/1. My thanks to Dr Andy Hunter for assistance with Scots language as well as his invaluable contributions as a singer and educator over the years to both myself and many others.

13 Embelton, Ian. World Pipe Band Championships streaming from BBC, www.rspba.org/html/news-detail.php?id=360 [accessed 13 March 2015].

14 See for instance the leading news site for piping, www.pipesdrums.com.

15 Piping Live! festival, www.pipinglive.co.uk.

16 An Commun Gaidhleach, www.ancomunn.co.uk.

17 The Royal Scottish Pipe Band Association, www.rspba.org.

18 See comments published by Keith Sanger: http://pipingpress.com/world-championship-winning-pipe-bands/history-of-the-pipe-band-and-the-worlds/ [accessed 17 August 2015]. This topic, amongst others, awaits further historical research.

19 See for instance the interactive map of pipe bands throughout the world at www.pipe-band.com.

20 See for instance www.youtube.com/watch?v=k3MzZgPBL3Q.

21 Personal communication, Morag Grant.

22 See for instance www.folkagainstfascism.com.

23 BBC Annual Report, 16 July 2013, www.bbc.co.uk/bbctrust/news/press_releases/2013/annual_report_ sc.html [accessed 9 May 2014].

24 www.thistleradio.com.

25 www.celticmusicradio.net.

26 www.youtube.com/watch?v=93-nZHGdMfA.

CHAPTER 3

Auld Lang Syne

'Auld Lang Syne' (lit. 'long time since') is the most ubiquitous Scottish song in the world. Yet a 2012 poll on BBC Radio Scotland[1] revealed that fewer than 40 per cent of Scots polled knew its meaning. The title acts as a synecdoche for the wider message of the song, which says that friendship remains despite change and the passage of time.[2] The phrase itself 'auld lang syne' was part of the culture of Scotland long before the eighteenth century and first appears in 1568 in the *Bannatyne Manuscript* (McLean et al. 2015). In almost all the hundreds of versions of this song in many languages throughout the world, this is the underlying sentiment which has appealed to many people of different cultures, race and faith. It is now sung in Scotland and throughout the world on 'Hogmanay', 31 December, as a symbolic song at the turning of the old year into the new. It is used in this way as a cultural trope in many Hollywood films from around the 1940s onwards. The song encapsulates a sense of social bond, loyalty and connection which, quite probably because of its universality, appealed to Robert Burns.

It appears in a number of versions before Burns' publication in *The Scots Musical Museum* (Johnson, 6 vols, 1787–1803), but in typical Burns fashion, he added two verses to the traditional version he learnt from oral tradition. The tune and words even appear in various forms in the original *Scots Musical Museum* and have appeared in hundreds of other arrangements across the world since that time.[3] In volume 1 (1787), for instance, there is a version published by Johnson from Ramsay entitled 'Auld Lang Syne', which includes an entirely different tune and a different set of more lyrical and complex verses which makes it essentially a different song altogether. Then in volume 5 (1796), Johnson publishes Burns' version which has essentially the same words that are known today, but to an older, different and very beautiful tune, that is arguably more authentic than the one commonly sung today.[4] Burns then goes on to publish a version with George Thomson in 1799 in his *Select Collection of Original Scottish Airs* (see Thomson 1793), which is set to the tune familiar to most people today. All this is before we even get out of the eighteenth century: and this is nowhere near a complete record of 'Auld Lang Syne's genesis. What it does show, however, is the sheer complexity and mythologisation that surround this song, which in a sense stands as a useful metaphor for the complex invention of history in Scottish music. In this way, 'Auld Lang Syne' also acts as a synecdoche for the mythologisation and invention of Scotland and Scottish musical history, which is the subject of this chapter.

Scottish Musical Beginnings

Very little is known of music in Scotland prior to the ninth century. In general, the lack of source material led Farmer (1929, 1947) to postulate theories of musical practice that were based upon better evidenced Irish sources. Problematically, this view suggested that Scotland was ethnically and culturally homogenous, which has never been the case. Bronze Age culture in Scotland is now thought to have been part of a Europe-wide web of exchange with elements of shared language and culture. So to talk about Scotland as a culturally or ethnically distinct nation, or even region in early history is the product of enlightenment ideals. Certainly even by the sixth century Scotland had developed four distinct racial populations:

> By the sixth century the area of modern Scotland is thought to have been inhabited by peoples now known as the Picts in the east and north-east of the country, the Dál Riata in the region of modern Argyll, Britons in Strathclyde and Anglo-Saxons in the Lothians. From the mid-ninth century the Picts and Dál Riata appear to have been united in some way under Cinaed mac Ailpín to form the new kingdom of Alba.
>
> (Clements 2009: 5)

Early Scottish people were a mix of both indigenous peoples and those who had travelled in from elsewhere in Europe and Scandinavia. Much of the evidence for early culture is derived from modern place names, from Pictish stones and crosses and from well researched archaeological evidence of lifestyles and material culture. The Gaelic name for Scotland is 'Alba', pronounced with a silent 'a' in-between the 'l' and the 'b' as in the Gaelic language. Scottish Gaelic is a distinct language which is similar to Irish Gaelic. The language of Scottish Gaelic is one of the main surviving Goidelic languages usually grouped along with Irish Gaelic and Manx. The other main Celtic languages today are Brythonic which includes Welsh, Breton and Cornish languages. There have been various categorising schema by linguists for these strands of old Celtic languages, including insular/continental and P-Celtic/Q-Celtic where distinctions rest upon word order and pronunciation. What is clear is that the Celtic languages survive in a geographical spread along the western fringes of Europe, including the key countries and regions in Brittany, Cornwall, the Isle of Man, Ireland and Scotland. It is no coincidence therefore, that the majority of the Celtic music festivals are found in these places, with the largest annually being the France's Festival Interceltique[5] at Lorient in Brittany. Closely rivalled by Glasgow's hugely successful Celtic Connections festival held in January each year.

Some of the earliest evidence of musical culture in Scotland is from the ninth and tenth centuries and includes stone carvings of harps or harpists, horns, pipes or pipers, or surviving musical instruments including the following:

- the Midhowe broch whistle (c. 200 BC–AD 100);
- the Burghead horn mount, a surviving decorated metal ring which is considered part of a horn because of a suspension ring found on the ring which indicates that it was used as a 'blast horn' rather than a 'drinking horn' (c. AD 800–900);
- the carved stones of Aberlemno in Angus, number three cross depicts two horn players and a roimboid harp (c. AD 750–850);
- the carved harper and triple piper on St Martin's cross, Iona (c. AD 750–800);
- the triangular carved harp on the Aldbar cross slab in Brechin Cathedral (c. AD 850–950);
- the Ardchattan cross slab from Etive which depicts at least a harper and piper (c. AD 900–1100);
- the harper carved on the Duplin cross of Forteviot (c. AD 800);
- the Monifieth cross shaft which depicts a carved harper (c. AD 800–1100);
- the harp and cymbal players on the Nigg cross slab (c. AD 750–850).

(See Clements 2009)

Some of these carvings and instruments are in and of themselves beautiful objects, regardless of their historical and cultural significance. But what they do tell us is that in early history, people living in what we now call Scotland had a vernacular musical culture which included harpists, horn players, triple pipes and, although not visually depicted, singing. Various discussions of these carvings all agree that much of the iconography on carved stones is Davidic and basically Christian, even though many of the carved stones demonstrate pre-Christian Pictish culture in the process of adopting elements of Christianity. What is interesting though is that the representations of harpists (for instance on the Duplin cross and Aldbar cross slab) are associated with the biblical iconography of David demonstrating the high status of the harp and harpists in early society. However, it is important to remember that at this time 'Scotland' did not yet exist. It was really later on in the thirteenth century that Scotland as a distinct country emerged through civic and territorial relationships as one of the leading scholars of early Scotland, Professor Dauvit Broun, explains:

> Scotland as a single country and people that we might recognise today emerged in the thirteenth century through the growing importance of royal authority for those with property and possessions. By the mid-thirteenth century the kings of Scots, who had for centuries been regarded as the ultimate authority in their realm, began to see themselves as of equal status with the king of England. Previously the concept of ultimate royal authority has been identified with geography. The king of Scots identified with the mainland north of the Forth, which was a perceived as an island divided from the rest of Britain by the Firth of Forth. This division can be seen vividly in Matthew Paris's map of Britain (around 1250). By the mid-thirteenth century a new idea of kingdoms as sovereign entities had been born. This meant that kingdoms were now seen as areas of jurisdiction with their own legal system. It was in this context that Scotland was first thought of as a sovereign, united country in a way we would recognise today.[6]

Unusually amongst nations, Scotland has had an unbroken popular sense of national identity from that time until today (Williamson 2009). Since the late seventeenth century, Scottish music has been regarded in cultural discourse as a distinct 'national music' and, despite the huge variety of different traditions, is still discussed as 'Scottish traditional music' because it is a category term that makes sense to those who perform it.

There is not, and never has been, any 'British traditional music'. Partly because of the emphasis on nationalism in traditional music since the enlightenment and partly because 'Britain' was always most readily deployed as a political identity of convenience and imperialist ambition, always secondary to the national identities of the English, Scots, Irish, Welsh, Manx and others who lived in it. Paradoxically, the only music that could reasonably be argued to be identified as 'British traditional music' and that has simultaneously become the single most potent musical symbol of Scotland, is the bagpipe tradition. It has acquired this symbolism for various reasons, principally amongst them, the use of pipers and pipe bands in the British Army in myriad campaigns of British Empire building throughout the modern period. Modern bagpipes, played on the shoulder with three drones and the melody-producing chanter, were really an invention of the eighteenth century and popularised worldwide by the British Army. Therefore, the closest to what might be termed British traditional music is the Scottish bagpipe tradition, as it is the only one genuinely used in the service of any British identity.

In early Scottish history there are pipes, however. The earliest evidence, such as that at Saint Martin's cross on the Isle of Iona, suggests that triple pipes were the earliest form of bagpipes. These are generally a mouth-blown instrument with several cylindrical cane or reed tubes with reeds cut into the body of the tube, the mouth acting as the reservoir of air. Extensive practice-based research recently suggests that this triple-pipe tradition could have been similar to the surviving performing tradition of the Llauneddas in contemporary Sardinia. In fact, Brown suggests that the addition of the bag to already pre-existing triple pipes in Scotland was an obvious idea and the transition from triple pipes to bagpipes probably happened in the fourteenth century, as bagpipes became established in Scotland (Brown 2006).[7]

Early Modern Scottish Traditional Music

The key social event in Scotland in the early modern period[8] which had a profound impact upon Scottish life was the religious Reformation of the mid-to-late sixteenth century. The influence of the Reformation in Scottish musical life was to start to divorce spiritual life from vernacular life, including music. In sixteenth- and seventeenth-century Scotland, traditional music was of course most often found as dance music, but evidence from personal tune books and manuscript collections demonstrates that Scotland had a rich tradition of musically literate musicians who did not see traditional music as distinct from other genres such as religious or art music; a compartmentalisation so ingrained in contemporary culture. In Scotland, the Reformation was zealous largely because of the influence of John Knox, whose leadership encouraged successive generations of ministers and leading individuals either discouraging or banning music, not just from the kirk (Scots lit. 'Church'), but also in community life too. Scotland did however support a network of busy music schools often run by town councils, and over many decades these existed in early modern Scotland in towns and cities such as Aberdeen, Ayr, Cupar, Dumbarton, Dundee, Edinburgh, Elgin, Glasgow, Inverness, Irvine, Lanark and St Andrews. Boys were trained in musical literacy, singing and instrumental playing up until the age of about fifteen, and they would form the choir for the local church where the music master was usually also the precentor (Johnson 1972: 9). In the seventeenth century organs, bagpipes, fiddles, drama and sophisticated choral music were all deemed to be devious influences on the people which would stand in the way of their direct communication with God, and were therefore banned.

We know that in the sixteenth and seventeenth centuries there was a range of home-made instruments as well as professionally constructed ones. *The Complaynt of Scotland*, published in 1548 in Edinburgh, details some of the homemade instruments, including the trump, the corne pipe, the pipe maid of ane gait horne (the stock and horn) and the reed or whistle which was a small whistle formed from an 'excavated elder branch' (Johnson 1972: 88). These various instruments existed alongside the bagpipes which the material record shows existed in forms as variable as the localities they were produced in (for a more detailed discussion see Cheape 2008). Constructed from hard native woods such as pear wood, these bagpipes often had two drones instead of the more familiar three which we know today were a late-eighteenth-century innovation.

This oppressive Reformation zeal that had held sway over Scottish social life in the seventeenth century really disintegrated quite quickly at the start of the eighteenth century. However, interestingly, in the Highlands and Islands, or in the *Gaelteachd* (lit. 'the Gaelic-speaking area'), many of the older orders of Gaelic poets, musicians, *filidh*, doctors and other high status individuals, did make the transfer to Protestantism as clergy (Newton 2003: 3). Although Protestantism had reached the Highlands and Islands in the sixteenth, seventeenth and early eighteenth centuries (notably in Argyll), it was only in the 1780s with the advancement of a grassroots Evangelical movement, which coincided with the first really widespread Clearances, that Protestantism had its greatest impact in the Highlands and Islands of Scotland (Newton 2003). Opposition to Protestantism, and to the ministers that evangelised it in the *Gaelteachd*, did emerge in music, with many dance tunes and songs written to complain and satirise the clergy, such as '*Coma Leam am Ministeir*' ('I don't care about the minister'), '*Diel Stick the Minister*', and songs such as the Argyll Gaelic song, '*Am Ministeir 's Am Bàillidh*' ('The minister and the bailiff') (Newton 2003: 6).

Mrs MacLeod of Raasay

(traditional arr. S. McKerrell)

Figure 3.1 The traditional reel 'Mrs MacLeod of Rasaay'

It is also in the sixteenth century where we find the first mention of the reel as a form of particularly Scottish dance music. Today, the reel can be simply defined as a tune type in cut common tempo (a 2|2 time signature) with regular patterns of four free-flowing, swung quavers per beat. In Scotland, the quavers tend to be performed in an approximately long-short-long-short pattern within each beat. This tune type is first mentioned in the proceedings of a 1591 witch trial at North Berwick (Lamb 2013). The reel itself has gathered over decades scholarship that supports the idea of it as an indigenous Scottish dance form (see for example Gelbart 2007: 31). One of the most archetypal reels in Scottish traditional music is the very old tune 'Mrs MacLeod of Raasay':

Track 6. A reel, 'Mrs MacLeod of Rasaay' (see companion website: www.routledge.com/cw/mckerrell).

Herder, Ossian and the mythologisation of Scotland

A German named Johannes Gottfried Herder (1744–1803) was the first to coin the term *volkslied* or 'folksong' in an essay about Ossian and song in the collection *Von Deutscher Art und Kunst: Einige Fliegende Blätter* ('Of German Style and Art') in 1773.[9] He was influenced by Scottish and English collecting that had already begun, such as Bishop Percy's collection of songs from Northumberland. Herder is for me, the first figure in the conscious scholarship of traditional music, and the person who begins the coagulation of nature, nation, folk and music to suggest that the traditional music embodies the natural, true spirit of the national character. However Gelbart has challenged this, suggesting that there were a number of other Scottish writers in the 1760s and earlier, who produced a discourse of nationalism, nature and its relationship to Scottish traditional music before Herder (Gelbart 2007). These include English and Scots writers of the eighteenth century such as James Beattie, Joseph Ritson, Bishop Percy and, of course, James MacPherson. However, it is probably not too bland a generalisation to suggest that the scholarship of traditional music really only took off in the early nineteenth century, and it was only at this point in history that Herder's writings were becoming known in Britain (Gelbart 2007: 105).

It was Herder who established the principle motivation for the literate elite to collect traditional culture, through his invention and consolidation of the idea of the spirit of the nation (the *nationalbildung*) which he felt could be found in its purest form amongst the oral songs and poetry of the 'peasants' in the country. This idea of the authentic spirit or national culture existing amongst the illiterate members of society became extremely powerful in eighteenth- and nineteenth-century Europe and inspired hundreds of antiquarian upper-class men and women to go out and collect, or to compile from previously published material, the folk songs, sayings and culture in their own countries. The term 'folklore' was not coined until 1846, in a letter by William John Thoms, an English antiquarian, to the *Athenaeum*.

However, this might have been problematic in Scotland, because Scotland by the mid-eighteenth century was amongst the most literate nations in Europe. This was achieved through the widespread influence of Church-led education in Reformation Scotland. Protestantism ideally centred on the individual's relationship with God, and so the Church felt that it was useful for children to learn to read – ideally the Bible. However, importantly, the Reformation was conducted in Scotland mainly in English and Latin, which left Gaelic society largely Catholic. This meant that the songs, tunes and folklore of the Scottish people were remembered, transmitted, popularised and altered in *both* written and oral form. By the opening of the nineteenth century, educational reforms, capitalism and the remarkably fast urbanisation of Scotland led to an explosion in publication of traditional music, poetry and literature. Sir Walter Scott was key in this period, both for inventing a Celtic romanticism, but also largely responsible for inventing the English language novel. Scotland has consequently always had the reputation amongst scholars of traditional music and song as one of the most bookish nations on earth.

Ossian

One of the key factors in the rise of romantic nationalism in the whole of Europe, and in the rest of the English-speaking world, was the incredible popularity of James MacPherson's *Ossian*, a published book of 'translated' ancient Gaelic oral poetry, brought to the attention of the aristocracy by a highly entrepreneurial schoolteacher from Perthshire – James MacPherson, the 'rude bard of the North'. This small book and its successive publications in the 1760s were crucial in forming a sense of 'Celtic romanticism' of Scotland's past and for powerfully embedding this sense of Scottishness in the minds of the elite across Europe. The interesting fact is, however, that although there was, and continues to be, controversy around how much of MacPherson's material was invented and how much was genuine oral poetry, it is undeniably true that the so called 'translation' was in fact based upon elements that were genuine ancient oral epic poetry. Scotland has a rich heritage of Gaelic epic poetry that was orally transmitted and recorded in the minds of bards over several hundred years, from medieval through early modern and even into the modern period post-1750. The central features of the Celtic romanticisation of late-eighteenth- and early-nineteenth-century Scotland include:

- identities founded upon an imagined, rural and noble past;
- the music and poetry of harpists (clarsairs). Usually focusing on epic poetry that contains something of the essential 'das volk' of the national peoples;
- wandering noble bards, of high status who hold a disappearing (or disappeared) high vernacular art;
- a sense of an authentic national culture founded on a purity of race.

These mythologies were crucial in forming the sense of Scottishness, Welshness and Irishness in opposition to the dominant Englishness, through those involved in constructing romantic nationalism in the nineteenth century. The reason they are so important to understanding traditional music is that this sense of a romantic, often feminine, national Other in relation to the dominant imperialist notion of England, profoundly influenced the type of music, and the way in which it was presented throughout the nineteenth and twentieth centuries. Another reason why it is important to understand this conceptual time is that it founded a sense of racial nationalism.

This form of nationalism has scarred humanity, and was an ideological part, ultimately, of the grotesque, inhuman acts of the Great War and the Second World War through the twisted ideology of National Socialism. It is true to suggest that the earlier work of folk music antiquarians and collectors was used as partial justification by the Nazis for their campaigns against Jews, homosexuals, Roma, blacks and other racial and ethnic groups. Indeed many in the Nazi party saw Herder as the 'fountainhead of the whole nationalist movement' (Atkins 2010: 19). Nazis, fascists and the extreme right have always appropriated folk and traditional music as their own, in order to embody racist and highly problematic notions of the national self. Goebbels was particularly keen on folk music and utilised it as Nazi propaganda (Machin and Richardson 2012). More recently this has occurred in England, with the British National Party issuing compilation albums featuring tracks from English folk musicians, included against their will. There has been a strong reaction against this.[10] The relationship between traditional music and the nation has always been close and problematic, and it is therefore important to understand how the romantic nationalism of the late eighteenth and nineteenth centuries affected our own understanding of traditional music today. The legacies of MacPherson's *Ossian* are important and in some (more ephemeral ways) are still with us.

In the 1760s MacPherson published several volumes of epic poetry which were, he claimed, from oral sources and gave the histories of Fingal (Fionn) and his son Ossian, c. twelfth century. They were part of a wider movement of romanticism and are essentially unreadable today. The language is flowery and to the modern reader feels archaic. Even in MacPherson's time, however, he intended the language to be deliberately archaic to demonstrate the oldness of the texts. He was not alone: a number of other texts were published in the eighteenth century that mythologised Scottishness, Welshness and Englishness, such as Ritson's celebrations of 'Robin Hood' (1795) and Welsh mythologising from Edward Lluyd and William Pughe (1690–1790s). It is true to say, however, that the presentations of Scottish, Irish and Welsh mythological texts of epic poetry were deliberately countercultural tropes which stood in opposition to the sense of Englishness. London dominated Scotland, Wales and Ireland politically and militarily throughout the eighteenth century. The poems that MacPherson had already 'translated' from Gaelic were published in 1760 as *Fragments of Ancient Poetry, Collected in the Highlands of Scotland, and Translated from the Galic or Erse Language*. The Gaelic Homer had arrived.

MacPherson himself was also part of the success of the Ossian mythology. He was an educated middle-class Highlandman, whose family had fought on the Jacobite side of rebellion in the mid-eighteenth century. Johnson suggests that Jacobite songs were not really popular in eighteenth-century Scotland, but were the product of nationalist composers largely between 1790 and 1820 (Johnson 1972: 4). There is no doubt, however, that MacPherson was skilled in his adaptation of Gaelic epic poetry, and his production of a coherent text owes much to his own style of English which emphasised the artful and otherness of the epic poetry. He had come into contact with the Edinburgh literati and through them with Horace Walpole and Thomas Gray, who were enthusiastic about the poetry. MacPherson was entrepreneurial and managed to leverage his success with the publication of his poems to transform himself from Highland school teacher to Westminster political aide, becoming deeply involved in the East India Company.

The principal reason why MacPherson's 'translations' of Gaelic epic poetry into English were so important was that in the mid-eighteenth century, the Gaelic Scots living in the Highlands and Islands represented an important cultural Other to the English, and also to Scots-language and English-speaking Lowland Scots. It was not unusual in the early eighteenth century for Lowland Scots making a trip into the Highlands to make a will before they departed (Burt in Gelbart 2007: 29). The idea of a 'primitive' race of Gaels, living quite close to home (an 'internal Other') was important for London- and Edinburgh-based aristocracy: the English needed the idea of the 'noble savage' in the North in order to create their own, morally and intellectually superior conception of themselves. The same process has been identified in relation to the Welsh and the Irish, not to mention the exotic Other which was to become a defining trope of Western societies in the nineteenth century. One product of this was the increasing trend in the late eighteenth century for 'Scots' songs and tunes, often composed and performed by Englishmen for English audiences.

The final published version of Ossian's poems are derived from real Ossianic poems in the cycle of Irish Gaelic poems from the later Middle Ages about Fionn MacCumhaill, the captain of the Féine, serving Cormac King of Ireland, in the third century AD. It is worth remembering that during the medieval and early history of Scotland and Ireland, poets and high-status musicians travelled freely between these countries within an autonomous Gaelic-speaking region in the northwest of Europe. Irish poems travelled to Scotland through shared medium of Gaelic and often the authentic Scottish bards (*filidh*) were trained in Ireland in the middle ages. In Scotland, the key difference in defining Scotland came with the Jacobite final failure in 1745 (Culloden) and the growth of trading and urbanisation of the 'British' Empire in the late eighteenth and nineteenth centuries. The Irish Gaelic and Scottish Gaelic traditions were very similar, however one of the distinguishing differences was that in Scotland, the eighteenth- and nineteenth-century collectors of traditional Gaelic poetry and song included women (Byrne 2010).

When one considers the idea of 'poetry' in the seventeenth and eighteenth centuries (and indeed into the nineteenth), it is important to realise that amongst Gaelic society this was almost exclusively an oral tradition, often where the poems were sung in complex metre to particular tunes and where the *filidh* had a high status in society. The most prominent amongst these women poets was Mairi nighean Alasdair Ruaidh (Mary Macleod 1615–1705) who was in the service of the MacLeod's of Dunvegan. Other key female poets included Mary MacPherson (Mairi Mhòr nan Òran 1821–98).

Figure 3.2 Portrait of James MacPherson by Sir Joshua Reynolds (1772) (by kind permission of the National Galleries Scotland [Acc. No. PG 1439])

Before Culloden, bards and oral tradition were treated with some disdain amongst the educated Lowland Scots society. For instance, Thomas Blackwell, a professor of Greek at Marischal College in Aberdeen published in 1735 *An Enquiry into the Life and Writings of Homer*. In this view, Blackwell focused on social context and the life of the ancient Greeks. Culloden and the Jacobite demise changed this view of Gaelic bardic society: they became, 'the last poets of a noble but doomed cause' (Trevor-Roper 2008: 84), and the 'noble savage' was born.

This came within a wider European movement, begun by Herder and the discovery of the *Nibelungenlied* (1755), a text of ancient Germanic racial origins, used in various imaginings of German nationalism including Wagner's *Ring Cycle* and Nazism. Despite being widely criticised in the 1760s in London, MacPherson's poems were a raging success on the European continent. They were seized upon by many key figures including Herder, and his pupil Goethe (influential in the 'Sturm und Drang' movement), Napoleon, etc. The controversy continued into the late eighteenth century and set up a very important trope for the coming romantic nationalism in nineteenth-century Scotland. The reason that these poems were so important to the identity of Scots and Europeans was that if the whole thing was a fake, then the noble savage image and national identity of Scotland at the time was founded upon crumbling pages – and, furthermore, there would not be an authentic Scottish literature. However, the overwhelming romantic movement of that time gathered up Ossian and Fingal and swept them along on a tide of imagined history. The importance of the Ossianic and Fenian epics to the nationalist imagination in Europe cannot be overstated:

> Ossian became the way for Europeans to look northward to find the savage in their midst, and MacPherson made sure that the savage they found was a noble one. The influence of Ossian across Europe need hardly be reiterated. It fired the imaginations of the German and French Romantics, from Herder to Napoleon to Brahms. It turned Scotland into a particularly popular tourist destination . . . and [through reinterpretation and later mythologizing of a natural and indigenous Other] would make possible an idea of folk music, described in specific, classifying terms, set apart from art music.
>
> (Gelbart 2007: 62–4)

As cultural nationalism began to gain ground in Edinburgh (and London), there was controversy surrounding any foreign influence on Scottish and English music. The most famous of these was the attribution that an Italian, David Rizzio, who worked in Edinburgh for two years, was responsible for much of the character of Scottish music. The attribution of this Italian's name was made by William Thomson (a Scottish singer-composer who travelled to London to publish and perform in the 1720s), who published the *Orpheus Caledonius* in 1725. Later, a well-known Scots composer, James Oswald, published in the 1740s various *Collections of Curious Scots Tunes* in London, attributing some tunes to Rizzio (Gelbart 2007). Rizzio was murdered in 1566 for reputedly being the lover of Mary Queen of Scots, and was known to have performed music at the Edinburgh court. The attribution of Italian origins to Scottish music was met with consternation amongst those attempting to stake out Scottish culture as a national entity with distinct and natural characteristics. Robert Fergusson, the poet and author wrote an 'Elegy on the Death of Scots Music' in 1792 which included the following lines:

> Now foreign sonnets bear the gree [prize]
> And crabbit queer variety
> Of sound fresh sprung frae Italy
> A bastard breed!
> Unlike that saft-tongu'd melody
> Which now lies dead.

(Fergusson in Gelbart 2007: 36–7)

Edinburgh was the hotbed of continental art music in Scotland, with Italians such as Nicolo Pasuali, Giusto Tenducci and Francesco Barsanti all making a living performing and teaching. Art music in seventeenth-century Scotland only really took hold in the musical life of Edinburgh, and to a lesser extent in Aberdeen and other cities. But there was a strong link between the compositional and performance of art music between Bologna and Edinburgh, largely due to the influence of key aristocrats in the 1680s onwards (Johnson 1972: 12).

Enlightenment Scotland and Traditional Music

The eighteenth century in Scotland was a time of transition in many ways, social changes brought about by the spread of capitalism into Gaelic culture changed Highland life forever; intellectual dialogue in the Lowlands established Scotland as the leading centre of enlightenment philosophy in the world and crucially; Scotland lost her status as an independent nation, subsumed into the United Kingdom in 1707. In 1603 Scotland had lost its monarchy when James VI, 'King of Scots' (Protestant) became King of England and Scotland (two states under one monarchy). Incidentally it was James the VI and I who gained control of large parts of Ulster and started the plantations in 1607. Scotland had previously tried to create its own Empire through a complete disaster of a scheme in the 1690s where many Scots nobles lost their wealth and subsequently aided the English in the Union of the Parliaments 1707, where many Scots nobles were effectively bailed out (see more in Chapter 4).

In eighteenth-century Scotland, two features of musical life were quite different to today. Firstly, the categories of 'folk' or 'traditional' and 'classical' or 'art' music were not yet formed and there was much porosity between various genres of music. Particularly noticeable in the fiddle tradition, many fiddlers of traditional Scottish music were trained also to perform art music, a situation which is gradually re-emerging amongst some of our most talented musicians today. Secondly, Scottish traditional music was still a functional music culture across the Highlands and Lowlands where local teachers and performers regularly played for dancing in a variety of contexts from the home to the ballroom. If one were an eighteenth-century Scottish fiddle player, it would make very good sense to be able to perform anything from bourrée to a local reel. Traditional tunes and minuets existed alongside one another in the repertoire of eighteenth-century Scottish fiddlers, but evidence from personal manuscripts, society minutes, letters and oral tradition all support the notion that the canon of traditional music at this time was overwhelmingly more dominant in Scottish culture than the art music tradition (Johnson 1972). The most significant fiddlers (and in some cases composers) from this period included Niel Gow, his son Nathaniel, William McGibbon (1690–1756) and Charles McLean (1712–65) all of whom were trained in the art music performance practice of the day making them eminently more employable.

With the exception of these notable fiddlers and elite musicians, 'traditional music' was largely an oral tradition passed amongst people by singing and playing. In the South of Scotland, vernacular songs included love songs, ballads telling the stories of Scottish culture and society, dance tunes, parodic songs, agricultural songs and many more genres. In the Highlands and Islands of Scotland, Gaelic culture and kinship remained strong despite the transition from agrarian to capitalist forms of social structure during the eighteenth century. The musical forms of eighteenth-century Gaelic Scotland were different to those found in the Lowlands, and revolved around clan society, work song and dance. As society changed, so did Scottish traditional music. The understanding of what traditional music was shifted from a functional meaning to a nationalist meaning. Traditional music effectively emerged as an idea in eighteenth-century Scotland more often discussed as 'folk music' or 'Scottish music', heavily linked to nature, the national spirit and to some important mythological constructions of Scottishness. Nature and 'naturalness' were absolutely central to the eighteenth-century conceptions of Scottish and other traditional music and vernacular culture. At the beginning of the eighteenth century, what discourse there was around 'Scottish music' was only really beginning to develop. However, Scottish 'national music' was 'natural' and represented a primarily social function (for dance, funerals, weddings, etc.) where Scottish people and their music were a part of nature. Later in the 1780s and '90s, Scottish music as a form of national music, emerged as the 'natural' essence of the racially distinct people.[11] In this new way of thinking, nature shifted to become the opposite of civilisation, and the 'nature' and the 'naturalness' of Scottish traditional music became the justification for the substantial shift towards the search for origins and collection which was only just beginning.

It is also this transition beginning in the 1760s onwards where we find the idea really take root of traditional music, or 'folk music', as the music of the people. Before this, national music (which was more the terminological locus of musical discourse in England, Scotland, Ireland and Wales in the eighteenth century) was assumed to have been written first by the mythological bards and then the minstrels – all high status individuals who were ascribed with the composition of many of the key tunes and songs. The first to explicitly declare this was the egalitarian Professor of Moral Philosophy and Logic at Marischal College in Aberdeen – James Beattie. He is one of the first enlightenment thinkers to make explicit the romantic link between national music and a racial nationalism:

> There is a certain style of melody peculiar to each musical country, which the people of that country are apt to prefer to every other style. That they should prefer their own, is not surprising; and that the melody of one people should differ from that of another, is not more surprising, perhaps, than that the language of one people should differ from that of another.
>
> (James Beattie in Gelbart 2007: 89)

Before the idea of traditional Scottish music as the 'music of the folk' and thus springing directly from a national race, there were many origins theories of Scottish music including:

- It was widely held in the seventeenth and eighteenth centuries that Scottish music owed its distinctive character to the wandering ancient bards and minstrels who sought patronage in medieval Scotland. This mythology was based on partial truth in that there were in the medieval period a number of high-status bards, particularly in Gaelic society who roamed, seeking patronage from various aristocratic houses. That they were responsible more generally for inventing Scottish music is related to the association of these characters with nature and the natural order of pre-enlightenment life.
- George Thomson in his *Select Collection* suggests that really, Scottish music 'took its rise among real Shepherds' around the River Tweed (Thomson 1793).
- David Rizzio was widely suggested in the early eighteenth century as the progenitor of Scottish 'national' music – a view highly controversial given his Italian origins.
- James I was also thought by many for a long time to have composed the essential characteristics of Scottish music in the eighteenth century.
- The monks of Melrose were credited by some aristocratic writers with the invention of Scottish music (Gelbart 2007: 90).
- Many writers starting with Charles Burney suggested that Scottish 'national' music was very similar to Chinese 'national' music and theorised a shared heritage in the ancient Greek music. This problematically orientalist and elitist idea now seems ridiculous, but was widely subscribed to in the early nineteenth century and tenaciously kept appearing in writings inspired by cultural evolutionism right up until the mid-twentieth century when cultural relativism really began to replace universal evolutionism in scholarly discourse on traditional musics, and the discipline of ethnomusicology emerged (see Chapter 9 for a more detailed discussion).
- Samuel Bayard has suggested that the entirety of Anglo-American traditional music is derived from the oral tradition of around 55 tune families – and that all traditional songs and tunes currently or previously known in Scotland, England, Wales, Ireland, America, Canada, and any other Anglophone nations, are derived from these basic *ideas* of tunes (see Chapter 9).

This period also saw the beginnings of music publishing in Scotland, which began properly in Edinburgh in 1725 with the publication of William Thomson's *Orpheus Caledonius*. Key publications of the eighteenth century in Scottish music include: Allan Ramsay's *Tea-table Miscellany* (1723); James Oswald's *The Caledonian Pocket Companion* (1745); and William Napier's *A Selection of the Most Favourite Scots Songs* (1790). However, the key publication of Scottish music of the eighteenth century, which was to have a profound influence upon the construction of what became national music, is *The Scots Musical Museum*, a three-volume collection of music published in Edinburgh between 1787 and 1803 by James Johnson (1754–1811). The collection contains over 600 tunes and songs, of which Robert Burns contributed about a third. This is the most significant historical source of Scottish traditional music and continues to be used as a sourcebook of songs.

George Thomson was an active member of the Edinburgh Musical Society, the pre-eminent musical institution in Scottish art music in the eighteenth century. Thomson was responsible for persuading continental composers including Pleyel, Kozeluch, Haydn, Beethoven, Weber, Hummel and Henry Bishop to arrange classical versions

Figure 3.3 Portrait of Robert Burns by Alexander Nasmyth (1787) (by kind permission of National Galleries Scotland [Acc. No. PG 1063])

of Scottish traditional tunes (Johnson 1972: 42). Johnson suggests that the 1770s were the highlight for art music in Edinburgh society largely because of the presence of key continental musicians and composers including Johann Georg Christoff Schetky, Domenico Corri, Franceso Barsanti, Johann Friedrich Lampe, Nicolo Pasquali and the 'great castrato' Tenducci (Johnson 1972: 13). The Scottish Earl of Kelly was the pre-eminent Scottish-born art music composer of the late eighteenth century. Corelli and Handel were the favoured continental art music composers in the early-eighteenth-century Edinburgh music scene (Johnson 1972: 34–5).

Robert Burns

A key figure in the eighteenth century, and across the history of Scottish traditional music, is Robert Burns (1759–96), who very quickly after his death assumed an iconic status both at home and abroad. Today, Burns' poetry and song and his character as an individual have been mythologised and re-invented countless times since his death in 1796. In some senses Burns stands as a trope for Scottishness and to examine how he has been understood at different times in history is to examine the state of cultural nationalism in Scotland.

Burns was born into a farming family in 1759, in Alloway. He was a complex person who had many voices. There is no doubt that he was one of the greatest poets and song writers in European history and his work ranges from thick, localised Scots to high 'Johnsonian' English. He is celebrated throughout the world as a poet, but it is his songwriting, and arrangement where he made his greatest contribution to Scottish traditional music. He celebrated Scottishness and Scots language and as well as being a fine wordsmith was also a good fiddler. His work resonates today because of his brilliance at capturing universal emotional resonances and his ability to marry meaningful text with attractive melodies. He is unusual in the sense that he was exceptionally good at lyrical composition as well as poetry, which often do not go hand-in-hand. One of the reasons we know about Burns' work is that he was a prolific author and published many song settings as well as poems in his own lifetime. He published his *Poems Chiefly in the Scottish Dialect* in 1786 and crucially for Scottish traditional musicians contributed about half of the total 600 songs in James Johnson's *Scots Musical Museum*.

Burns wrote many wonderful songs, but one of the best loved is 'My Love is Like a Red, Red Rose'. Unashamedly sentimental, this song is one of the best-known Scottish songs, probably only superseded by 'Auld Lang Syne'. The text demonstrates Burns' brilliant ability to capture universal emotional metaphors and one of the key metaphors in the song is that of the red rose. As well as signifying love through the colour of the flower, the red rose also signals the dual nature of human love – the flower representing the beauty and passion of love and the thorns symbolising the pain that is so often felt between those who are in love, or have loved. Burns extends the metaphors in the song through his use of lines that evoke the permanence and depth of love that can be experienced, suggesting that his love will last until the rocks melt with the sun. The song in total captures in very few words and through its melody much of the immanent feelings of being in love and has as a consequence been recorded many times. My personal favourite is the recording by the late Scottish singer Davy Steel.

Track 7. 'My Love's Like a Red, Red Rose', sung by Davy Steel (see companion website: www.routledge.com/cw/mckerrell).

> O my Love's like a red, red rose,
> That's newly sprung in June:
> O my Love's like the melodie,
> That's sweetly play'd in tune.
>
> As fair art thou, my bonnie lass,
> So deep in love am I;
> And I will love thee still, my dear,
> Till a' the seas gang dry.
>
> Till a' the seas gang dry,
> my dear, And the rocks melt wi' the sun;
> And I will love thee still, my dear,
> While the sands o' life shall run.
>
> And fare-thee-weel, my only Love!
> And fare-thee-weel, a while!
> And I will come again, my Love,
> Tho' 'twere ten thousand mile!
>
> (Sung by Davy Steele, *Songs of Robert Burns, vol. 4*)

Figure 3.4 Portrait of the fiddler Niel Gow by Henry Raeburn (1787) (by kind permission of the National Galleries Scotland [Acc. No. PG 160])

At the same time as Burns was delighting the aristocracy and high society in Edinburgh, Niel Gow (1727–1807), the fiddler from Strathbraan in Perthshire, was also making a very good living from performing for dances at home and elsewhere throughout Scotland and in London. Burns met Gow in a pub in Dunkeld in 1787 where they allegedly swapped tunes. Both were the pre-eminent figures of eighteenth-century Scottish traditional music. It was at this time, just as Burns and Gow were establishing their reputation through performance and publication, that Scottish traditional music was really beginning to be published properly.

The end of the eighteenth century saw some very important collections of traditional music and song published, not least because it was at this time that the idea of the 'nation' and the romanticism of the social elite found expression in their efforts to collect the traditional music around them.

Gow and the birth of the fiddle

With such strong European influences on Scottish traditional music, it is no surprise that many of the art music techniques brought to Scotland by Italian musicians rubbed off on Scottish traditional musicians. In particular, the key fiddler in enlightenment Scotland, Niel Gow who, as well as having an unusually spelled first name, was considered the pre-eminent fiddler of his day. He was paid to play throughout Britain, but earned his living as the fiddler to the Duke of Atholl at his home in Perthshire.

His legacy through composition has been significant for Scottish fiddling, but he also shifted the musical styles in Perthshire and the North East of Scotland through his technical innovation.

The eighteenth century has been regarded as the 'golden age' of Scottish fiddling and Gow and his sons John and Nathaniel (1763–1831) in particular continued his performance traditions and compositional talents through publication and service for the aristocracy. Gow was born in Strathbraan, near Dunkeld, and worked most of his life for the Duke of Atholl earning on average about £5 per year. He was renowned both for his style of fiddling, which was particularly sought after for high society dances, and for his invention of the 'up-driven bow' technique in Scottish fiddling (Π v v v). This is a difficult manoeuvre where the player draws one long down bow and three short, but loud, up bows. In the eighteenth century it was common for fiddlers to play traditional music with cellists (sometimes referred to as 'bass fiddle'), and there was much greater porosity between musical genres such as traditional, or classical music than there is today.

Gow is probably best remembered for his compositions (between 50 and 80), and for his meeting with Robert Burns in 1787 at the Inver Inn. There has always been some cross-attribution of fiddle compositions between Niel and his son Nathaniel, and the provenance of many of the most famous tunes is still debated. Some of his most famous include 'Farewell to Whisky', written in 1799 after a particularly bad harvest led to a ban on whisky production, and 'Welcome Whisky Back Again', written the following year, when the ban was lifted.

Track 8. 'Niel Gow's Lament for the Death of his Brother Donald', performed by Bruce MacGregor, www.youtube.com/watch?v=WObU8jGOEtM (see companion website: www.routledge.com/cw/mckerrell).

Listening guide: Pay particular attention to the characteristics that you think make it traditional music and/or classical music. Is there a difference you can hear? What sort of assumptions do you make about traditional music or classical music for the fiddle? Pay particular attention to identifying double stopping, ornamentation, the internal structure, vibrato and the use of rubato.

Romanticism and Scottishness in Traditional Music

One of the key effects of the romantic nationalism that swept through Britain and consumed much of the nineteenth-century discourse around Scotland, was that in seeking out the pure, rural, older forms of culture as the natural and authentic national culture, the romantics created them as Other. This was a shift from the early-to-mid-eighteenth century, where the naturalness of Scottish traditional music and vernacular culture had been very much a part of the conception of music as a mimetic functional activity. In other words, prior to the enlightenment, traditional music was a form of social activity for dancing, weddings and celebrating that essentially reflected rules and patterns of living that existed in nature. The shift from the 1760s onwards involved the recasting of nature through rationalism, positivism and enlightenment thought as an opposing humanity; the nature–nurture dialectic emerged at this time. Romantics invoked the naturalness, rurality and oldness of (aspects of) Scottish traditional music as evidence of its supposed purity and thereby refashioned their own literate, urban and largely upper-class identities in contrast to their own internal low Other.

Walter Scott and the (re-)invention of Scottish music

Sir Walter Scott's *Minstrelsey of the Scottish Border* (first published in February 1802) was a key publication in what became the romanticisation and mythologising of Scotland. It is a collection of Border Ballads supposedly drawn from oral tradition by Scott. Scott was incredibly creative, and as well as having a profound effect upon the way in which we view 'Scotland' and 'Scottishness' through his fiction writing, the influence of his cultural mythologising has been tremendous. In his *Minstrelsy* there are many varied items of songs and ballads and, in common with many other nineteenth-century collectors, he saw himself as collecting the 'last leaves' of oral tradition. He had himself spent time recovering as a child from polio where he heard many traditional ballads from his grandmother and was taught to read by his aunt Janet.

We know that Scott did in fact make several trips into the Borderlands in Teviotdale and Liddesdale, and that as Sherriff of Selkirk, would have had the opportunity to meet many ordinary citizens. He also drew on many of his friends and family for material. The collection of songs and ballads does therefore reflect in some ways the oral tradition at the end of the eighteenth century in the Scottish Borders, however Scott often invented stories or altered them to suit his own purposes. The only ballad we know for certain Scott got directly from a singer is 'The Fray of Suport', from 'John Graham of the Nook', also known as 'The Lang Quaker' who was an itinerant mender of watches. Scott went to meet him with Robert Shortreed in Liddesdale in the 1790s, who describes his singing as 'the awfuest and uncoest howling sound I ever heard'.[12]

The importance of this collection, however, lies in its commercial success. It established Walter Scott amongst the Edinburgh literati of the early nineteenth century and established his reputation ahead of his massively popular Waverley novels. The world that Scott created in this collection, with sprawling and copious stories and mythologising (often in footnotes) was influential during the nineteenth century for many collectors and publishers who came after and, therefore, for the construction of Scottishness we have inherited today. For Scott, as for many other romantics of his time, the hills were unchanging, the people proud and fierce, the traditions ancient and noble, and the resulting publications in this period construct all of these ideas in song and in their accompanying introductions and notes.

Romanticisation also had other effects on the instrumental music and performance of many forms of traditional music including everything from straightforward invention to subtle adaptation and subversion of older oral traditions. For example, Iain MacInnes has shown how some of these romantic ideals altered the piping tradition through the agency and patronage of the Highland Societies of London and Scotland (MacInnes 1989). He has shown how the period from the first bagpipe competition in 1781, sponsored by the Highland Society of London, until the 1840s was one of experimentation, invention and change. The Highland Societies of London and Scotland held great power over the performing community, who were in the main working-class pipers, largely through their financial incentives and social position. They instigated the romantic full costumes for pipers and invented many rules and musical conventions for their competitions, some of which still remain today. These competitions took place in an atmosphere of feverish excitement and the pipers played against romantic 'Highland Glen' backdrops. The gentlemen of their committees decided who could compete and often what they would play. Prizes and patronage were substantial and at that time often represented a livelihood for these pipers, and therefore, the competitions attracted the top pipers of the day. These players were required to provide written scores of piobaireachd in order for the judges who did not have access to the oral culture of piobaireachd and light music performance to determine whether or not the piper had 'gone off the tune'. In this way, the Highland Societies of London and Scotland bred a sort of standardisation of piobaireachd, and controlled via their higher social status and financial power, the performance of the leading pipers in Scotland. This sort of control of the performing community from above eroded the oral nature of transmission because they sought 'scientific' notations of piobaireachd which in turn changed forever the way in which the music was taught.

However, many pipers in the nineteenth century, and into the twentieth century, still relied heavily on oral transmission simply because they could not read music. Interestingly, their influence extended to the physical construction of the instruments too. MacInnes notes that the bagpipe as we know it, with three drones, was not completely standardised in Scotland even by the early nineteenth century, and demonstrates through competition records that the two-drone bagpipe finally went out of fashion in the early 1820s and was banned by the Highland Societies because it 'required less exertion for inflation' (MacInnes 1989: 90). In these ways, the romantic nationalist instincts of the landed elites in the nineteenth century had a profound effect both upon the performing community themselves and the music that they played.

Summary

We have seen that Scottish traditional music cannot really be considered one cohesive repertoire, set of practices or aesthetic, and that the forces that have shaped it are diverse and often with very long historical antecedents. Scottish traditional music, like many forms of music, lives most fully in our lives when people are playing, listening, teaching or talking about it. This sense of doing gives us a deep feeling of belonging, which is why the social life of traditional music is so important. Scottish cultural life is increasingly varied, but has always been deeply literate and historically-aware. That is perhaps why there has been so much mythologizing and debate about the authenticity and nature of Scottishness, and what traditional Scottish music can and might be. However, there are certain trends or tropes that we can draw out from our brief examination of just a few of the diverse social situations in which Scottish traditional music acts as a social force. The first of these is a deep sense of nationhood and the national constructed through Scottish traditional music. This includes a strong stream of discourse and sense of belonging to an alterior Other, to the idea of Britain, English and Britishness. The second is the long institutionalisation and sense of structure and control that has permeated much of the social life of Scottish traditional music. The third is the notion of Scotland as a magical, otherworldly place belonging both to ordinary human beings and to the fantastical fairies, changelings and the mystical Other. Many traditional cultures in Northern Europe have this supernatural influence but it is perhaps most strongly expressed in Scottish ballads and Gaelic culture. These three constructs, alterior nationalism, institutionalisation and the supernatural, for me constitute at various times and in different contexts and balances, part of the special significance of Scottish traditional music and traditional culture more broadly. What is unique amongst neighbouring traditions such as Ireland, Brittany and Wales is the degree to which Scots themselves have mythologised, re-imagined and manufactured their own past and musical identities, reinventing their belonging and identity through multiple generations.

Notes

1 Poll results broadcast on BBC Radio Scotland Hogmanay programme (31 December 2012).
2 I am indebted to the musicologist Morag Grant for discussion of this song and other aspects of Scottish music, and whose exhaustive study of the song and its cultural reception is due for publication in book form in the near future.
3 The National Library of Scotland has now made this important collection of Scottish traditional music available digitally and it can be accessed online at http://digital.nls.uk/special-collections-of-printed-music.
4 More detail on the various versions and sound examples of the tune can be heard at http://burnsc21.glasgow.ac.uk/online-exhibitions/auld-lang-syne/.
5 Festival Interceltique: www.festival-interceltique.com.
6 Broun, Dauvit, personal communication, 18 April 2014.
7 See also Smyth (2007).
8 Usually taken to mean roughly the late fifteenth century to the late eighteenth century, i.e. representing the transition from medieval to modern and enlightenment society.
9 Although even this point is the subject of substantial debate in German scholarship, see Gelbart (2007: 5; 102–110).
10 See for example www.folkagainstfascism.com.
11 See Gelbart (2007), Chapter 2 for a detailed discussion of this concept.
12 Personal communication, from 'Walter Scott and the Rich Ballad Traditions of the Scottish Borders', a talk delivered by Lucy MacRae and Kaye McAlpine of the School of Scottish Studies, University of Edinburgh. See also the useful online resources at www.blogs.hss.ed.ac.uk/minstrelsy-tryst/.

PART II

Scottish Traditional Music

POLITICS, PEOPLE AND PLACE

CHAPTER 4

The Politics of Scottish Traditional Music

The issue of Scottish identity is for some a simple matter. When viewed from the personal level ethnicity is often the deciding factor. However, in scholarly terms where one attempts to gain a broader understanding, Scottish and British identities are highly ambiguous and contested. With the exception of the Highland bagpipe tradition and their British Army imperialist musical canon, there is no such thing as a 'British traditional music'. Part of the complexity of writing about Scottish traditional music and Scottish social life is that it is intertwined in very thick strands with British history, making both political and personal identity complex. Robin Cohen points out that 'Britain' is partly such a problematic term because it has supported, 'at least 16 different political entities – including the Commonwealth and Free State of England, Wales and Ireland (1649–54), the Commonwealth of Great Britain and Ireland (1654–60), the United Kingdom of Great Britain and Ireland (1801–1922) and the United Kingdom of Great Britain and Northern Ireland (since 1922)' (Cohen 2000: 577). That ambiguity really takes root in the eighteenth century with the Union of the Parliaments in 1707 and the upsurgence in Jacobitism. The Union with England and Wales was a good deal economically for Scotland but a bad deal culturally because it meant that, almost uniquely within Europe, Scotland became a stateless Kingdom, a nation with power. For Scottish traditional music and musicians, this led to numerous socio-political groups and causes that give us a rich heritage of songs and tunes, but real problems attempting to string them together in a single narrative. Today we are in a time of transition with the re-establishment in 1999 of the Scottish parliament, after 300 years, and the consequent rise of a Scottish socio-political confidence.

The politics of Scottish traditional music have almost always been a mix of egalitarianism, outward-facing nationalism and various brands of Protestant socialism. Combinations of these key religious and political ideologies have at times been prominent in Scottish traditional music, and there has also been a small but significant history of communism and internationalism in Scotland. The key trope, however, in Scottish traditional music and arguably in Scotland's political history has been egalitarianism, or equality amongst human beings. Scotland's version of egalitarianism is quite simply about the unconditional value of equal worth amongst people, regardless of economic or social status. This strand of political ideology has run strongly in Scottish music for 300 years and we can find it alive and well in the lyrics of songs from Robert Burns to Dick Gaughan. In the statistical world of real elections and opinion, Scottish voters were slightly further to the left of the typical UK voter with a strong allegiance to the UK Labour Party throughout the twentieth century, but since devolution in 1999, the Scottish National Party (SNP) have emerged as the dominating force in Scottish politics. Murray Pittock suggests that *The Scotland Act* passed in 1978 was the first messy attempt at legislating for devolution (Pittock 2013), followed in 1979 with a referendum for a devolved Scottish Assembly. This was doomed to failure, as the legislation for the referendum ensured that unless more than 40 per cent of the total eligible Scottish electorate voted for independence, it would not happen. In the event, a majority did vote for Scottish devolution in 1979, but the absolute total who voted 'Yes' was only 33 per cent of the eligible electorate and consequently did not meet the legislative requirement; thus the devolved Scottish Assembly never materialised.

The subsequent introduction of the experimental Poll Tax in 1989, a year ahead of England, was 'deeply unpopular' (Pittock 2013). But the eventual victory against this new form of tax also bolstered the nationalist case in Scotland which, when combined with the market capitalist ideologies of Thatcher and her government in the 1980s, were ironically key to the growth of Scottish nationalism and partly responsible for the Scottish cultural renaissance of the 1990s. This cultural renaissance can be seen as one of the immediate consequences of the failure of the 1979 Assembly vote in Scotland and it began a creative renaissance in the 1980s, first in literature and then in music and art.

Figure 4.1 'The Massacre of Glencoe' (painted 1883–86) by James Hamilton (1853–94) (by kind permission of Glasgow Life/Glasgow Museums)

The politics of eighteenth-century Scotland were quite different from those of the nineteenth or twentieth centuries. Liberalism went hand-in-hand with the heady ideological and philosophical milieu of enlightenment Edinburgh, whereas the rapid industrialisation and urbanisation of the nineteenth century brought forward a very strong commitment to socialism and increases in the voting franchise. In the twentieth century, Scotland increasingly found itself disconnected from the London-based UK government and the emergence in 1999 of the first Scottish parliament since 1707 was a turning point in Scottish political life. The subsequent election in 2007 of the Scottish National Party as the devolved government of Scotland has bolstered the voice of Scotland's traditional musicians, often through social media. Scottish traditional musicians and audiences played a key part in the upsurge of the left immediately following the Second World War and in the anti-nuclear movements in the 1950s and '60s, and most recently voiced strong nationalist sentiment in the lead up to the referendum on Scottish independence on the 18 September 2014. However, the community of Scottish traditional music is still broadly a social democratic one that in general abstains from direct radicalism. When viewed over the long perspective throughout the modern period, the principal political achievement of Scottish traditional music and musicians has been to voice a simple sense of socially shared Scottish egalitarianism.

Jacobite Song

In the seventeenth century, religion in Scotland was a very powerful force. Powerful in that it divided quite distinctly the Catholic Highlands or *Gaelteachd* from the Protestant Lowlands and from England. In cultural terms, too, Gaelic Scotland in the Highlands and Islands had much greater contact with other northern European seafaring nations and islands such as Ireland, the Orkneys, Shetland and the Scandinavian countries. Musically, this religio-cultural divide in the seventeenth century was important because it directly divided the political loyalties and culture of the mainly Catholic Highland clans from Protestant Lowland civic society, at that point still governed from Edinburgh.

After the Union of the Crowns in 1603, Scotland and England shared a monarch but not a parliament. King James VII (of Scotland) and II (of England) was a Catholic and ruled Scotland and England from 1685 to 1689. He was a part of the Stewart dynasty and was supported by most of the Scottish Highland clans. The most prominent political clan was the Campbells of Argyll who were ruthless and shrewd political operators stepping between their Gaelic, Highland neighbours and their Lowland and English trading partners. The Earl of Argyll as leader of Clan Campbell was instrumental in 1688–89 in bringing about the deposition of Charles VII and II and installing William of Orange (a Dutchman) who was staunchly Protestant and an obvious supporter of pro-Reformation. This allowed them great powers over extensive territories in the Highlands. However, the majority of the Highland clans still supported the Stewart monarchy, these people were known as Jacobites (coming from Latin designation of the exiled James, *Jacobus*).

The first campaign in support of the Stewart cause was led by John Graham of Claverhouse – the Viscount of Dundee – in the spring of 1689. He is commemorated in the song 'Bonnie Dundee', contributed by Sir Walter Scott ('the wizard of the north') and in the pipe tune 'The Lament for the Viscount of Dundee' which is a lovely *piobaireachd* with a variety of styles of interpretation still regularly played today. This rebellion against William of Orange was defeated and Dundee was killed in the action. However, Jacobitism lived on, and there were many, particularly in the predominantly Catholic *Gaelteachd*, that supported the Stewart kings and the next skirmish was in

Figure 4.2 Score for the piobaireachd 'The Massacre of Glencoe'. Music reproduced here by kind permission of the Piobaireachd Society, www.piobaireachd.co.uk

1690 between Dundee's forces and government forces at the Haughs of Cromdale. This led to a very famous song and pipe tune called 'The Haughs of Cromdale' which is still played as a 4|4 march today. At the same time, the Irish Jacobites suffered a bloody defeat in 1690 at the Battle of the Boyne, where they were defeated by pro-government forces. This battle is still commemorated by Orangemen in both Scotland and Ireland as a victory, and has played a significant part in the construction of Protestant–Catholic sectarianism in both countries.

Many other songs and tunes were written to celebrate key events and Jacobites during the eighteenth century, including well-known tunes such as 'John Roy Stewart'. After this period of Jacobite uprising in the late 1680s, the government re-imposed military rule in the Highlands and this led to one of the most notorious and tragic incidents in Scottish history, the Massacre of Glencoe. This massacre grew out of Campbell loyalties to the new Protestant monarchy. William demanded that all the Jacobite clan chiefs swear an oath of loyalty to him by the 1 January 1692. That the chief of the Glencoe MacDonalds – Alasdair MacDonald (McIain) – did not go down to swear allegiance was used as a reason by their old rivals, the Argyll Campbells, to massacre almost the entire Glencoe MacDonalds. This led to the famous piobaireachd, 'The Massacre of Glencoe', which uses attractive arching melodic lines to express the grief and violence of this massacre (see Figures 4.1 and 4.2).

The eighteenth century opened with a concerted effort by the Scottish parliament to force a union of the English and Scottish parliaments, which eventually happened in 1707 establishing that highly ambiguous political entity – the United Kingdom of Great Britain. However, if we consider some of the initial complexities of eighteenth-century life in Scotland, we can begin with the Union of the Parliaments.

The reasons behind the union of the parliaments were largely commercial ones that benefitted the Scottish upper classes who composed the membership of the Scottish parliament, and there was considerable opposition to the union from the Scottish people. The parliamentarians (commissioners) in Scotland were heavily in debt because of the failure of the Darien scheme, established by the 'company of Scotland' in 1695. This was an attempt by the Scottish parliament to establish a trading empire, similar to those of the Dutch, English or Portuguese, who had already established highly profitable imperial trading companies throughout the world. The Darien scheme threatened English trading interests and was very expensive. Its failure cost the Scottish nobility in the region of £300,000, around a quarter of Scotland's cash liquidity. Of the 2,000 or so people who sailed to Panama, only about 300 came back. The scheme almost bankrupted the country and led directly to one of the key incentives of the 1707 Act of Union with England – the 'equivalent', a sum of £398,000, paid directly to the Scottish nobles, of which approximately 58 per cent went to those who had lost money in the Darien scheme.

In addition to the failure of the Darien scheme and the other three disasters for the Scots in the 1690s – the Scottish famine of 1695–1700; rising tariff barriers against Scottish goods; and the Nine Years' War – further political problems emerged in the early 1700s which moved the political classes. Not least of these was the Act of Settlement that declared that the British throne could only pass to the protestant, royal family of Hanover, ironically despised mostly by Scottish nobility for the English parliament's failure to consult them, and not for its inherently sectarian intent. In addition to the large 'equivalent' paid to the Scots, there were cash bribes of around £20,000 paid to various key noblemen which ensured that the Act of Union passed into law in 1707. As Christopher Harvie has said, 'resentment of the Union continued to fester in the north . . . the English forgot about it . . . almost completely' (Harvie 2002: 113). Robert Burns wrote a key political song in 1791 about the bribing of

Scots nobility who, despite the broad unpopularity of union with England, went ahead regardless. The song is usually known today as 'Parcel O Rogues in a Nation':

> Fareweel to a oor Scottish fame,
> Fareweel oor ancient glory;
> Fareweel ev'n tae oor Scottish name,
> Sae famed in martial story.
> Now Sark rins over Solway sands,
> An Tweed rins to the ocean,
> Tae mark where England's province stands-
> Sic a parcel of rogues in a nation.

> What force or guile could not subdue,
> Through mony warlike ages,
> Is wrought now by a coward few,
> For hireling traitor's wages.
> The English steel we could disdain,
> Secure in valour's station;
> But English gold has been our bane-
> Sic a parcel of rogues in a nation.

> O would, or I had seen the day
> That treason thus could sell us,
> My auld grey head had lain in clay,
> Wi' Bruce and loyal Wallace.
> But pith and power, till my last hour,
> I'll mak this declaration;
> We're bought and sold for English gold-
> Sic a parcel of rogues in a nation.

In 1714, George I (a German of Hanover) accepted the Anglo-Scottish (British) crown which gave Jacobites more cause for resentment and further reasons for a rebellion of which the next substantial one took place in 1715. The failure of this revolution and the subsequent 1719 revolt ensured that any further revolutionary action by Jacobite-leaning Highlanders against the British Hanoverian government would have to include the military involvement of France. Significantly, the Scottish Gaelic population was Catholic, which served to strengthen their ideological bond with France and to divide them further from the Protestant Lowland Scotland. As relations between France and the United Kingdom worsened the politics of Scottish Jacobitism gained strength and by 1744 Britain was at war with France. Charles Edward Stewart ('Bonnie Prince Charlie', 1720–88) then residing in France, was convinced that if he went directly to the Highlands and Islands of Scotland he would be able to persuade the Jacobite clan chiefs to support him and that this support allied to the problems between France and the UK could lead to an invasion from both the Highlands of Scotland and from France in the South.

He sailed in a small fishing boat into Loch nan Uamh in Moidart on 25 July 1745. Ultimately, his campaign would be a disaster for the Highlands and Islands and he would narrowly escape and return to Italy to die in exile. This 1745 rebellion and the final battle of Culloden had massive implications for Scottish traditional music, not least of which were widespread military rule in the Highlands and Islands, the erosion of Gaelic culture including the music of the pipes and, eventually, the clearing of the people to make way for more profitable sheep on the land.

Charles Stewart features in a large legacy of Gaelic songs, poetry and fiddle and bagpipe music, tunes such as 'My King Has Landed in Moidart', 'Charlie's Welcome', 'The Roses of Prince Charlie', all celebrate the man himself: other related tunes, such as 'John Roy Stewart', celebrate other Jacobites who were involved in the almost successful Jacobite uprising of 1745 (*Bliadhna na Thearlaich* Gaelic lit. 'the year of Charlie'). It was during his march from Glenfinnan towards Edinburgh that Charles' army outwitted General Sir John Cope, who decided to occupy Inverness rather than take battle, leading to satirical songs and tunes about 'Johnny Cope'. The Jacobite army only turned back in resignation from Derby in December 1745 because they realised they could not completely take over the Hanoverian regime in London, only 120 miles further south. As the Jacobites retreated into Scotland and to Inverness, so the Hanoverian forces mustered and came north. On 16 April 1746 the two armies met at Culloden moor, four miles east of Inverness, where the Jacobite army was slaughtered by a tactically superior army under the command of the Duke of Cumberland. This defeat and the consequent flight of Charlie is also commemorated in song and poetry, and really led to a complete change in the lifestyle of the Highlands and Islands and the destruction of the clan system. There are many songs dealing with the Jacobite revolution, which came from Robert Burns and other notable figures in the eighteenth and nineteenth centuries such as James Hogg and Lady Caroline Nairne.

As Gibson has successfully argued, it is a common misconception that the bagpipes were banned or entered a decline after Culloden (Gibson 1998). The instrument, however, and many social activities that underpinned Gaelic culture were discouraged by the occupying Hanoverian forces in the Highlands and through the Act of Proscription in 1746. What is not disputed, though, is that the social way of life in the *Gaelteachd* did change and the clan system of family-based hierarchy, patronage, power and dispute resolution had altered forever. Clan chiefs were becoming more modern and outward looking, and with the ever more pervasive shift to the cash economy they needed increased rents from their land. By the end of the eighteenth century these social changes led to the formation of the Highland Societies of London and Scotland and the Falkirk Tryst, the first ever bagpipe competition in 1781 held at the Masonic Lodge in the Back Row of Falkirk over three days, setting the scene for the pipes as a pseudo-romantic nationalistic symbol. This was all done in the spirit of preservation of the time, stemming from enlightenment principles and the rising romantic movement. These and other competitions based on them were attractive as they offered large financial rewards or even a full-time job as piper to the gentry.

Whigs, Tories and Romantics

The Reform Act of 1832 changed Scottish society forever. The electorate rose from 4,500 to 65,000 and thus politicians had to begin to take more notice of the needs of the general population experiencing rapid urbanisation and industrialisation. Whigs and Tories were the dominant political parties in Scotland from the seventeenth to the nineteenth century and the Reform Act was passed under a Whig government. The Whigs were associated with the Protesters (Presbyterians) and the Tories with the Anglican Church, whilst both parties supported constitutional monarchy and the aristocracy. There are several famous Scots songs that discuss the Whigs and Tories, known as pipe tunes, for example 'Tullochgorm'.

Scotland went through significant political transformation during the nineteenth century. The growth of labour movements (including Chartism, trade unions and the Co-operative movement) and the power of the people led to changes in society that affected mainly the patronage of pipers. However, the second half of the century saw the total dominance of Scottish politics by the Liberal Party, which was associated with respectability, self-improvement, sobriety and education, all values that Scottish middle classes embodied. This has been claimed by some writers to be one of the reasons that Scottish culture died a death in nineteenth-century anglicisation and English assimilation: by incorporating many Scottish institutions into UK life, Scottishness was subsumed. The split of the General Assembly of the Church of Scotland in 1843, when the Free Church was formed in opposition to the absolute veto by congregations of their ministers, was part of a massive reduction in the social influence of the Church in Scottish life. Control of education and poor relief was transferred to political parties in London and this was a huge blow to the nation's sense of identity. In addition, the lairds and chieftains were sending their sons to be educated at English public schools and universities, thereby furthering the process of anglicisation. The Glasgow Law Amendment Society was formed by business leaders in the West of Scotland to promote changes in Scots law to move it closer to English law.

Pipers and drummers were significant in the imperialism of the nineteenth century, particularly through the British Army, which offered a new home for pipers in the numerous Highland regiments. This further cemented the place of Scots within the anglicised British Empire and many Scots were in prominent positions of authority throughout its colonial reaches. Sir Walter Scott led a resurgent romantic movement with his Waverley novels and 'Tales of a Grandfather' in investing

> the Scottish past with a magical appeal and satisfied the powerful emotional needs for nostalgia in a society experiencing unprecedented changes. Scott was a brilliant pioneer in the invention of tradition . . . which helped to develop a new set of national symbols and icons while at the same time renewing others of venerable antiquity in the contemporary image of Victorian Scotland. The tartan and kilt of the Highlands had been appropriated even before 1830 as the national dress. But its adoption was given further impetus by the heroic and well-publicized deeds of the kilted regiments in the Empire, by the growing number of Caledonian Societies in the emigrant communities abroad with their pipe bands and tartan dress and, not least, by Queen Victoria's love affair with the Highlands . . . . Highlandism had now been given wholehearted royal approval and tartan recognized as the badge of Scottish identity . . . At the same time, Scottish landscape painting developed a fascination with 'the land of the mountain and the flood'.
>
> (Devine 1999: 292–3)

The Kailyard writers also were included in this romanticising Victorian movement in the latter half of the nineteenth century and had mass appeal with bestsellers such as *Beside the Bonnie Brier Bush* (Ian Maclaren, published 1894) and extremely sentimental publications like this one tended to add to the notions of a rural past, in which the bagpipe and its players often had prominence.

Marxism, Red Clydeside and the Revival

Ewan McVicar claims that neither Robert Burns or Hamish Henderson ever wrote an original tune, but that they re-fashioned older tunes and their genius existed in the composition of wonderful lyrics (McVicar 2010: 10). However, although there is

Figure 4.3 Sketch of Hamish Henderson by Timothy Neat (by kind permission of the artist)

certainly truth in this assertion, and his suggestion that up until the folk revival the composing of Scots song was largely the composition of lyrics to pre-existing tunes, there is no doubt that part of the reason for this phenomenon has long been the ease of communicating and remembering new songs. This task is made easier if one already knows the tune, and in the case of some very famous Scottish songs, the pre-existence of the tune has undoubtedly been a factor in the rapid popularisation of songs. One of the most famous of these is Hamish Henderson's 'John MacLean's March' composed in 1948 for the John MacLean Memorial Meeting in St Andrew's Hall, Glasgow. John MacLean (1879–1923) was the leading figure in communist 'Red Clydeside', a popular hero amongst left-wing workers in the heavy industries of the West of Scotland, particularly during the First World War. He was a powerful Marxist orator who was even nominated at one point the Soviet consul in Glasgow (1918). Glasgow came close in this period to a de facto radical workers' revolution, but as Harvie suggests, although there was a serious industrial problem and conditions for a genuine Marxist revolution in Glasgow were evident, there was a crucial lack of 'a consistent and developing pattern of working-class resistance and leadership' (Harvie 1998: 17). MacLean was an important figure for the left in Scotland, giving rise to this celebratory song by Hamish Henderson. The song in both sentiment and style presaged much of the coming folk revival:

'John MacLean's March' (words H. Henderson, 1948. With kind permission of the Henderson estate).

Hey Mac did ye see him as he cam in by Gorgie,
Awa ower the Lammerlaw and north o' the Tay?
Yon man is comin' and the hale toon is turnin' oot,
We're aa' sair he'll win back tae Glasga the day.

The jiners and hauders-on are marchin' fae Clydebank,
Come noo an' hear him, he'll be ower thrang tae bide.
Turn oot Jock and Jimmie, leave yer cranes an' yer muckle gantries
Great John Maclean's comin' back tae the Clyde.

Argyle Street and London Road's the route that we're mairchin'
The lads frae the Broomielaw are oot tae a man.
Hey, Neil, whaur's yer hoderums, ye big Hielan teuchter?
Get yer pipes, mate, and march at the heid o'the clan!

Hallo Pat Malone, I knew ye'd be here, son
The red and green, my lads, we'll wear side by side,
The Gorbals is his the day and Glasgae belangs tae him,
Noo great John Maclean's comin' hame tae the Clyde.

It's forward tae Glasga Green we'll mairch in guid order,
Will grips his banner weel, that boy isna blate,
Aye there man, that's Johnny noo, that's him, aye, the bonnie fechter
Lenin's his fere, Mac, and Leibnecht's his mate.

Tak tent when he's speakin' for they'll mind whit wis said here
In Glasgae our city and the hale world besides.
Tha's richt, lads, the scarlet's bonnie, here's tae ye Hielan' Shonie!
Oor John Maclean has come hame to the Clyde.

An weel when it's ower, I'll awa hame tae Springburn,
Come hame tae yer tea noo, John, we'll soon hae ye fed!
It's hard wark the speakin', an I'm sair ye'll be tired the nicht,
I'll sleep on the flair, Mac, and gie John the bed.

The hale city's quiet noo, It kens that he's restin'
Hame wi' his Glasga freens, the fame and their pride.
The red will be worn, my lads, and Scotland will rise again,
Noo great John Maclean has come hame tae the Clyde[1]

This song was well known amongst Scottish revivalists and is still sung regularly today. However, it is dwarfed by another of Henderson's well-crafted songs, 'Freedom Come All Ye', which has come to symbolise for many Scots and others too, a sort of socialist-egalitarian dream of international equality and tolerance. The Scots language of this song rewards some study, the most difficult words are explained in brackets.

'Freedom Come All Ye'[2] (lyrics Hamish Henderson, c. 1960, sung to the traditional pipe tune, 'The Bloody Fields of Flanders'. With kind permission of the Henderson estate).

Roch the wind in the clear day's dawin   (Roch = rough)
Blaws the cloods heelster-gowdie ow'r   (heelster-gowdie = head over heels)
the bay
But there's mair nor a roch wind
blawin
Through the great glen o the warld the
day.

It's a thocht that will gar oor rottans   (thocht = thought; gar oor = make us
                                                sick; rottans = rats)

A' they rogues that gang gallus, fresh and gay *(gang = go along; gallus = cheeky and bold)*

Tak the road and seek ither loanins *(loanins = pastures)*

For their ill ploys, tae sport and play

Nae mair will the bonnie callants *(callants = young men)*

Mairch tae war when oor braggarts crously craw *(braggarts = braggers; crously craw = arrogantly crow)*

Nor wee weans frae pit-heid and clachan *(clachan = small village)*

Mourn the ships sailin doon the Broomielaw. *(Broomielaw = Ship dock in Glasgow)*

Broken faimlies in lands we've herriet *(herriet = harried)*

Will curse Scotland the Brave nae mair, nae mair;

Black and white, ane til ither mairriet *(mairriet = married)*

Mak the vile barracks o their maisters bare

So come all ye at hame wi freedom,

Never heed whit the hoodies croak for doom *(hoodies = sinister carrion crows)*

In your hoose a' the bairns o Adam

Can find breid, barley-bree and painted room. *(barley-bree = a malt liquor similar to whisky)*

When MacLean meets wi's freens in Springburn *(Springburn = district of Glasgow)*

A' the roses and geans will turn tae bloom *(geans = wild cherry trees)*

And a black boy frae yont Nyanga

Dings the fell gallows o the burghers doon. *(dings = knocks)*

The Folk Revival

Like many aspects of our lives, the end of the Second World War brought significant changes to our world. This was combined with an increasing pace of change, as technology, social attitudes, new economic realities and cultural liberalisation seeped through Western societies influencing our culture and way of life. The post-war period brought about the most radical shift in the participation, production and consumption of traditional music in England, Ireland, Scotland and Wales principally through the commodification of traditional music through the folk revival. This process, begun in the 1950s, has led to a complete shift in the way we understand traditional music, transforming the majority of traditional music into a form of commercial music, effectively adopting the markers of popular music, leaving only small pockets of participation in traditional music as a form of cash-free social music making, and thus changing its sound and ideology forever (see for instance Cowan 1991; Munro 1996).

The folk revival in Britain and Ireland was initially a political movement that gradually attracted more followers not just through the countercultural revivalist spirit, but also simply because of the aesthetic enjoyment of traditional music. By the end of the 1960s, the revival was a widespread movement driven by a young, urban group who were to varying degrees left of the political centre. Some of the key changes to traditional music in the 1950s and '60s were the formation of numerous folk clubs, the creation of an educated audience, the re-mythologising of authenticity and the advances in PA technology which eventually enabled the professionalisation of folk groups and consequent growth of recordings. Throughout the 1950s and for much of the 1960s the folk revival was a folk song revival, where young, urban singers looked to aging, rural and often traveller singers for authentic versions of folk songs. This concern for establishing authentic versions of songs was central to the folk revival as it had been to the 'first' Edwardian English folk revival. By establishing authoritative song texts and performance practice, young revival singers in the 1950s and '60s were constructing a strong sense of vernacular national identity that was central to both the political left and Scottish nationalism. The revival did not produce the same sense of Welsh, English or Irish nationalism, largely because of differing socio-political situations, whereas Scotland already had an established Scottish National Party (established 1934) which had been gathering support in the 1960s and would eventually lead to the first Scottish referendum in 1979. The narrative surrounding English nationalism was still in the mid-twentieth century dormant and confined to a very small minority of those on the extreme far-right, but which has in more recent times emerged, better organised, to appropriate English traditional music for their political cause (Lucas 2013; Spracklen 2013).

For the majority of revivalists in the mid-twentieth century, the location of authenticity in the performances of older, rural singers was at the heart of their re-imagination of personal, local and national identities. In England, Ireland and Scotland, many of the so-called 'source singers' were drawn from the traveller community, who genuinely had an unbroken transmission of traditional song stretching back many years. Their status as an internal Other to the settled, mainstream population also underlined their authority as members of an unbroken 'carrying stream', and it was at this time when much of the contemporary language of traditional music emerged from metaphorical references to the past performed authentically in the present: 'the living tradition'; 'source singers'; and 'revivalists'.

The first major event of the Scottish revival was the first People's Céilidh organised by Hamish Henderson on Friday, 31 August 1951 in Oddfellows Hall, Edinburgh. This was founded out of political beliefs as an alternative to the heavily European elitism of the Edinburgh Festival, which had begun in the city in 1947. The People's Céilidh was a reaction against the festival – whose organising committee was described by Henderson as 'the Edinbourgeoisie' (McVicar 2010: 33) – as the programme at the time reflected nothing of its location and could have been sited anywhere in Europe with an audience of Western art music. Henderson introduced the People's Céilidh as a nationalist project to introduce indigenous Scottish culture to the largely urban middle-class audience. Eventually, this antidote to the more formal festival later became known by its now-familiar title, the Edinburgh Fringe Festival (and is still very popular today). Norman Buchan describes the first céilidh and its impact:

As I went into the Oddfellows Hall the bloody place was packed, feet were going, and it was Jimmy MacBeath singing 'The Gallant Forty-Twa'. Hamish had assembled these people. Jessie Murray sang 'Skippin' Barfit Through The Heather'; . . . Flora MacNeil was singing 'The Silver Whistle (An Fhideag Airgid)' – beautiful! I'd never heard anything like this. John Strachan was singing about forty verses of a ballad . . . An amazing night for people who'd never heard them before! It swept me off my feet completely.

(Norman Buchan in McVicar 2010: 32)

The key moment and significance of this festival was the performance in 1953 of the traveller singer Jeannie Robertson, brought down from Aberdeen to Edinburgh and introduced to Edinburgh audiences by Hamish Henderson. The People's Céilidh ran annually from 1951 until 1954 when it was effectively stopped by the influence of the Scottish Trades Union Congress because of the perceived threat of communist influence in the festivals.

The fundamental shift in the ideology and character of traditional music from highly localised, social activity to commodified, self-conscious and professional musical genre depended upon these distinctions between compartmentalised groups largely predicated upon authenticity. In some ways, this was the inevitable consequence of the massive post-war social upheaval, and in others a reaction against the immediately preceding austerity in post-war Britain. And for Ireland too, the need to define the national consciousness was perhaps less strong after thirty years of home rule, but nevertheless young people in the 1960s had been shaped by an extremely poor nation where memories of the political struggle against English oppression were still alive. Therefore one of the central genres of this leftist movement to emerge in the 1950s and '60s was protest song.

Protest Song

Protest songs are a form of overtly political song that actively narrate opposition to a particular perceived injustice. In Scottish music, protest songs have been around for a very long time and usually perform a sense of opposition and injustice to London-centric UK policies, nuclear weapons or social policies that have had detrimental consequences for ordinary Scots. These include: protests about Hanoverian oppression of the Jacobites and Highland culture; anti-Union, anti-Royalist (and Republican) and anti-English-rule songs of Scottish nationalism from the eighteenth century to the present day; nineteenth-century weavers' songs of protest; the anti-nuclear song of the 1960s from the Campaign for Nuclear Disarmament (CND); protests at the UK poll tax, trialled in Scotland by Margaret Thatcher's government; feminist songs about the subjugation of women in Scottish and other societies; and other instances of particular protest that have emerged in Scottish song, for example 1980s songs about South African apartheid, such as 'Mandela Danced in the Square' by Ian Davison. Songs such as 'I'm the Man that MUF-Fed It' by Nancy Nicholson (one of Scotland's most notable protest songwriters in the tradition) plays on the acronym MUF, used by the Atomic Energy Authority for 'material unaccounted for', which was cleverly worked into the chorus of this parodic protest song.[3]

One of the key musical sites of radical protest in Scotland was the Borrowstounness (Bo'ness) near Falkirk. *The Rebels Céilidh Song Book* was an important local publication published by the Bo'ness Rebels Literary Society in the late 1960s (n.d.). Inside the first page are two quotes that speak to the publication's strongly nationalist intention. The first is from Hugh MacDiarmid:

The rose of a' the world is no' for me,
I want for my part
Only the little white rose of Scotland,
That smells sharp and sweet
–And breaks the heart.

The second quote, attributed to William Wallace, runs as follows: 'Do with me what you will. Scotland shall yet be free' (Anon., [1968?]). The 1950s witnessed a fervent political activism amongst many in the Central Belt of Scotland. Hamish Henderson's People's Céilidh was a turning point for young urbanites who were introduced to the traditional music of the Scottish travellers, Gaelic song and piping. Yet further east of Edinburgh, in Linlithgow, Borrowstounness (Bo'ness) and in Glasgow, there was a more politically radical movement led by Morris Blythman (aka 'Thurso Berwick'), and others. The important legacy of these politically motivated revivalists was mainly educational, although some could argue that the radicalism of the 1950s and '60s led directly to the upsurge in Scottish nationalism in the decade that followed and to the 1979 referendum. However, Scottish nationalism in the 1970s was also due in part to the UK economic decline and unemployment under Wilson and Callaghan's Labour governments. The Ballad and Blues club model of Lomax in London was exported by Blythman to Glasgow, where he set up a folk song club in Alan Glen's Academy, and by Norman and Janey Buchan in Rutherglen High School. Many key revivalists and singers came out of these clubs, including performers that continue to pass on their own repertoires today. Singers like Andy Hunter, Gordeanna McCullough and Ann Neilson were all pupils at these schools and developed a lifelong commitment to Scottish traditional music, both as performers and teachers.

There has been a strong and consistent feminist strand of Scottish musical culture since the revival, and one of the vehicles for this has been women's vocal groups and choirs. Groups such as Stravaig, Eurydice, Sisters Unlimited and most recently the Hidden Lane Choir in Glasgow. There are quite a few songs about women's role in society and some of these are feminist songs, such as Nancy Nicholson's 'They Sent a Woman'. Another feminist song, 'The Lament of the Working Class Hero's Wife', deals with the theme of women's solidarity in the face of unequal power in the traditional marriage. In this case, the song also satirises the role of the socialist revolutionary with a very Scottish phenomenon of down-to-earthiness.[4]

'The Lament of the Working Class Hero's Wife'

O the wains are greeting and the sink is leaking
And you're standing in the pub wi' your Youngers Tartan Special,
And you say you're educating all the younger generation
Of your left wing politics and that's a fact.

Chorus

I ken I'm the wife but I'll no be your skivvy
You may be a man, but what can you give me?
Cuts in houses, cuts and bruises,
That's no the story for a bloody life of glory!

O you say that the solution is a left wing revolution,
But your drinking money's pockled fae the family allowance;

Your Marx and all your Lenin does nae help me with the cleaning
And I've had to put my wedding ring into the pawn

Chorus

Well I really canna take it, so you're going to have to make it
On your own, 'cos I'm going with the bairns and our belongings
And we'll maybe go to Maggie's or to Effie's or to Aggie's
Cos we've got a lot of sisters that'll help me through!

(Henderson and others 1982)

Race, Ethnicity and Whiteness in Scottish Traditional Music

Traditional music in Scotland is almost exclusively the domain of white, middle-class 'creatariat'.[5] In fact, the whiteness of the participants, audiences, musicians, listeners, educators and entrepreneurs involved in Scottish traditional music is so total, that it appears to have been accepted as a tabula rasa of this form of cultural production – an unexamined aspect of the mental model of Scottish traditional music. If that is the case, why should we think about whiteness, and what are the effects of this socio-cultural homogeneity within the tradition? There are three particular issues facing the traditional music communities in Scotland today that relate to their whiteness and are important both for the health of the tradition but also to the perception of traditional music in the wider public. These issues revolve around (1) the cultural autonomy for traditional music, (2) the appropriation of traditional music by the far-right and (3) the creative health of the musical tradition.

In terms of the creative health and cultural autonomy, the folk revival in Scotland from 1951 through to the end of the 1960s was a powerful time of political activism, musical innovation and experimentation. The 1970s brought a growing professionalisation of Scottish traditional music and culminated politically in the election of Margaret Thatcher as the prime minister of the UK in 1979.

The years 1979–90 are generally regarded as a dark period in Scottish cultural life, both because of the election in Britain of another London-based government that very few Scots had voted for, and also because of the increasing London-centricity of arts and media, where very few Scottish voices ever made it onto television or radio. Part of the cultural reaction to this political disenfranchisement in the 1980s was the new Scottish cultural renaissance in music, literature, art and film which emerged in the following decade to offer Scots both cultural forms rooted in their own vernacular experience and political messages grounded in democratic socialism that differed substantially from the further right-of-centre, more conservative policies and practices of the Westminster establishment. Scottish traditional and popular musicians were crucial in this flourishing of Scottish culture in the 1990s. When Scots heard for the first time in 1987 the pop duo the Proclaimers singing in a Scottish accent, this simple act made a powerful impact upon their cultural confidence:

> singing not in a generic Americanese but proudly and defiantly in their native Scots. It was a Eureka moment. The Proclaimers were one of a small number of important Scottish bands in the 1980s who were laying down the foundations of what would eventually develop into a full-blown Scottish musical renaissance . . . all of these Scottish musicians drew heavily from an indigenous

folk tradition. This folk tradition is the unsung hero . . . of the Scottish cultural renaissance. The folk tradition, through its songs, ballads and poetry, has helped keep our language and identity alive, at a grassroots level, from below, when all around was a standardised English, and a generic British identity promoted from above.

(Williamson 2009: 56–7)

Following the resurgence of Scottish cultural confidence in the 1990s and the steady stream of literary, artistic and musical awards made to artists working, presenting and performing in Scotland, Scottish traditional music began to emerge in public policy and moved from mostly local contexts to an art-form of national importance with the ensuing state-sponsored funding and public policy. In the late 1990s there were a number of key developments that demonstrated the emergence of Scottish traditional music and traditional arts more widely into the national cultural (and political) life of Scottish public life. It is no coincidence that along with the re-opening of a Scottish parliament in 1999 for the first time in 300 years came the acceptance of the first students in Scottish traditional music on the new BA (Scottish Music) degree at the Royal Scottish Academy of Music and Drama in 1996 (now Royal Conservatoire of Scotland); the first public acknowledgement of the value of Scottish traditional music in the social benefit of the Feis movement in 1996 (Matarasso 1996), the recognition of the importance of traditional arts by the Scottish Arts Council and their replacement, Creative Scotland; and the many further examples of institutionalisation and recognition of Scottish traditional music that has gathered momentum since the late 1990s (McKerrell 2014).

One of the decisive moments in the political life of Scottish traditional music was the performance by the well-known traditional singer Sheena Wellington of Robert Burns' 'A Man's a Man for a' That' at the opening of the Scottish parliament in 1999 (for a useful examination of this event within the wider musical context of the time see Bold 2006). Scottish traditional music had arrived, taking the centre stage in both private and public Scottish cultural life.

Today, it is fair to say that Scottish traditional music is more closely constitutive of Scottish political nationalism than ever before. By 2014, the year of the Scottish referendum on independence, almost all public political statements from Scottish traditional musicians advocated a free and independent Scotland and the grassroots music scene had not been so politically active since the 1960s' folk revival and CND movement. Even though a majority of Scots opted to stay in the union with England, Wales and Northern Ireland on 18 September 2014, almost all commentators have agreed that the political spirit and activism that the national referendum debate awoke in Scotland was an extremely positive outcome. Scottish culture and Scottish traditional music since the late 1990s has emerged into a renaissance where there are many more artistic voices audible in the public sphere, and many of those voices are political voices calling for all manner of change, often through the medium of song. And accompanying this renaissance has been a growth of experimentation with Other musics in Scotland, hybrid musical collaborations by bands such as India-Alba and Salsa Celtica have diversified and extended the total conception of Scottish traditional music to a more plural cultural space. Scots have always used traditional song as both a medium for expressing and constructing political views, but also as a means of creating a common bond between those that sing them. This is in my view the real power of political song; that it provides a sort of relational empowerment where those who sing and those that listen bond to one another in the performance of shared values and aspirations.

Notes

1 Lyrics adapted from the John MacLean archive, available at www.marxists.org/archive/maclean/works/march.htm © Crown copyright 2012 [accessed 29 August 2013].

2 Lyrics adapted from the Education Scotland website and various recordings: a prescriptive score is available at www.educationscotland.gov.uk/scotlandssongs/secondary/thefreedomcomeallye.asp © Crown copyright 2012 [accessed 30 September 2014].

3 See for example the performance at www.youtube.com/watch?v=MdRtA2MEevg.

4 There is an excellent version online, sung by Alison McMoreland, at www.youtube.com/watch?v=anKqdABd17s.

5 Although this term is still not widespread, it does seem to capture the changing discourse and social compartmentalisation of the production and publicness of Scottish traditional music in the twenty-first century.

CHAPTER 5

The People of Scottish Traditional Music

Music is now often thought of as a largely social practice undertaken by people with other people. Historically, however, music was considered an object, with the emphasis upon the musical work and, particularly in the classical canon, upon the composer. This view of music as an object has almost entirely dominated the historiography of Scottish traditional music. That approach takes music as a thing which exists most fully in the texts and sounds we hear, read and perform. Such a reductive view of music as an object has led to the disappearance of people from histories and discourses about music. Since the post-war period, scholars of music have reconsidered and largely rejected this narrow view of music-as-object, in favour of a more active and human conception of the role of musicians and audiences in music, and even what music might be.

One classic definition of music (in ethnomusicology) is that of John Blacking, who characterised music as 'humanly organised sound' (Blacking 1973). His writing, and that of other ethnomusicologists, has firmly focused attention on the ways in which people make, listen to, transmit, organise and understand music within its socio-cultural contexts. This is a profoundly relativist understanding of music as a human activity that emphasises the insider's cultural understanding. However, in recent years there has been a reappraisal of this approach which has facilitated our understanding of the intercultural and affective power of music across cultures without denying the cultural specificity of local traditions. Increasingly, questions about traditional music in particular are focusing not only on music's role in social processes of identity construction and cultural authenticity, but also in our shared understanding of representation of minority groups, cultural tourism, economic and educational benefits and music as intangible cultural heritage. This is of course partially the consequence of globalisation which is leading to a greater visibility of local traditional musics around the world, but also reflects a change in the social structures within the communities that perform, teach, listen and consume traditional music. It is reflected in changes to the economic basis for sustaining indigenous cultural activities such as the rapid professionalisation of Scottish traditional music in the last few decades, and in the ways in which we engage with music online and both as consumers and as a community of friends who share a common interest in traditional music.

In this chapter we will examine who performs, teaches, listens to and consumes Scottish traditional music, and what we can say about them and how this once geographically defined musical tradition is now increasingly deterritorialised (understood as something we do rather than a geographically-defined music) and digitally mediated. We will examine how people conceive of Scottish traditional music and what that might say about them and their place in the world. In so doing, we will gain a better understanding of what music means within this particular community of practice (Wenger 1998) and how it acts as a social practice as well as an object of human attention. Scotland itself is a busy cultural place. The Scottish Household Survey is the principal source of national statistical evidence of cultural participation with a very large cultural participation sample size of around 9,000 to 10,000 people annually. It shows that women are more culturally engaged than men and perhaps unsurprisingly also consistently demonstrates through time that the wealthier, younger and better educated, the greater one's engagement in culture. The 2013 data show that 31 per cent of respondents attended a 'live music event', which broadly includes traditional music and popular music including rock or jazz, but excludes classical music and opera. Only 7 per cent of respondents reported attending classical music or opera in the previous year (Scottish Government 2014). These figures are very general but do give a picture of participation in the arts which shows that those who are actively involved in traditional music are far more enthusiastically engaged in cultural participation than the general populace.

Those involved in Scottish traditional music have been portrayed in different ways in different times, largely as a product of the interests and aims of those authors writing about them. In the eighteenth century, Scottish traditional music did not really exist as a concept, but the idea of 'national music' had taken hold, and the music was beginning to be discussed as a means of understanding the *nationalbildung* (or 'authentic spirit of the nation' – see Chapter 1). In this conception, the people came from the land and their national character was constructed and reflected in the indigenous folk song – one of the reasons why this racially-bound conception of traditional music flourished alongside racial and ethnic nationalism up until its demise in the world wars.

Music was critical to this endeavour in that it allowed widespread mythologising of vanished harpers, bards and minstrels to construct a fantastical Scotland that never really existed, but that was a powerful trope for collectors and class-bound constructions of Scottishness. Indeed, the power of this sense of romantic nationalism in the nineteenth century led directly to the 'Celtic Twilight' movement in Scottish traditional music towards the end of the nineteenth century, which believed in 'last leaves' (Henderson 1964: 49) collecting of oral tradition before it finally vanished under the weight of urban and industrial progress. It was a powerful idea and manifested itself finally in the establishment of many of the key institutions of Scottish music such as An Comunn Gàidhealach (the Gaelic Association, founded in 1891), who still hold the annual Mod for Gaelic music-making competitions; the Piobaireachd Society (founded in 1909), whose membership have traditionally been drawn from the non-performing community; and the Clarsach Society (founded in 1931), whose efforts produced the first working instruments for Scottish harp players. Just over the border in England, we know that analogous work, such as Peacock's 1805 tune collection, Bell's *Rhymes of Northern Bards* (1812) and significantly, William Chappell's *National English Airs* (1838), were adding momentum to the romanticism of the Border region and Northumberland. Evidenced by committees such as the 'Ancient Melodies Committee of the Newcastle-upon-Tyne Society of Antiquaries', founded in 1855 to compile the last-leaves of Northumbrian music (Barker 2004: 165). This sense of a disappearing cultural heritage combined with a deep-seated romantic nationalism merged into the notion of a Celtic Twilight, and was a powerful motivation for late-nineteenth-century writers to objectify and construct fanciful versions of Scotland and the Scots.

In the twentieth century, much of the revivalists' conception of Scottish music depended upon the cultural 'purity' of the Scottish traveller community because of their separation from mainstream urbanised society lent them, and their songs and stories, a cultural authority with which to construct a revival of indigenous Scottish culture. In the twenty-first century, as Scottish traditional music moves into a newly commodified and commercial space which I would argue is now primarily digitally mediated, we have emerged into a context where traditional musics from all parts of the world are understood in relation to other types of music rather than their historical origins. Drawing on Slobin (Slobin 1993), Nicholas Cook terms this shift the 'relational turn' in music (Cook 2012) noting that intercultural relations in many ways are now more significant to understanding local musical traditions than any indigenous provenance itself.

This type of relational analysis is both much needed in today's digitally mediated world, but more than that, it offers an opportunity for engaging through music in community construction and developing traditional music as an economically sustainable cultural industry, understanding both where the music comes from, but also how we relate to others who want to listen, perform, watch, dance, produce, participate in and consume traditional culture. It understands music through the human encounters between individuals and groups, emphasising not only belonging and authenticity, but crucially how those identities are related to the identities of others elsewhere in the world, and their music. To do this requires one to understand music not as a noun but as a verb; something that we do. Christopher Small and Thomas Turino have written about the power of music as a social process (Small 1998; Turino 2008) and, as they point out, it is when we consider how people *music* themselves that the relational understanding becomes most powerful because it mobilises music as a social force which helps us to unite, resist, repel, attract and even love each other. As Cook suggests, one of the most significant aspects of any relational analysis of music is that it shifts music from being the object of study to a social process that aims 'to create relationships between its spectators' (Cook 2012: 195). This idea explains one of the most fundamentally important reasons for making music; that it offers a means for creating belonging and improving relations between ourselves as human beings.

Surveying the Community of Practice

How then can we explore the relationships and relational values of the people who through a shared interest form a Scottish traditional music community of practice? And when we examine the people and groups involved in Scottish traditional music as a social phenomenon, what might that tell us about its value and potential in contemporary society? These questions are complex but in part can be examined by talking to and surveying the people bound together as listeners, performers, consumers, fans, dancers, teachers, pupils, retailers (or even scholars) of Scottish traditional music. One means of doing this is to gather evidence about who is participating in Scottish traditional music and how they interact, value and conceive of it. Between March and August 2014, I ran an online survey in order to gather evidence about the people involved in Scottish traditional music. The survey was conducted entirely online and was a purposive sample in that only those who had an interest in Scottish traditional music were sampled (those without were filtered from the results). I deliberately targeted the community of practice through web fora, my own website, mailing lists, and publicised the survey via BBC Radio Scotland, where I appeared on the *Travelling Folk* show on 15 May 2014 to encourage participation. I also posted notices about the survey on some key websites (including www.footstompin.com, www.thesession.org and others), to encourage those with an interest in Scottish traditional music to take part. The resulting sample size (excluding those who did not express an interest) was 275. In the survey, respondents were asked to comment on six interrelated and important conceptual areas that are key to understanding the relations within and without the Scottish traditional music community of practice:

- class, gender and age of sample;
- performance;
- education;
- transmission, consumption and reception;
- definitions and perceptions;
- politics and policy.

From this survey we begin to get a picture of the people who participate in Scottish traditional music today, their shared sense of what it means to them in their lives and how they relate to others. There are of course many different people who respond to all types of survey, but there are clear patterns available and these are often important because of what they can tell us about shared values and relationships. These in turn, can offer us evidence for how we might best focus our attention in terms of teaching, transmitting and supporting music as a social activity.

Gender and class in Scottish traditional music

Johnson notes that in the seventeenth and eighteenth centuries each instrument had a specific gendered status:

> Of these, recorder, flute, violin, and cello were played only by gentlemen; gamba and keyboard instruments were played by both sexes, the latter becoming increasingly 'female' as the century progressed; and cittern was played only by ladies ... for the 'male' instruments are the sociable ones which fit together into orchestras and chamber ensembles, whereas the 'female' instruments are lone and harmonically self-supporting .... A male/female distinction also held in singing, for ladies typically sang solos in their own homes, while gentlemen sang together away from home – glees in the tavern, or choruses of Handel's oratorios in the concert hall. For women, music-making was an individual activity; for men, it was a group activity.
>
> (Johnson 1972: 24)

The results of this survey demonstrate that the people involved in Scottish traditional music are split very evenly between men and women, they are international in that they live in many parts of the world, and 63 per cent of them are over forty-five years old. This is not surprising when one considers that many of those who actively identify with Scottish traditional music would have emerged in the revival of the 1960s. Gender however is the socially constructed understanding of biological sex and musical instruments are still heavily gendered. When I have canvassed students on this, one finds this to be the case: typically bagpipes, drums and brass instruments are socially perceived as masculine instruments whereas harp and often fiddle are constructed as feminine. As in other cultures of course these instruments are open to gender change; the banjo was widely considered as a genteel feminine instrument in the nineteenth century and its transformation at the hands of Earl Scruggs and his musical inheritors transformed it into a masculine bluegrass instrument. Similarly, the harp, once decidedly a high-status, masculine instrument played by bards in Gaelic court culture, is now perceived as a feminine instrument in Scotland. Whilst it is fair to suggest that participation today in Scottish traditional music is a roughly evenly distributed activity between men and women, much of the repertoire, aesthetics and values follow general contemporary social conceptions of gender. Music is however extremely effective at subverting and redrawing gender distinctions in society. Further research into this area has the potential to help us to understand better how Scottish gender relations are constructed, how they have changed through the years and how music can be used to move towards a fairer society (see for instance Alferov n.d.; Goldstein 1991).

Class, education and ethnicity

There has been discussion of the terms 'traditional music' and 'folk music' and their relative meaning and signification in different cultures for many years. In this sample, once excluding 'other' responses, 60 per cent of respondents felt there was no difference and 40 per cent felt that those terms were not interchangeable. They are extremely well educated with 73 per cent of them holding an undergraduate degree and about 40 per cent even holding a postgraduate qualification. Of the total respondents, 80 per cent perform in public and 38 per cent do so at least once a week. They are a very active musical community who regularly play music together as part of their normal lives. Once begun, they continue Scottish traditional music as a lifelong interest, which correlates with the age profile; about a quarter of all respondents have been performing Scottish traditional music for more than thirty years. Only 18 per cent of respondents do not perform, which is much lower than in other genres (see Hibberd 2009 and below). Mostly people today engage in Scottish traditional music at the pub, in their houses, communities and through attendance at festivals and concerts.

Most people have at one time in their lives paid for some sort of instruction in Scottish traditional music, but a significant proportion of 37 per cent have not and almost 60 per cent of all respondents did not receive any instruction in Scottish traditional music at school, which almost directly correlates to the group of over forty-five-year-olds whose musical experience at school (with one or two notable exceptions) would have been almost entirely based in the Western classical tradition. Only 6 per cent feel that there is currently good or excellent provision in schools for Scottish traditional music but, perhaps more interestingly, the largest proportion of 42 per cent indicated that they did not know, against slightly fewer (39 per cent) who reliably suggested there was too little Scottish traditional music in schools.

When it comes to participating in and learning traditional Scottish music, most people use a wide variety of sources for learning new tunes and songs including, most commonly, hard copy music collections, commercial albums, pub sessions or singarounds and from friends and family directly. They are active consumers, as three quarters of those surveyed purchase recordings several times a year or more regularly. Scottish traditional music is now predominantly digitally mediated and 69 per cent of respondents indicated that they use digital communications to access information about Scottish traditional music in their area. Seventy-one per cent of them pay to go to a live gig at least several times a year or more often, and a staggering 90 per cent of all respondents to the survey go to hear live Scottish traditional music several times a year or more often. This demonstrates just how actively engaged this community of practice is, and how central live performance is to Scottish traditional music more widely.

Perhaps most surprisingly of all, 95 per cent of all respondents felt that the statement 'Scottish traditional music should be old' was either completely irrelevant or only very slightly relevant. This is an astonishing shift in attitudes towards Scottish traditional music, when one considers the ideological foundations of the folk revival which hinged upon bringing the old, and thereby authentic, practice of the Scottish travelling community and the older tunes and songs from the eighteenth and nineteenth centuries back into common circulation. This is the most significant result of this survey and indicates a fundamental shift in what Scottish traditional music represents for its own community of practice.

The two most significant statements relating to how respondents define Scottish traditional music were that it should be 'orally transmitted' (73 per cent) and 'composed in a traditional style' (68 per cent). This shifts the definition of Scottish traditional music firmly onto its relational characteristics. The community itself is suggesting that the nature of oral transmission of songs and tunes and the shared sense of a sonic aesthetics are at the heart of what it means to participate in Scottish traditional music. The survey also revealed that there is almost wholesale rejection not only of the importance of 'oldness' to Scottish traditional music, but also a firm rejection of the salience of dance or the nationality of the composer. This is not surprising in that much of the output of Scottish traditional music today is music made for listening as a form of commodified music placing a distance between the audience and the performers.

The demise of any nationally defined component in the understanding of Scottish traditional music is of course more complex than this survey would suggest, however, as the terms of the question outline it, most people rejected any link between the nationality of the composer and the resulting evaluation of the Scottishness of Scottish traditional music. This does not really speak to ethnicity because, as is understood in contemporary society, ethnicity is acquired and race is inherited. To be ethnically Scottish is to learn and immerse oneself in the culture, language and habits of Scots; one cannot be racially 'Scottish' as no such racial category exists. There is clearly an ethnicity to Scottish traditional music however, although what this survey suggests is that that ethnicity is not defined by where you come from, but understood by how one learns to play and sing and a set of particularly Scottish aesthetic values shared by people within the Scottish traditional music community of practice.

Participation, cultural policy and politics

On the very important area of how people engage with each other in this community, we know that Scottish traditional music amongst many other local and ethnic forms of traditional music is now primarily digitally mediated. However, given the limitations of this questionnaire, and of the sample size, we can know that two of the most common ways in which people participate in Scottish traditional music is through weekly informal sessions and through active engagement with online recorded performances (both audio and video). There is also a high degree of relative engagement via social media, with at least 43 per cent of respondents discussing Scottish traditional music with others at least once a week or more often. When one steps back and considers the community and their social connectedness, about half of those surveyed said that they physically meet and perform with others, discuss via social media *and* watch or listen to Scottish traditional music on social media at least once a month.

The closest statistical evidence with which to compare this data comes from the results of the Scottish Household Survey Culture and Sport Module 2007/2008 (Scottish Government 2009). This was a more detailed survey of cultural attendance, participation and value in Scotland than is normally conducted in the Scottish Household Survey and does break down responses by musical genres. It shows that in that year, 38 per cent of the 6,763 respondents had attended a musical event in the past year. The survey also shows that Scottish traditional music (11 per cent) was more popular than classical music (7 per cent), live DJ events (9 per cent), opera (5 per cent) and jazz (4 per cent). Discounting non-musical forms such as the cinema or theatre, Scottish traditional music was only superseded by 'other live music events' which is largely popular music such as rock and pop. This evidence, combined with the evidence from my own survey underlines the unusually high degree of socialisation and commitment in this community of practice, and also suggests that Scottish traditional music has a significant agency in people's lives, allowing those that count themselves to be part of the community to feel a strong sense of belonging, given their frequent participation. This also has ramifications for policy and practice in that it provides evidence for the claim that Scottish traditional music might be one of the most effective cultural activities for the production of that slippery yet desirable quality of community cohesion.

These statistics support the notion that money spent on access and education in Scottish traditional music might be money well spent, with a high return of social connectedness, allowing those that gain access a lifetime of cultural engagement, often at very little cost. About half of all those surveyed had received some state funding, either individually or as part of a group. This is presumably a much lower figure than the amount of state subsidy given to classical music in Scotland and the UK as a whole. Unsurprisingly therefore, the largest proportion of respondents at 47 per cent felt that Scottish traditional music does not receive enough state support. The government data on funding for Scottish traditional music vis-à-vis other musical genres when compared with the small amount of data we have on attendance and participation by musical genre would also tend to support this view. However, there was a sizeable proportion of 40 per cent who were not sure, and 9 per cent of people agreed with the proposition that Scottish traditional music receives adequate funding in Scotland. This combined with the very high level of education amongst the respondents, suggests that public awareness of the spending of Creative Scotland and of local authority support is confined to a narrow section of society.

Politically, the respondents to this survey felt that Scottish independence was a desirable thing, but perhaps not as fervently as one would expect amongst those with a deep involvement in Scottish vernacular culture. Only 53 per cent of respondents reported that they supported independence, with 21 per cent undecided and 15 per cent firmly against. The results of the nationwide referendum on independence in Scotland held on 18 September 2014 found over two million Scots (55 per cent) against independence and 45 per cent of voters in favour of independence, with an exceptionally high turnout of 85 per cent of the possible electorate. The lack of a greater proportion of respondents who are committed nationalists tells us something quite important about Scottish traditional music today. When one considers this against the other factors reported about what constitutes Scottish traditional music today, it adds further evidence to the claim that nationalism as a cultural trope has faded from people's understanding of why traditional music matters. Furthermore, the character of the public debate on Scottish independence in 2014 was almost entirely devoid of appeals to cultural nationalism. As well as being a deliberate campaign policy of the Scottish Nationalist Party, the absence of cultural appeals to nationalist impulses across the public debate tells us something about the place of culture in Scottish society today. It suggests that musical culture within Scotland is now considered part of the personal domain, something that creates a sense of belonging and identity, but not necessarily a national one. This is supported by the evidence from the survey which suggests that the oral transmission and traditional compositional style are key defining factors in their understanding of what Scottish traditional music is. Neither of which are nationalist qualities of music. Scottish traditional music is seemingly a musical community where the interpersonal relations and aesthetics count more strongly than any sense of national identity.

Tradition and modernity

One of the central defining binaries of all traditional and folk musics from around the world is the internal aesthetic and relational discourse around tradition and modernity. Expressed often musically, and in the reception of traditional music in reviews, fora, magazines, between friends and in multimodal album covers and liner notes, the tension between the traditional and the modern or contemporary has been both crucial to those that place themselves at the heart of the tradition, at the boundaries of traditional practice or beyond. But a perspective of traditional culture that places it in binary opposition to commercial culture has been too simplistic for some time. This dichotomy was, and still is in some people's minds, the countercultural relationship that actually gives the value and affective power to traditional music and culture. It speaks to them as an antidote to contemporary capitalism that allows them to express their more authentic values, mostly situated in a more leftist, communitarian worldview. But speak to younger musicians and fans of traditional music and one senses a different, more complex relationship with both traditional culture and late modern capitalism. Traditional music specifically allows many to connect and to forge quite specific identities for themselves that are a new, more deeply felt form of authenticity, in essence an experience of branded authenticity.

Sarah Banet-Weiser (Banet-Weiser 2012) has successfully argued that brand authenticity is a powerful framework for understanding culture and identity in contemporary capitalist cultures which moves beyond the problematic binary exchanges of Marxist economic analyses of culture. In her examination of brand culture in the late modern

West she outlines a kind of relational cultural sociology of brands where she demonstrates how we might move beyond the binary assumptions of traditional versus modern or old versus new to a more realistic conception of how we conceive of traditional music. She suggests that:

> As a relationship based on exchange ... branding cannot be explained as commodification or as the mere incorporation of cultural spheres of life by advanced capitalism . . . . We cannot productively think about brand culture, or what brands mean for culture, without accounting for the affective relational quality – the *experience* – of brands . . . . Far more than an economic strategy of capitalism, brands are the cultural spaces in which individuals feel safe, secure, relevant, and authentic.
>
> (Banet-Weiser 2012: 8–9)

If one accepts that musical participation and traditional music in particular can be conceived of as a form of relational commodity, then how we listen to and perform and what we say about music all contributes not only to our own sense of belonging and authenticity, but also to how we project this to others. In this sense then musical participation becomes a form of social branding, or of social belonging; what you listen to and perform codifies your identity, and in today's digitally mediated world it does not depend upon where you were born, the colour of your skin or your accent. This is often discussed in terms of 'cultural capital' (Bennett et al. 2009; Bourdieu 1984). We are essentially free to choose a social identity that suits our values and our sense of who we are (or want to be). Traditional music therefore embodies certain relational values that are important to many involved in the community. Those values can be mobilised to tell others what we value, and many within the community of practice, as shown in the survey results, value the active, often countercultural, socially engaged nature of Scottish traditional music: a form of music that values oral transmission and acoustic instruments over notation and synthetic sounds; an educated elite that identify with egalitarian values, the homemade and independence of thought over the dominant neo-liberal capitalist, mass produced political hegemony of today's culture. But as a social practice, it is a weak one. These values may be inscribed into the ways in which people participate, in the pub, often every week, sharing and singing traditional music and song, but they do not translate into strong forms of social action. Scottish traditional music, much like the popular 'world music' genre, is well suited to late modern capitalism in that identifying with these musics allows people to be a 'branded Other' and thereby enhance their cultural capital. Avidly consuming and supporting capitalist relations via the economic exchange of musical 'brands' whilst also symbolically raising a hand in protest to signal that they object to the polarising, destructive forces of late modern capitalism – a sort of weak anti-capitalist protest from the inside, without any material significance.

This was the real success and result of the powerfully successful Anglo-American folk revivals of the 1960s. They were hugely successful in attracting young, middle-class urban participants, who then created the network of folk clubs, venues, record companies, audiences and fans which supported the increasing commodification, branding and professionalisation of traditional music, sometimes turning it into that more commercially recognisable brand – 'folk music'. This development of a classed sense of traditional or folk music, particularly within Anglo-American society, matters because of people's increasing emphasis that culture matters, because people make social judgements and 'class' each other partially upon your cultural 'assets'. Social class matters, and it has been empirically shown that in the UK today that the cultural capital of music, although unevenly distributed, is constitutive of class (Bennett et al. 2009). Therefore, counting oneself part of the community of practice in traditional Scottish music matters, not just because of what it does for your sense of belonging, but for what it says to others about your identity and your class. Traditional music (and 'folk music') today construct both positive community social life yet also construct middle-class cultural capital and form the basis for highly commercial economic exchange. The exchange value of Scottish traditional music lies both in the authenticity and affective power of the music but also in the cultural capital that it affords participants. By participating in Scottish traditional music, we are both saying something about our aesthetic preferences and also constructing a particular social structure that informs our, and others, views of class and social identity.

CHAPTER **6**

The Place of Scottish Traditional Music

[The] New Europeanness is neither a process nor a product of centralization or canon formation. It is in no sense of a definition singular, and it shows no signs of being refracted into core repertoires.... the musical landscape of New Europeanness is one of borders rather than of centers ... as sites of exchange and passage, rather than exclusion. This is not the musical geography of Europeanness as it unfolded from the late Middle Ages until the mid-twentieth century, which was dominated by centers ... Tradition is up for grabs.... Drawing from the past, however selectively, enriches the ways in which the present is given new meaning.

(Bohlman 2011: 262)

Scotland has a distinct and perhaps unusually well-defined physical landscape. There is no ambiguity about where it is, despite the centuries of socio-political change and cultural discourse. The physical Scotland sits at the top of Europe, above England and Wales and beside the island of Ireland. It has only one physical border with England; its remaining borders are with the North Sea and the Atlantic Ocean. The place of Scotland is however a different matter. Place is not physical, nor is it tangible, but it is observable. Place is the mythological construction of landscape, and musical places allow us to feel a sort of shared emotional belonging, a relational affect that unites us as listeners. It follows therefore, that the musical place of a certain area or landscape is constructed largely in the audience, and that there are therefore myriad mythological constructions of the musical place of Scotland. Narrowing that down to the mythological sonic construction of Scotland in traditional music might still mean that there are an infinite number of possible Scottish 'places' in the minds of the global citizenry. However, it is possible, as with any aesthetic domain, to gain a deeper and meaningful understanding by examining the shared understandings of musical place, or the 'unnuanced' (Cook 2001) meanings, sometimes called cultural tropes, at work in the musical construction of Scotland.

It was Michel Foucault who proposed the study of the ways in which people use object, technology, thoughts and conduct in order to transform their way of being in the world; to alter their state of mind, emotion or communication.[1] All sorts of people throughout the world regularly disappear into their own personal imaginary and mythological places through the use of music as a technology of the self. The significance of place is therefore that it allows us to understand the meaning of traditional music and its relationship to particular regions, towns, landscapes and countries in people's everyday lives, both as a 'technology of the self', but also as a means to gain insight into the socially shared meaning and aesthetics of Scotland and its place in people's imaginations. In ethnomusicology a great deal of work has gone into understanding the 'soundscapes' around us, both in terms of the musical sound and humans' interaction with their environments. Raimond Murray Schaefer's *The Tuning of the World* (1977) was one of the earliest books to deal with the musical and sonic construction of place, and this close examination and its consequences for our understanding of the social life of music has continued from various disciplinary perspectives (see for instance Leyshon et al. 1998; Smith 1994; Stokes 1994). Increasingly, scholars are attempting to understand not just how once common soundscapes are in danger of vanishing because of globalisation and industrial development, but are also examining the types of acoustic soundscapes, or acoustic ecologies that exist within various different places. Part of this concern has been a reassessment of the importance of studying sound and how we hear and its semiotic significance in everyday life. This emanates from a concern amongst ethnomusicologists and others that music studies has been too 'visual' with an over-reliance on the score and the resultant ways in which this prioritises Western, diatonic musical understanding over indigenous and vernacular musical systems (Feld 1981; Feld and Fox 1994).

There are, as previously mentioned, myriad potential musical places within Scotland which do not require one to be physically located there, or for that matter to even have ever been to that place. However, these days Scotland is often thought about in terms of four large overlapping regions: the Highlands and Islands, the Central Belt (including Edinburgh and Glasgow), the North East and the Borders. In this chapter we will examine how Scottish traditional music in particular constructs and mythologises the place of the Scottish Borders.

The Musical Place of the Scottish Borders

> From the moorlands and the meadows
> To the city of the shadows
> Where I wander old and lonely comes a call I understand
> The clear soft notes enthralling
> It is calling ever calling
> 'Tis the spirit of the open in the dear old Borderland.[2]

Driving through the Scottish Borders can be a beautiful yet desolate experience. Cold moorlands, dying light, isolated headlamps and late nights can all be transformed with music that can alter your perception of the particular landscape in which you are travelling. There are albums for every occasion, however, whilst passing through the

Borders; the one I most enjoy is the 2008 release *Windward Away* by the singer Archie Fisher. The songs on this album come from, and are homologous with, the landscape, and the romanticism of the lyrics construct a very particular sense of place for me as a listener. However, one does not have to physically go to a place in order to develop an understanding of it. The concept of place is mythologised in culture and can be both collective and individual. Sometimes hearing a song or a poem about a place can be very powerful and traditional music is arguably more tied to particularised landscapes than other musics. Archie Fisher is one of Scotland's greatest singer-songwriters, and in many of his songs, he evokes a carefully constructed sense of place and emotion of the moors, hills, rivers, towns and people that make up the Scottish Borders. This sense of place is personal to each listener, and yet as this chapter shows, there are key conceptions of place that resonate through time. Understanding the cultural resonances and intertextual themes that have been performed through time allows us an insight into the shared sense of musical place of the Scottish Borders. It is my contention (and others') that although mythological, there are cultural places that are well established mythologies carrying particularised identities and emotional characteristics constructed in song, poetry and music. In this way, the cultural place of one song, artist or repertoire can be critically understood in relation to historical and contemporary communal identities in musical discourse.

Intertextuality in the music of the Scottish Borders

Hearing the meaning of a song is of course as much an act of creation as are performance or composition, because it is in the act of hearing that we construct semiotic meaning and make sense of the musical text and its cultural intertextuality. Roland Barthes stresses that 'it is the reader of myths himself who must reveal their essential function' (Barthes 1993: 129). Understanding place is of course deeply personal (as in a 'technology of the self') yet often the meanings we share can help us to recognise that certain motifs or tropes have been prevalent through time and help us to recognise the influence of song and poetry upon our communal perceptions of landscape. In particular, references to names of specific localities can be very powerful aural landmarks that help construct communal mythologies of place and signal particular emotions and meanings. As Fisher puts it, 'I think the traditional songs I like singing are the ones that are visually most creative, that paint the strongest pictures . . . . To name a place in a song will generate an image'.[3]

Within the border between Scotland and England there are a number of historical dualisms that have been present in much of the writing about that region, that can have been absorbed into the place of the Scottish Borders. There are three principal historical places in the Scottish Borders that emerge in song and literature, including the rough and unlawful 'debatable lands' of the medieval Border Reivers;[4] the romantic (and sometimes nationalist) place of the rolling hills of the Borders; and the daunting supernatural landscape of Border Ballads where otherworldly beings help to dictate community morality. These three places can be found in music and song, literature and poetry, as well as in contemporary commercial heritage constructions of the Scottish Borders. They are key to a strong regional identity, distinct from both the national identities of Scotland and England. For over five centuries, the Scottish–English borderlands have formed an in-between space between two nations, with shifting borders and malleable allegiances. Key figures such as Sir Walter Scott, James Hogg and Hugh MacDiarmid, as well as the core repertoire of the traditional Border Ballads, have been influential in constructing a Scottish national identity from this landscape. And because the landscape itself has been central to competing mythologies and power struggles, the Border people have engendered a strong regional identity with fascinating local characters and landscapes prevalent in their music. Speaking with them can leave you with a strong impression of Borderer first and Scottish/English second, as the Borders remain, 'a single and coherent space that spans the political boundary between England and Scotland' (Gray 2000: 15; see also Barker 2004: 164).

Scottish national consciousness has tended to rely on the nineteenth-century romanticism of key figures in the invention of Scotland. The most prominent of these is Sir Walter Scott, a major nineteenth-century romantic novelist and socialite, who appropriated Border landscape and traditions to invent a national mythology of nostalgia in a romantic landscape:

> [Scott] invested the Scottish past with a magical appeal and satisfied the powerful emotional needs for nostalgia in a society experiencing unprecedented changes. Scott was a brilliant pioneer in the invention of tradition ... which helped to develop a new set of national symbols and icons while at the same time renewing others of venerable antiquity in the contemporary image of Victorian Scotland.
>
> (Devine 1999: 292)

Sir Walter Scott produced a landmark collection of Border Ballads, published in February 1802, entitled *The Minstrelsy of the Scottish Border* (Scott 1802). He became in the nineteenth century a highly influential novelist but was at this time the Sheriff of Selkirk, and on his judicial tours of the Scottish Borders, he collected many versions of songs sung particularly in Teviotdale and Redesdale. Many of these found their way into his *Minstrelsy*, which was his first real attempt at profitable commercial publishing and was remarkably successful. He gave particular importance to ballads that mentioned specific places in the Scottish Borders and through his editorial commentary he made explicit connections between the landscapes mentioned in the Border Ballads and their physical existence, mapping the narratives of the Ballads onto the physical landscape of the Scottish Borders (MacRae 2014). He was an active place-maker, who used the Scottish Border Ballads to construct a particularly strong sense of place and cultural nationalism.

Later in the nineteenth century, the Kailyard writers were a group of late Victorian writers who extended this romantic link between the landscape of Scotland and a lyrical romantic affect through mass appeal with bestselling novels such as *Beside the Bonnie Brier Bush* by Ian Maclaren, published in 1894. Extremely sentimental publications such as this tended to add to the notions of a rural past, in which instruments such as the bagpipe, and musicians such as harpers, were prominently reinvented as symbols of a romantic and culturally distinct national mythology. One of the key tropes to come out of the deep mythologisation of Scotland and Scottishness in the long nineteenth century was the creation of an imagined Other-within: a sort of idealised notion of the romantic pre-industrial, rural working class with closely guarded songs, stories and poetry handed down 'unsullied' in an authentic oral tradition. This of course was almost entirely fictitious but a necessary element of the romantic nationalism so thoroughly ingrained into the Scottish and British psyche in the nineteenth century. Indeed, this romanticism spearheaded by Scott led to the 'Celtic Twilight' movement in the later nineteenth century.

Scott, Chappell and other myth-makers were part of a wider European movement (clearly visible with the clarity of hindsight) whose efforts had tangible effects on the traditional musics of the European Other-within. Scott's vision of nationhood and Scottish culture rely upon the landscape and ballads of the Scottish Borders. In his work there is a strong element of mythologising a Scottishness in its fullest sense, much of his nationalism in poetry and song relies on a Border identity (Lamont and Rossington 2007). For instance in his 'The Lay of the Last Minstrel', a narrative of loss and belonging is told, of one of the last wandering harpist bards. At publication in 1805, the poem was very popular (with sales of 27,000)[5] and received positive reviews, underscoring the power of these mythological constructions of place in the early-nineteenth-century imagination.

> O Caledonia! stern and wild,
> Meet nurse for a poetic child!
> Land of brown heath and shaggy wood,
> Land of the mountain and the flood,
> Land of my sires! what mortal hand
> Can e'er untie the filial band,
> That knits me to thy rugged strand!
> Still, as I view each well-known scene,
> Think what is now, and what hath been,
> Seems as, to me, of all bereft,
> Sole friends thy woods and streams were left;
> And thus I love them better still,
> Even in extremity of ill.
> By Yarrow's streams still let me stray,
> Though none should guide my feeble way;
> Still feel the breeze down Ettrick break,
> Although it chill my wither'd cheek;
> Still lay my head by Teviot Stone,
> Though there, forgotten and alone,
> The bard may draw his parting groan
>
> (Extract from 'The Lay of the Last Minstrel' by
> Walter Scott [1805] [Cameron n.d.: 60–1])

This poem is unusual in some important ways: primarily, harps (and harpers) were historically centred in the Highlands of Scotland and around Perthshire at Atholl, in use as a high-status instrument in Gaelic court culture and were not a common instrument within the Borders of Scotland (Sanger and Kinnaird 1992: 93, 145; Newton 2009). Scott is making an explicit link between the race and the landscape, and in so doing constructs a sense of racial nationalism, so prevalent in the rise of European nationalisms in the nineteenth century. The minstrel is undertaking a journey, a familiar artistic theme across cultures, but in doing so, the minstrel is grounded in the stones, hills and rivers of the Scottish Borders which are presented as timeless and stable against the temporality of the 'feeble way' of the minstrel. In this poem by Scott we have many motifs at play that are associated with the Borders, in particular the mythologising of the Border landscape as national idea; the fashionable myth of his time of the 'last leaves' whereby the minstrel stands as a metaphor for the death of authentic, oral tradition; the myth of the homecoming after an arduous journey in typically cruel Border weather; and, the myth of the supernatural, particularly strong in Border poetry and ballads.

In this last respect, it may be that in song, the Yarrow valley in the Scottish Borders is the most otherworldly and consistently supernatural place in Scotland. This cannot simply be attributed to the physical landscape of Yarrow, but its pre-eminence as a site of otherworldliness in song is indisputable. Traditional ballads such as 'The Cruel Mither' and 'The Dowie Dens O Yarrow' and literary figures such as Scott, Hogg and even William Wordsworth (child of Cumberland just over the Border), all construct Yarrow's eerie qualities. J.B. Selkirk (1832–1904) was born in the year of Walter Scott's death and was a published poet whose 'Song of Yarrow' emphasises the strong sense of lonely, eerie otherworldliness of Yarrow. In this poem, Yarrow's waters are 'murmuring', and 'pouring a lonely music through the heather'. The stream is given human qualities of speech in it sings a 'lonely song' of reminiscence, and he emphasises the timeless nature of the Yarrow water, very much an elaborate art poem of the style fashionable in the nineteenth century (Selkirk in Cameron n.d.: 77–9). Similarly, in the very old Scottish ballad 'The Dowie Dens O Yarrow', the theme of the supernatural dream comes through strongly in the dream of the narrator. This dream is one that combines the supernatural with the sorrow associated with Yarrow and the violence of the Border region in a classic 'Romeo and Juliet' trope. In the ballad, the Lady who 'lives in the North' has been courted by nine noblemen, but falls in love with a young man called John from Yarrow:

O mither dear I ha'e dreamed a dream
An' I wish't may prove nae sorrow
I dreamed I pu'd the heather bell
On the bonnie braes o' Yarrow.

Three he slew, and three withdrew
And three lay deadly wounded
But in behind cam' her brother George
An' pierced his body thorough.

(Traditional)

This unsuitable match is disdained by her mother, and although the boy from Yarrow manages to kill the nine armed men sent to kill him in Yarrow, he is murdered by the lady's brother George. In a dream, she goes on a journey to Yarrow and sees her John slain as a bloody corpse in the valley but she wraps him up in her yellow hair and carries him home. She then lies down in her bed and dies of a broken heart. The narrative contains strong elements of the supernatural in the use of a dream and the significance of the number nine (used mostly for counting objects or men), and the division of those men into threes, both strongly associated with the supernatural. The number three usually signalling 'mystical significance' whereas the number seven is usually a measure of time or people, 'seven sons, daughters, brothers, sisters, knights . . . ' (Wimberly 1965: 330). The colour yellow in her hair signifies marriage and these strongly resonate with other supernatural signs that are weaved into the place of the Scottish Borders through the ballad tradition.

Other Border Ballads, such as 'Tam Lin' set around Selkirk, 'Thomas the Rhymer' set in the Eildon Hills near Melrose, and many others, contain numerous metaphors for water as supernatural, dangerous and other. In 'Tam Lin', his name and his supernatural transformations in the arms of Janet suggest water and associations as a water sprite (Niles 1977: 346). But as Niles suggest, the more important narrative in 'Tam Lin' is in fact the 'simple and essential . . . story of a man and a woman who survive' (Niles 1977: 347). And it is this theme that also comes across strongly in Fisher's songs: places like the Scottish Borders speak to us about the otherworldliness, inherent change and emotional transformation in life, yet they simultaneously allow for a sense of stability and reassurance amidst life's journey.

Taking the shine off the sublime

The other famous nineteenth-century name most closely associated with the Borders is James Hogg, the 'Ettrick Shepherd' (1770–1835). Hogg was known to be a novelist, short-story writer, essayist, musician, poet, journalist and songwriter, and considered himself to be the natural successor to Robert Burns, going as far as to claim the same birthday as the bard (Steel 1985: 2, 4). He played upon his image as the Ettrick Shepherd and even sported a plaid when in London to encourage this sense of the rural shepherd, which of course was playing to the sensibilities of the time (Mack 1993: 308). As Gilbert has shown, Hogg had a closer and more emic relationship with tradition than Scott (Gilbert 2006). This can be seen in his respect for singers and his informants who are regarded as active, important agents of culture. In this way, lessons can be learnt from Hogg: his was not a concern for historical origins or authorship; the objects of his interest were the affective properties, or, put another way, he was interested in what the songs said about human experience. This humanity and the landscape of the Borders are richly portrayed in much of his work such as the songs in *The Mountain Bard* (1807), *The Queen's Wake* (1813) and his most famous work and novel of morality, *The Confessions of a Justified Sinner* (1824).

I would suggest that for Hogg the morality of the people is as important as the landscape in which they live, to the construction of place. And the place of the Borders for Hogg is a frightening place. Filled with otherworldly goings-on set within a desolate landscape which dominates the meek humanity within it, his Borders juxtapose the supernatural fairies against the ordinary human. In so doing, Hogg becomes one of the first to cement the pragmatic aesthetic of the ordinariness that has become central to the identity of Scots. The otherworld and the fairies become a counterpoint to the ordinariness of everyday Scots. This sense of vernacular ordinariness, or pragmatism, is now a core Scottish trope. Hogg does much to construct this in work such as *The Queen's Wake*. In this epic poem, he attempts to romanticise the arrival of Mary, Queen of Scots in 1561 at Leith (Edinburgh) and the poem revolves around a battle of the bards. The bards are distinguished from each other as Gael or Borderer, and Hogg mythologises the use of tartan to distinguish clans in the poem. As well as cementing an old Scottish dualism of Highlander versus Lowlander, Hogg has here borrowed from Scott in inventing the link between ethnicity and sartorial style. In the poem, Rizio, the Italian, is presented as bard to Mary and tells a lay of Malcolm of Lorne, but he is not well received by the Scottish audience. In the poem, he constructs a disdain of the flowery lyricism of the European other through the narrator, demonstrating disdain for the foreign minstrel's art song:

The strain died soft in note of woe,
Nor breath nor whisper 'gan to flow,
From courtly circle; all as still,
As midnight on the lonely hill.
So well that foreign minstrel's strain
Had mimicked passion, woe, and pain,
Seemed even the chilly hand of death
Stealing away his mellow breath.
So sighed – so stopp'd – so died his lay, –
His spirit too seemed fled for aye.

'Tis true, the gay attentive throng
Admired, but loved not much, his song;
Admired his wonderous voice and skill,
His harp that thrilled or wept at will.
But that affected gaudy rhyme,
The querulous keys and changing chime,
Scarce could the Highland chieftain brook:
Disdain seemed kindling in his look
That song so vapid, artful, terse,
Should e'er compete with Scottish verse.

(Hogg 1819: 46)

In this poem, we can see Hogg actively constructing the ordinary and everyday aesthetic of Scottish poetry and song in opposition to the 'vapid, artful, terse . . . gaudy rhyme' of the bard. This is a central motif of the Scottish vernacular. Much Scottish traditional song is value-laden repertoire, thick with admiration for the ordinary, emphasis of the indigenous and disdain for the artful, fanciful and sophistry of the other. As Seamus Heaney put it, Hogg, and the Scottish people have 'the gift for taking the shine off the sublime' (Heaney 2003: 11). Contemporary performers and repertoire, and particularly professional traditional musicians, do not emphasise this dualism as much, but it lives on in songs and in singers' introductions to their material at festivals and folk clubs. Fisher's use of the aesthetic of the ordinary and of the harshness of the ordinary life (see below) can be read as an echo of Hogg's mythologising of the Borders. As a value, it is important to the construction of place, and forms part of a complex of dualisms that were particularly prevalent in the nineteenth century's fertile playground of invention.

Later in the poem, the tenth bard's song presents another key trope of the place of the Borders in the Bard of Ettrick's supernatural tale of the Borderlands. 'Old David' is one where the green doublets and white steeds of the 'fairy queen' emphasise the other-worldly nature of the Borders.

Fast spur they on through bush and brake;
To Ettrick woods their course they take.
Old David followed still in view,
Till near the Lochilaw they drew;
There in a deep and wonderous dell,
Where noon-tide breezes never blew,
From flowers to drink the morning dew;

There, underneath the sylvan shade,
The fairies' spacious bower was made.

(Hogg 1819: 121)

Eventually, the Bard of Ettrick, in a mythological and romantic historical X-factor-esque singing competition, comes in second to Gardyn of Deeside, who carries off the bejewelled harp. However, Queen Mary gifts another, simpler but magical harp to the Bard of Ettrick who then takes it home to the Borders. Like many myths of magical instruments such as those of the famous MacCrimmon pipers, the otherworldly instrument, gifted to the ordinary human can only ever sound musical in their hands. So Hogg goes beyond the temporal world, to mythologise a harsh, supernatural Scottish Borders which ultimately provides a contrast for the ordinariness of its Scottish inhabitants.

Nationalists, Reivers and place

Not far from the West Marches site of Kirconnell is the birthplace of Christopher Murray Grieve (1892–1978), known by his pen name Hugh MacDiarmid, one of Scotland's most important poets of the twentieth century. MacDiarmid singlehandedly began the Scottish renaissance in literature and poetry, reinvented the political nationalist movement and established Scots as an authentic and creative language in the twentieth century. He was always a controversial figure and, some would claim, racist if not certainly xenophobic towards the English. An ardent Scottish nationalist, MacDiarmid insisted on Scotland as a radical and free nation that he wished to see removed from the colonial imperialism of the United Kingdom. The place of the Scottish Borders for MacDiarmid was an inspiration that channelled the landscape into a sincere striving for a Scottish socialist state. This sense in which the landscape of the Borders fed his political ideology is cleanly stated in his essay, 'Growing up in Langholm', in which he makes the connection between place and nation:

> These were indeed the champagne days – these long enchanted days on the Esk, the Wauchope and the Ewes – and the thought of them today remains as intoxicating as they must have been in actual fact all those years ago. I have been 'mad about Scotland' ever since . . . .
>
> My earliest impressions are of an almost tropical luxuriance of nature – of great forests, of honey-scented heather hills, and moorlands infinitely rich in little-appreciated beauties of flowering, of animal and insect life, of subtle relationships of water and light, and of a multitude of rivers, each with its distinct music.
>
> (MacDiarmid in Miller 1970: 166–7)

MacDiarmid's poetry is filled with the landscape of the Borders and the history of the 'raidings and reivings' (Miller 1970: 164) that served as a source of creativity, but one which he turned into a fierce political will. Indeed, Lyall suggests that the childhood landscape of Langholm and its powerful agency as a 'secret reservoir' of inspiration gave MacDiarmid the foundation for his poetry and politics (Lyall 2006: 69). So just as others, such as Scott and Hogg, used the landscape to serve their own sense of romantic nationalism which MacDiarmid deplored, he mobilises the landscape, and the Calvinist people that live in it, as a key to his lifelong radicalism. For both MacDiarmid and many of the traditional Border Ballads, the mythology of the Border Reivers has left a grain of independence and toughness in the place of the Borders. And although his complex identity as an internationalist, republican radical went far beyond the simple notions of struggle and independence of the Border Reivers, he acknowledges them in his exploration of selfhood, in the poem 'Kinsfolk' of 1931:

> Reivers to weavers and to me. Weird way!
> Yet in the last analysis I've sprung
> Frae battles, mair than ballads, and it seems
> The thrawn auld water has at last upswung
> Through me, and's mountin' like the vera devil
> To its richt level!
>
> (MacDiarmid in Lyall 2006: 68)

The fearsome Border Reivers have been a significant theme in the traditional music of the Border Ballads, and they continue to lend a strong sense of independence to Border identity. For example, witness the adoption of the name for a local (now defunct) professional rugby side; Mark Knopfler's song 'Border Reiver', on his 2009 *Get Lucky* album, in which the truck referred to in the song is the tough and durable 'Albion Reiver' of the 1960s and '70s; and a small line of commercial flummery dedicated to very tangible markers of Reiving such as 'I'm a Border Reiver' t-shirts. Historically, in fact, Reivers as outlaw cattle-raiders had a very familiar knowledge of the landscape and used it to their advantage in evading government efforts at control. The sixteenth and seventeenth centuries saw a system of Wardens given control over the Marches of the Borders, which were divided into the East, Middle and West Marches. They appear to have had little control and to have been constantly frustrated in their efforts to pacify the indigenous Borderers, as complaining letters from local Wardens to their political masters demonstrate.[6] John Gray describes how the violent, terrorising history of the Border Reivers was useful for nationalist propaganda on both sides of the border and ironically led to a place with a stronger regional than national identity, where the population was forced into a life of 'subsistence and resistance' by the actions of two larger, distant powers (Gray 2003: 25). The mythology of Border Reiving has a secure basis in historical fact and is amplified and transmogrified in traditional song, as can be heard in the independence and wiliness of Borderers in ballads such as 'Jock O the Side' and 'Kinmont Willie'.

In this latter ballad, the arrest of Kinmont Willie leads to a rescue attempt by the 'bauld Buccleuch' who goes to the rescue of the notorious Reiver across the border with England. The events surrounding the border serve as a metaphor for independence on the Scottish side, where lords like Buccleuch actively defend Reivers because they are Scottish, even when they are noted raiders. These ballads became important in the nineteenth century largely because of the growth of the national idea, stimulated by MacPherson's Ossian and Scott's own agenda, and were collected and presented to the public in an active attempt to mythologise a national identity, where thieves and Reivers were presented as heroic in the cause of defending 'auld Alba'. But the sense of place that exists in these ballads shows that nationalism is only part of the story. Ballads set in the Borders demonstrate various motifs including the nationalist tendency, but also the romantic hero, the outlaw, the supernatural moral foil to human society and the eerie desolation of the landscape.

The Borderlands of Archie Fisher

Archie Fisher is a internationally renowned singer and guitarist who has been a professional musician for fifty years. He has a large audience in traditional music particularly in the UK and throughout North America. His professional life has paralleled the folk revival and the subsequent commercialisation of traditional Scottish music and his encyclopaedic knowledge of traditional music and nuanced approach to song and poetry make him a formidable interviewee (McKerrell 2011a). He is one of seven siblings, three of whom – Archie and his sisters Cilla and Ray – became professional singers. The family can trace their roots to the Isles of Barra and Vatersay in the Outer Hebrides and to the Scottish Borders, where he now resides. He was born in 1939 to Morag (Marion) and John Fisher (1891–1957) and raised in Partick, Glasgow. Fisher's career began in the 1960s and this scene has been richly documented by Stephanie Smith in her PhD study of the Fisher family (Smith 1988). She describes the early years of Fisher's musical development within the fertile and optimistic Glaswegian folk revival scene of the 1950s and '60s. Her fieldwork with the Fishers documents an appealing and refreshingly pre-commercial folk scene in industrial Glasgow. Significantly, Fisher is acknowledged by his peers as a highly influential figure, the late Hamish Imlach suggesting that 'Archie was certainly the first professional folksinger in Scotland' (Imlach in Smith 1988: 145). His performing and decades of touring in the UK and North America has given Fisher a strong following who regularly turn out for his touring dates at home and abroad. His repertoire encompasses many traditional songs as well as his own compositions, and I believe his work as a lyricist-poet is as significant as his performance.

Probably the key construct in Fisher's songs is of the romantic place of the Borders. This is clearly stated in his compositions and in his song 'River and the Road', which encapsulates the key dualism of love and loss which grows within Fisher's landscape of the Borders and emanates through all of his songs.

Figure 6.1 Portrait of Archie Fisher (reproduced by kind permission of Archie Fisher)

Often when I think of you I see a Border river
Changing with the melting snows, both there and gone forever.
You're the river I'm the road, that runs along your ridges,
Giving you the right of way and always building bridges.

. . .

For everywhere the Heron flies the winding river follows
And in turn she claims the skies, then stalks along the shadows
And often when I think of you, I see a Border river
Changing with the melting snows, both there and gone forever.

(Fisher 2008)

In the sleeve notes to his 2008 release *Windward Away*, Fisher actually says that the title of this song refers to 'two perennial love theme images intertwined and eventually unravelled' (Fisher 2008: n.p.). He constructs a strong sense of being at once at home with the familiar landscape of the Borders, and simultaneously suffering the loss of emotional transience from relationships as part of a life fully lived in the romantic Borders. It is desolate and harsh in the same way as the older Border Ballads, or the poetry of Scott and Hogg, but differs in a key respect: how that conflictual energy is channelled. Fisher takes dualisms such as transience and home, love and loss, river and road, man and woman, and uses the emotional energy to romanticise the landscape of Borders. In this way, he manages to fill the Border landscape as an affective space within which we can reconcile the tensions in our emotional lives, and allows us to feel love and loss as communal and individual at the same time.

Another of Fisher's key place-making tools is his metaphorical use of water as unknowable or supernatural. Rivers 'as changing as a woman', 'dark waters of . . .', and in many songs, the shifting nature of rivers, as shown in 'Tam Lin', above, embodies the changing nature of life. He is working in a long tradition, that specifically within the Borders has

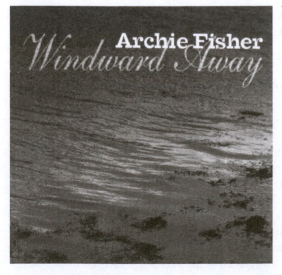

Figure 6.2 Archie Fisher, *Windward Away* album cover

given water both protective and dangerous connotation depending on the context of the story. For instance, in the Border Ballad 'Kinmont Willie', we see the river and the weather as meaningful within the story, emphasising the narrative of danger in verses such as:

Then on we held for Carlisle town,
And at Staneshaw-bank the Eden we cross'd;
The water was great and meikle of spate,
But the never a horse nor man we lost.

And when we reached the Staneshaw-bank,
The wind was rising loud and hie;
And there the laird garr'd leave our steeds,
For fear that they should stamp and nie.

And when we left the Staneshaw-bank,
The wind began full loud to blaw;
But 'twas wind and weet, and fire and sleet,
When we came beneath the castle wa.

(Traditional, in Reed 1991: 33)

And later in the ballad, the Eden river is a place of welcoming and sanctuary for Kinmont Willie, and Buccleuch, as they safely swim across it to evade Lord Scroope. This is a motif that repeats in other Border Ballads, for example in 'Jock O the Side', when Jock-O-the-side, against all common sense, continues into the river Tyne in a rescue attempt:

Sae now the water they a' hae tane,
By anes and twas they a' swam through;
'Here we are a' safe', says the Laird's Jock,
'And, poor faint Wat, what think ye now?'

They scarce the ither side had won,
When twenty men they saw pursue;
Frae Newcastle town they had been sent,
A' English lads, right good and true.

But when the land-sergeant the water saw,
'It winna ride, my lads,' quo' he;
Then out he cries, 'Ye the pris'ner may take,
But leave the irons, I pray, to me'.

(Traditional, in Reed 1991: 40)

Listening to or reading the traditional Border Ballads, the sense of the otherworldly and of the romanticism is reimagined in Archie Fisher's songs. For example, in one of the oldest ballads, 'Thomas the Rhymer', 'true Thomas' is beguiled by 'a lady bright', who comes 'riding down by the Eildon Tree'. This lady turns out to be the queen of the fairies, with all the requisite attributes; a 'skirt o the grass-green silk', 'mantle O the velvet fyne', 'rosy lips', and a 'milk-white steed'. She presents true Thomas with a series of three options for a journey. There are clear echoes of these themes in Fisher's songs and his particular mythologising of the Borders. The queen of the fairies is presented in this ballad as a figure of great allure and it is significant that in Fisher's songs there is a strong trope of women as unfathomable and as otherworldly. He often deals with women metaphorically, relating them to water, rivers and ships and the consequent changing nature of water reveals their unknowability:

Lost love has the everlasting flow,
Of a never ending river.
And it's not an easy reckoning,
But sometimes I have the notion.
That womankind, in her heart and mind,
Is a tall ship on the ocean.

(Extract from 'Windward Away', title track from Fisher 2008)

The texture of his guitar accompaniment can also be heard as a homology for flowing water. In the song 'Windward Away', the guitar accompaniment is typical of his performance style. It is strongly strophic with an on-beat emphasis, and a richly-textured diatonic harmonic background to support his (often) nostalgic vocal delivery. This guitar style of fingerpicking is something that has been crystallised over decades for Fisher. Elements of his guitar style reflect varied influences, but his early technique was largely self-taught. He also spent time in India in the winter of 1965–66 where he undertook about six weeks of sitar lessons, which Smith suggests is evident on his first solo album *Archie Fisher* (XTRA 1070) made in 1968 (Smith 1988: 147). Fisher's use of the guitar was influenced by the American group the Weavers and by an American banjo player, Ralph Rinzler, who initially showed him how to pick the instrument. But like many in the early days of the folk revival, he learnt a lot through trial and error and trying to emulate recordings of Skiffle and early folk singers from America like Woody Guthrie. A quote from Norman Buchan who was a leading influence on the Scottish folk revival through his Rutherglen Academy Ballad Club, demonstrates well the inquisitiveness of Fisher's generation of Glaswegian revivalists:

I had been doing work in this field [of folk music] . . . at my own school, as a schoolteacher, secondary school. I had started a ballads club, and we went out and did occasional *what you now call gigs* at various organizations and associations and music clubs, in which I talked about folk material and the children sang [emphasis added] . . . . And I went to a school called Hyndland, in Glasgow, where they had a music club. And I spoke about the material and people sang . . . . But a couple of nights after that, there's a knock at the door, and two young chaps were standing there. They turned out later on to be called Archie Fisher and Bobby Campbell, who more or less said, 'Where did you get this stuff from?' And I said, 'Well, what do you mean?' And they said, 'Well, we were listening to you talking at Hyndland two nights ago and we would like to get some of this stuff' . . . . Archie, all this concealed talent within him for instruments, and performing, and the big voice from Ray.

(Buchan in Smith 1988: 82–3)

As well as revealing a musical tradition in transformation this quote reveals the inherent exploratory attitude of the young revivalists. Presumably, what Norman Buchan would have called a session or a singaround was, in the 1950s and '60s, in the process of transformation and revival through the efforts of the young. Part of this change was the commodification of sound and the adoption of key markers of popular music from the United States. This ethos of experimentation and inquisitiveness was central to the early Scottish revivalists and it produced some innovative approaches to singing and accompaniment that were to lead to the later instrumental revival in the 1970s.

In the song 'Borderlands', Fisher uses a poem written by the poet Roger Quin that deals with the place of the Scottish Borders. As a listener, this song is nostalgic and evokes strong dreamlike imaginary of the Borders, deeply resonant with the historical themes of dreams and journeys which are key themes of the historical mythology of the Scottish Borders. Quin (1850–1925) was born into a poetic family in a house overlooking the graveyard where Burns was buried (Cameron n.d.). He published one large volume of poetry entitled *The Heather Lintie* and spent much of his life 'walking the countryside and fishing its rivers' (Cameron n.d.: 94) from which presumably his love of the landscape was derived. The motif of the dream is one that is used in 'Borderlands' and of course one that has long significance in all art and in the songs of the Borders themselves. In Fisher's performance of 'Borderlands' we have some key motifs of the Scottish Borders mythologised in song.[7] The supernatural, the journey, the dream, the timeless nature of the landscape, the opposition with the city. The text, given here in full, is worth understanding as perhaps the richest evocation of the musical place of the Scottish Borders:

> From the moorlands and the meadows
> To the city of the shadows
> Where I wander old and lonely comes a call I understand
> The clear soft notes enthralling
> It is calling ever calling
> Tis the spirit of the open in the dear old Borderland.
>
> But this grim huge city daunts me
> Its wail of sorrow haunts me
> The nameless figure tossed amidst the human surf that beats
> Forever and forever in a frenzy of endeavour
> Along the cool barriers of this never-ending stream
>
> But I'll leave it in the morning
> Slip away without a warning
> Save a handclasp from the friend that knows the call that leads me on
> In the city's clang and clatter
> One old man the less won't matter;
> And no one here will say me nay, or care that I am gone.
>
> By Caddonfoot I'll linger
> It has charms that stay the singer
> And from the bridge a painter's dream of beauty there I'll see
> But I'll leave it all behind me
> when the purple evening shadows find me
> Past the vines of Clovenfords to haunted Torwoodlee.

Fair Dryburgh and Melrose,
Touched by the wizard's spell, arose
And Bemersyde and Leaderfoot and Elwyn's fairy dene;
With the Tweed serenely gliding,
Clearly seen then shyly hiding,
Where Eildon raised their triple crest to sentinel the scene.

But alas the dream is over;
I awake now to discover
The city's rush and the bustling crowd and the din on every hand;
But on my ear Asoftly falling,
I can hear the curlews calling,
And I know that soon I'll see them in the dear old Borderland.
        (Fisher 2008. Copyright Archie Fisher. Reprinted with permission.)

The song itself is wonderful in its description, where the river Tweed can be shyly hiding and the city's 'clang and clatter' evoke a strong imagery (in the mind of this listener). Furthermore, and what is important to the construction of place, is that the landscape is invested with emotional content. This is the key to place-making in song; that the landscape becomes an *affective space* with which the hearer of the song can identify a particularised place. So that you can listen and identify a clean open place, that offers a freedom from the industrial urban landscape, where you can imagine Caddonfoot's bridge and feel its simple beauty, and the otherworldly places of Melrose and Dryburgh beyond. This turns the landscape into something far more powerful, and invests it with affect. The melody of the song also adds to the dreamlike and peaceful emotion of the place. A single melodic motif focused around one note is repeated at various pitches and adds to a sense of inevitability and simplicity, reinforcing the song's text, emphasising the stability and timelessness of the landscape. The contour of the melody is expressed as descending sequences in both melody and harmony, which add to this effect. The only move away from strophic diatonic stability is provided through the accompaniment on the guitar, which is a thickly-textured B-flat major chordal pattern that tends to emphasise the leading note in the finger-picking patterns to introduce some harmonic movement which I suggest can be read as contributing to the dreamlike and supernatural themes of the song. As in much traditional music, the accompaniment emphasises the textual meaning and affect of the song.

Unlike earlier artists such as Hogg, Scott and MacDiarmid, Fisher does not turn the beauty and affective qualities into a nationalist place; the landscape is constructed as an otherworldly but familiar place of homecoming and stability set against the temporal and changing nature of love and loss. This individualism and sense of place is timely and works well in the highly individualist society of late modernity. Indeed, it is hard to imagine the use of place for grand political aims in the twenty-first century, where national and individual identity is increasingly kaleidoscopic. Key to Fisher's songs and performing identity is a place in the Scottish Borders that reminds us of our own temporality by its beautiful, unchanging and (at times) desolate landscape, which at once serves to remind us of our own insignificance and also to provide a sheltering and emotionally stable backdrop against the vagaries of our own emotional lives. And so this is a landscape that is used not for a grand societal idea like nationalism or socialism, but for a shared sense of place which provides a mythological context in the service of our own emotional experiences, allowing a shared sense of belonging to the place of the Scottish Borders. This is what makes the mythologies of place so powerful for listeners. And this is why Fisher's songs have particular relevance for me and for other listeners; it is this relational sense of belonging that we are permitted to share in as listeners.

In his original composition 'Ontario Dust', Fisher's vivid imagery constructs a dualist notion of the temporal uncertainties of journeying against the stability of home in the Scottish Borders. The song is one of homecoming, to the Borders after a trip to Ontario in which the landscape of the Borders is at once cold, unforgiving, desolate, yet ultimately welcoming and familiar. Place is constructed firmly as emotionally stable and familiar, romanticising the everyday dogs, envelopes strewn on the floor, and even the 'long winter's night' as home. For these reasons, there is a clear resonance with the historical aesthetics of MacDiarmid and Hogg with their rejection of financial gain in favour of the pragmatist verncular aesthetic of Scottishness.

> In the grey of the gloaming I full-beam my lights,
> As the borderland settles a long winter's night.
> There's a glitter of frost and a crunch to my wheels,
> As I turn on the back road for home.
>
> The old dog that welcomes me whines by the door,
> There's a stack of brown envelopes strewn on the floor.
> And the stone cottage echoes to the click of my heels,
> And the message light blinks on the phone.
>
> The last mile I travelled to this journey's end,
> Surrounded with the faces and the voices of friends.
> There were bronc and bull riders with rodeo shoes,
> And I've still got Ontario dust on my boots.
>
> I empty my suitcase by the washing machine,
> With the traces of places to where I have been.
> And it's too late for coffee but I pour out the grounds,
> Sit down by a cold empty fire.
>
> I can hear in the distance, the surf of the road,
> The swish of the tyres and the rumbling load.
> As the sweet silvery waters of the Gala run down,
> And the half-empty moon's climbing high.
>
> And I'm six hours ahead of Canadian time,
> But my pockets still jingle with dollars and dimes.
> I'm back in my homeland, disturbing my roots,
> But I've still got Ontario dust on my boots.
>
> It's not in the journey or where you arrive,
> It's the place that you're leaving and if you can survive.
> All the good times and bad times you'll find in despair,
> When your lonesome and lost in a song.

Away to the North of the Lake Eyrie shore,
There's a box of crisp apples by an old farmhouse's door.
Wood smoke and coffee are sweet on the air,
And the radio's rambling along.

The creek of old leather's been whispering to me,
What I'd like to wear and where I'd like to be.
I'd rather have Wranglers than Armani suits,
And a layer of Ontario dust on my boots.

Well there is no forever or never again,
There's a here and a there and a now and then.
And we all take our turn of the moon and the sun,
And the stars as the world rolls around.

On a bright winter's morning I walk in the field,
A horse at my shoulder and a dog at my heel.
And I pull down the cap brim to hide from the sun,
That is melting the frost on the ground.

I can still feel the stirrups and the slack in the rein,
As the cutting horse rolls back and tosses her mane.
But the clear Border dew, on the green, grassy shoots,
Has washed the Ontario dust from my boots.
        (Fisher 2008. Copyright Archie Fisher. Reprinted with permission.)

In this song, as in much of Fisher's material, the guitar itself is a richly-textured diatonic platform for the singer's narrative, with the sense of stability in the place of the Borders underscored through the stable harmonic progression and constant fingerpicking. The guitar accompaniment in A-flat major can also be heard as a metaphor for the 'sweet silvery waters' of the Gala. In 'Ontario Dust', the feeling of homecoming and familiarity in the place of the Borders is strongly mythologised in sound. Whether it is the 'surf of the road', the 'crunch' of the wheels, the 'jingle of dollars and dimes' or the 'creak of old leather', the affective power of these aural similes is the dominant agency of place. Appropriately, the song was written after Fisher's return from Ontario where he was riding with a cutting-horse trainer. The 'cutting horse', referred to in the song, is a horse used for 'cutting' the cattle out of the herd for a specific reason such as branding. This cutting trainer describes training these horses as like, 'putting a saddle on a border collie's back'.[8] The theme of homecoming to the stability and safety of the Borders after a journey is central to this song as it is to the traditional Border Ballads such as 'Kinmont Willie' and 'Thomas the Rhymer', or Scott's 'Lay of the Last Minstrel'. This resonates with the historical construction of the Border hills offering a sense of 'belonging and safety' that extends back in poetry and song to the Reivers (Gray 2003: 29). However, in this twenty-first century journey, the two places in the song of Ontario and the Scottish Borders provide a suitable dualism with which to energise a feeling of home. There are still traces of the journeying home from Ontario such as the 'jingle' of dollars, or the dust on his boots, the feel of the 'slack in the rein', that we can share in. Finally though, we share in the finality of homecoming to the place of the Scottish Borders, which is provided by the 'clear Border dew' that washes the dust of the journey from his boots.

Some Endings

What the songs of Archie Fisher, the Border Ballads of oral tradition and the nineteenth-century romanticism of the ballad collectors all have in common is that they give their audiences a mythology of the familiar which transforms the familiar physical landscape into a shared affective place. That is why the mythology of place is so important in song and why the strands of otherworldliness, Reiver rabbles and desolate romantic landscapes are so important in song. They have a relational affect, which allows listeners to share in an emotional experience which unites people across time and space. Scott transformed the landscape into a nationalist place, Hogg to a radical political place and, perhaps appropriately in late modernity, Archie Fisher has constructed a very individual and romantic place in the Scottish Borders that draws on a long tradition of mythologising. The place that Fisher creates through song draws on many communal or shared mythologies of the Scottish Borders to link us with him in affective space, where we can share a sense of the Borders as otherworldly, romantic, desolate and familiar without contradiction. They allow us as listeners to hear the places constructed within song as affective landscapes which are filled with the emotional energy that results from the historically dominant themes or dualisms that are associated with them. It is not so much the physical attributes of the landscape that are important to musical place, but the emotional feeling that we share in as active listeners – the relational affect of the music. Furthermore, this sense of a relational affect is often created out of the conflictual energy inherent in these dualisms that provides the emotional affect for the listener. And this is the real usefulness of mythologising place in song and poetry; they let us reimagine those landscapes we know individually, into places invested with emotion in which we share common feelings, that persistently help us to reimagine and affirm our own shared sense of belonging to place.

Notes

1 See DeNora (2000) for an excellent introduction to the use of music as a technology of the self.
2 Extract from the poem 'Borderland' by Roger Quinn, adapted and performed by Archie Fisher on, Archie Fisher, *Windward Away* (CD, Greentrax and Red House Records CDTRAX329, 2008). Copyright Archie Fisher. Reprinted with permission.
3 Archie Fisher, fieldwork interview, February 2009.
4 Essentially the Reivers were local groups of raiders whose main pastime was looting, raiding and stealing cattle from the gentry and others within the Border region. The Reivers period has been characterised as 300 years of wars of independence on the Anglo-Scottish Borderlands (Gray 2003: 22).
5 See resources on Walter Scott at www.walterscott.lib.ed.ac.uk for more information [accessed 26 July 2010].
6 For a good example of this see a letter from Sir Cuthbert Collingwood, Deputy Warden of the Middle March, to Lord Walsingham in 1587 in (Reed 1991: 19).
7 A live performance can be heard via the Tobar an Dulachais digital archive at www.tobarandualchais.co.uk/play/93059.
8 Fisher, personal communication.

PART III

Theorising Scottish Traditional Music

CHAPTER 7

Mediatisation of Scottish Traditional Music

The mediation and mediatisation of Scottish music has been growing ever since the first broadside ballads and pamphlets were produced. My focus in this chapter is upon the exponential growth of its mediatisation since 1945. It is commonly observed that Scottish traditional music has always been a bookish culture. Very few traditional indigenous musics from around the world possess such a long literate history which has run alongside oral tradition, and with so many literary inclined aficionados. It is remarkable to think that the writing and notation of Scottish traditional music began properly as far back as the eighteenth century and that people today still regard oral tradition as one of its defining characteristics (see Chapter 5 in this book). Within the modern era too, Scottish traditional music has emigrated along with Scots to many parts of the new world, and indeed has now come back again, with musicians from Scotland and elsewhere, such as Nova Scotia, New Zealand, South Africa and Ontario, regularly sharing tunes and songs and moving around the world. Piping, for example, although heard in New Zealand as far back as April 1773, only began to gain a foothold in the 1860s, still remarkably early in the life of this newly colonised nation (Milosavljevic 2014). Many fine musicians and singers have emigrated to North America from Scotland, and very recently, this trend has been put into reverse, with professional musicians immigrating to Scotland from North America – particularly from Nova Scotia, Cape Breton and other areas. In many of these regions of the world there has always been a strong connection to Scottish culture which was the product of emigration, both voluntary and forced, and particularly associated with the Clearances from Highlands and Islands from the 1780s onwards.

The influence of Scots abroad in the early nation-forming phases of the New World is difficult to overstate and can be witnessed in the number of Scottish town and place names given to new settlements. There are today no fewer than 39 Edinburghs and

25 Glasgows around the world (Pittock 2013). Newton suggests that the influence of religion and the loss of Gaelic as the first language weakened musical transmission amongst the settler communities in North America (Newton 2003: 16), however there is much more that is shared between the musical cultures in Canada and Scotland. Crucially however, much of the discourse surrounding traditional music, and particularly Scottish-derived traditional music in Canada rests upon a one-way assumption that it was taken across the water by emigrants from Scotland, where it 'survived' essentially unaltered in rural communities, particularly amongst the maritime regions on the eastern seaboard. This mythology is, like most, based upon partial truth, but the main usefulness of this kind of essentialist historical mythology is to serve the debates around authenticity of musical sources and performers (in both Scotland and Canada) rather better than it does the understanding of vernacular music-making in the contemporary world (see for instance Bennett 1994).

One of the great benefits of this history of musical and community emigration and colonialism is that there are many voices that can claim authenticity of Scottish traditional music from different perspectives around the world. One does not have to be in Scotland, or ever to have been there, in order to become a Scottish fiddler or piper. This richness is now largely digitally mediated and as such has had its consequences in terms of how we access, conceive of and even perform Scottish traditional music. Digitalisation, however, has arrived on the back of several hundred years of print culture in Scotland and Britain and, more recently, after an explosion of musical discourse in the newspapers, pamphlets and magazines of the 1950s and '60s revival.

There have of course been many types of publications associated with Scottish traditional music, and these tend to be divided into two categories: first, publications dealing with the culture and reception of Scottish traditional music and, second, local or special interest publications devoted to particular instrumental or local traditions. One could also divide them into books with musical notation and books discussing music in its widest sense. The division of publications into local or special interest publications and broader cultural publications has the advantage of reflecting the communities of practice who contribute and consume these publications. Publications dealing with the broad cultural reception of Scottish traditional musicians and aficionados have included:

- *Sandy Bell's Broadsheet*
- *Broadbeat*
- *Folk Diary*
- *Scottish Folk Gazette*
- *Living Tradition*
- *FolkRoots.*

In the second category there have been numerous small publications, pamphlets and magazines devoted to particular instruments or locales that have always been common and these include examples such as *Sounding Strings* (Clarsach), *Box and Fiddle* (accordion and fiddle clubs), *Folk Around the Forth*, *Piping Today* and the *Piping Times* amongst many others. These titles have coexisted alongside other media, such as radio and television programmes including the *White Heather Club*, *Travelling Folk*, *Crunluath*, *Celtic Connections*, *Thistle & Shamrock*, *Pipeline* and many others dealing with Scottish traditional music. The importance in the post-war period of all these books, magazines, pamphlets, radio and television shows, articles, CDs, digital downloads, internet fora and websites that have mediated, and continue to mediate, Scottish traditional music to a distributed audience across the world, is that they construct the aesthetic and social semiotic discourses that are central to the social value of these musical practices. This process of mediation, which is essentially the communication of meaning by various different media, is increasingly important to all musics simply because more and more of our musical lives are mediated (Auslander 2008).

The process of mediatisation is different and it refers at heart to the increasing significance and power of the media in our shared understandings of how the world is, and what is 'real' in society. In so doing, I draw more on the social constructivist understanding of mediatisation as opposed to the institutionalist tradition. The constructivist position is one that 'highlights the role of various media as part of the process of the communicative construction of social and cultural reality' (Couldry and Hepp 2013). Applying this theoretical perspective to Scottish traditional music involves considering not only how and what music is mediated, but also why, and in what form it is mediated. Understanding this is important for traditional music, not least because the longstanding assumptions that live performance is 'real' and recorded performances are somehow 'unreal' are now being fundamentally challenged in an increasingly mediatised society. This means that much of the participation in Scottish traditional music as an activity is done by listening to music videos on YouTube; contributing and reading comments on internet fora or social media; streaming albums from online services; swapping tunes and notation via online discussion pages such as www.thesession.org, Facebook and www.footstompin.com; reading reviews of new albums, gigs and artists via online music magazines; and online newspaper pages or smartphone/tablet apps.

However, as Part II of this book demonstrates, those people involved in Scottish traditional music still have an unusually high participation in live communal performance, often in pub sessions or singarounds, at festivals or céilidhs. But the dominant use of digital media and the mediatisation that it brings has profoundly changed not just what, when and how we participate in Scottish traditional music, but even what we consider it to be. The concepts of authenticity and tradition and what they signify have changed, along with how we consume and produce Scottish traditional music. No-one today would seriously suggest that a digital recording of Belle Stewart singing a Scottish ballad such as 'The Berry Fields O Blair' was not Scottish traditional music, but go back even to the 1950s when Hamish Henderson first played back his field recordings to his traveller informants: they described the experience of hearing themselves on tape as 'like magic to them – hearing themselves come back out of this machine' (Duncan Williamson in Neat 2009: 221).

In other ways too, the mediatisation of Scottish traditional music continues to alter different constituencies' conceptions of what it is, and different media have different effects and affordances on the community. One of the ways in which we can make sense of this mediatisation and understand how it constructs and transforms culture is through an analytical approach that privileges the way in which narratives and people's voices are heard and constructed in musical discourse and discourse about music. When we listen to a ballad or a song there are often multiple voices telling the story, not just in terms of the direct speech within a song, but also in what we understand as the author's voice. Indeed, it is not just in song that we have different competing or complementary voices in the narrative, but this approach can also be extended through multimodal analysis to understanding the narratives and agency within instrumental music (see Chapter 8). The methods that are most appropriate today for studying these different voices and how they construct particular types of narrative come from the established methods of ethnographic and qualitative research combined with more contemporary methods such as critical discourse analysis and narratology. By understanding the choices and discursive effects that are performed in traditional music we can work towards a more insightful and empowering reading of contemporary texts and their mediated meaning in contemporary society. Performers too make particular choices about how they present themselves during performance, which changes with the medium. The 'sources singers' of the twentieth century with great reverence for oral tradition would often profess their intention merely to be a vehicle for the story of the ballad or song within an authentic 'carrying stream'. Today's singers are performing in a more highly mediatised context where authenticity as a social process demands a more layered performance and consequently they often insert themselves into the narrative either through the language they use or increasingly through visual and sonic choices in music videos or online performances. What has happened is that where once the singer was heard as the voice of narration from collective history, the performer now intrudes into the performance both as a narrator but also as a commodified persona, layering the complexity of understanding traditional music today. Where once a ballad may have been heard as a linear story, represented by a singer within their close personal community, now the internal narrative of the ballad is sometimes presented alongside the authorial presence of the singer, their public and commercial identity and vocal persona they represent within performance (see for instance the analysis in Chapter 8). If one accepts this picture of more layered narrative complexity, then it follows that the tools needed to understand traditional song today involve drawing upon analytical methods that allow for a plurality of perspectives on traditional song performance.

When analysing traditional or folk music, a strong argument can now be made that where that music is mass mediated for a distributed audience not confined to any one geographical location, the methods and approaches from disciplines such as media and communications become more useful in understanding the social significance of these texts. So much traditional music today is digitally mediated both online and via commercial recordings, television and radio, that in some cases (although not all) traditional music can be understood as a sub-genre of popular music. Clearly there are significant differences between traditional Scottish music and the mass-mediated popular music of Scottish bands like Belle and Sebastian or Travis, but few would seriously dispute now that the traditional music of artists such as Dougie MacLean, Capercaillie, Runrig, or the Scottish traditional music sung by Julie Fowlis in the Pixar movie *Brave*, or in the massively successful soundtracks to films such as *Rob Roy*, has not reached out to a mass audience across continents. Indeed, what is hugely encouraging in the twenty-first century is that in films like *Brave* and even more regularly on television through broadcasting from BBC Alba and elsewhere on the BBC, authentic traditional music and musicians are now representing Scotland in sound.

This is a long way from the kitsch and often fake representations of Scotland in light entertainment scores to films of the 1950s and '60s. And the consensus around the boundaries between popular music, folk music and traditional music are now more porous than they have ever been. The sorts of analytical tools needed for understanding these musical performances require analytical methods that take account of the commodified and commercial nature of the performances and their heavy mediatisation online and on radio and television. Adam Kaul draws a useful distinction between these two concepts in that commercialisation signals growth of economic exchange between performers and their promoters and audiences, whereas commodification is a deeper process that brings with it social transformation of the symbolic value of traditional music (Kaul 2007). Even smaller artists and bands today feel a strong necessity to have a website, digital albums and often videos online. This mediation of traditional music does not negate, and is not mutually exclusive with, face-to-face collective encounters in sessions or at festivals. It is important, however, that we are able to understand and analyse the multimedia in reaching an understanding of what Scottish traditional music means in the twenty-first century.

Voicing Folk in Tradition Today

One of the key reasons for this shift in mediation and the move from purely local, social music making to a partially mass-mediated traditional music has been the adoption of economic models from popular music in terms of touring, distribution of gig income, commercialisation of recordings and the shift towards professionalisation, royalties and rights (McKerrell 2011a). The other very significant change in the twenty-first century is the collapse of historically and geographically defined authenticity into authenticity in performance practice. This has had particular implications for the meaning of 'folk music' both in Scotland, Britain and in North America, and what is performed, how and to whom. The commodification of traditional music, as well as altering the socio-economic basis for the tradition, has also altered the very performative nature of authorial presence, performance and vocal persona. This shift can broadly be evidenced in the texts of traditional song, performance practices and contexts and their reception by audiences.

Figure 7.1 Julie Fowlis recording the score for the film *Brave* (photograph: Jonathan Prime)

In the 1990s, many of the intellectual enlightenment traditions that revivalist assumptions were based upon, were challenged both in scholarship by writers such as Appadurai (1996) and in public life, where multiple, often plural, identities emerged. Gary West, drawing on Zygmunt Bauman, acknowledges this phenomenon within Scottish traditional music, when he recognises that the metaphor of tradition as a 'carrying stream' is still useful today because it reflects this 'liquid modernity' we find in traditional music (West 2012). This is the result of globalisation and huge advances in communication, which allow people from all over the world to share in the production, consumption and reception of Scottish traditional music. Appadurai suggested that in terms of collective identities, historical origins were perhaps less important today than the mythologising and personal constructions that indviduals and communities make for themselves, which may or may not have any basis in fact. This newly emergent social context combined with the awakening by the historical community to the notion of 'invented history' (Hobsbawm and Ranger 1992; Trevor-Roper 2008) and the subsequent and substantial impact this had on the scholarship of Scottish culture (see for instance Gelbart 2007) has led to a reassessment of how Scottishness is actually constructed in cultural life, and of how the relationships between historical, textual sources impact upon contemporary identities.

Today there are two different directions in which bands employ the term 'folk' in the Scottish music world. One set of practices embodies the expansion of the popular music model and the appropriation of 'folk' as a term to re-position their authenticity by borrowing from the rootedness of age in traditional musics. Bands and artists such as Admiral Fallow, Rachel Sermanni, Drew Wright (Wounded Knee) and others represent this trend. They are effectively mass-mediated, commercial music typical of the ways of production, distribution and reception of popular musics. But the distinction between these self-consciously styled 'folk' artists and those who more commonly would be accepted as performing 'folk' or 'traditional' Scottish music, such as Shooglenifty, Tony McManus, Old Blind Dogs or Karine Polwart, is not simply a boundary of self-identity. The porosity between 'folk music' as a sub-genre of popular, mass-mediated music and 'traditional music' as a cultural genre with a claim to repertorial and stylistic authenticity, is increasingly porous and mediatised. Furthermore, there are well-known artists performing Scottish traditional music on the international stage and who are marketed as Scottish 'folk music', such as Diamh and Mànran, who are able to simultaneously engage in multiple identities, moving between mass media and intimate social musical contexts with ease, as David Francis suggests:

> I think we have a continuum of activity that professional musicians work along. So, at one end of the continuum you've got that highly commoditized image; the packaging up of the cultural objects . . . tunes and songs and so on. So people are doing that, but the same people that are up on stage at Glastonbury are also to be found working in community settings with people who are learning music, so that those musicians are actually the conduit from the well of heritage to the community and the public-at-large. There is a commitment from a significant majority of [traditional] musicians to see what they have, not as an individual possession, but as a collective possession, that they happen to commodify in that moment, but that doesn't mean that they can't use that material to share in an informal setting.
>
> (David Francis in McKerrell 2014)

In this way we see how the increasing commercialisation of traditional music leads to the commodification of authenticity and belonging. Financial exchange brings with it not just an exchange value and a commercialisation of music, but commodification in deeper ways. The very act of remunerating artists for public performance itself comes with a symbolic significance that goes beyond any transactional economic exchange; it subtly alters the cultural capital and social capital of those performance contexts too. The act of signing the contract, preparing, often travelling, performing for an audience and then sometimes capturing and distributing that performance through digital media involves a certain commodification of belonging and authenticity. The sense in which traditional musicians can perform a Scottishness, when it is broadcast or performed on the large stage, transforms the social semiotics of belonging and cultural authenticity. This is manifested in the discourse on stage, in album liner notes, newspaper articles, radio and television interviews and online fora amongst many others. The reception of traditional music changes both according to the medium, context and perceptions of the audience, and through time, the shared aesthetics amongst the community of practice changes their relationship with tradition itself.

What can be observed is that in Scotland the term 'folk music', once widespread in the twentieth century has absorbed much of the commercial signification through its widespread use by record company executives and as a commercial genre term. The semiotic plurality of that term is easily understood when one takes even a casual glance at what counts as folk for the big retailers such as Amazon or iTunes. Artists such as those mentioned above nestle alongside names like the Mamas and the Papas, Eddie Reader, John Martyn, Kirsty MacColl and Townes Van Zandt. The term 'folk', in Scotland and the UK at least, signifies a vague sense of acoustic music, or perhaps even simply a lack of the key markers of popular music: electric guitars, keyboards and drums. The term 'traditional music' is in greater use in Scotland to describe music that has some sort of connection to the oral tradition and to cultural expressions of authenticity. However, these terms are changed through their use in performative discourse so that in order to understand or define them involves examining their discursive use by musicians, audiences and fans in a variety of contexts. Scott Grills, drawing on Goffman, demonstrates how the careful analysis of the narrative framing of stage talk by 'folk musicians' is crucial to understanding how authenticity and belonging are constructed in 'folk' performances:

> However, like others who are situating public performances . . . folk artists may engage in misdirection, strategic reframing, lying, or other forms of intentional deception to enhance performance and modify audience definitions of the situation . . . . Folk musicians may be particularly attentive to situating their performance relative to the creation of markets and marketing opportunities more generally.
>
> (Grills 2009)

This demonstrates the value of attending to the discursive framing of traditional music, which can reveal the underlying strategies that performers and audiences alike employ to situate themselves and the music and to construct its social value. This process applies equally to instrumental music as it does to songs. Since the 1980s we have witnessed the gradual dissolution of dance music forms and structures in commercial traditional music. This has been most striking in some very recent music by bands such as Lau and KAN where the structural integrity of dance music forms such as jigs and reels have been complicated and transformed into exciting new musical structures often relying on additive rhythms and more complex structures in tunes. This change is sometimes signalled in how musicians themselves signify and promote their own composition, as in the hybrid forms of music in the late (and much missed) Martyn Bennett's oft-discussed albums *Bothy Culture* (1998), *Hardland* (2000) and *Grit* (2003). These albums fused traditional music into an electronic dance music genre and Bennett's own deep understanding of traditional music can be witnessed in his strong and fairly convincing case for his music to be marketed as electronic dance music. Given the considerable wealth of sonic material in these albums, which he sampled from the most authentic recordings of Scottish traditional music, Bennett's recordings do pose a challenge particularly to today's more hybrid neo-folk bands in Scotland. There is little doubt that Bennett's understanding of the traditional music of Scotland was exemplary. He trained in the traditional manner as both a piper and a fiddler and grew up with a mother who as well as being a fine traditional singer, particularly of Gaelic songs, is also an internationally renowned folklorist of Scottish culture (see for instance Bennett 1992). And as the pace of globalisation has increased, these discourses surrounding the very meaning of traditional music in the modern world have altered as people and ideas have circulated around the world. One of the key results of this has been the emergence in the opening years of the twenty-first century of the commercial genre of 'Celtic music'.

Scottish Music as 'Celtic Music'

The term 'Celtic music' is regarded with disdain by most performers I know of Scottish traditional music. However, it has been enthusiastically taken up by those with an interest in marketing or promoting Scottish traditional music both at home and abroad. As the international touring circuit opened up for Scottish traditional musicians in the 1980s and with the subsequent changes in professionalisation and marketing of Scottish bands, the logic of mediatisation and presentation have changed how these groups are perceived in other countries. In tandem with the emergence of a commercial genre of 'world music' came the invention of 'Celtic music' where bands deliberately altered their performative discourse and musical instrumentation to appear more ethnically and authentically Scottish to foreign audiences (McKerrell 2011a). More specifically, the term really took hold in Scotland with the establishment in the early 1990s of the radio show *Celtic Connections* on BBC Radio Scotland and the festival of the same name in Glasgow primarily located 'Celtic' music in Scotland within a decidedly commercial space:

> Whereas 'Scottish' may have been limiting for those creating radio playlists and festival programmes, 'Celtic' (in all its ambiguity) allowed for a multitude of interpretations and could be pushed much further than 'Scottish' or 'Irish' alone.
>
> (McLaughlin 2012: 71–2)

It is easy to see why: the 2015 Celtic Connections festival drew combined actual audiences of over 100,000 with gross ticket sales of over £1.1 million (*Inverness Courier* 2015). Aesthetically, the term 'Celtic' (usually pronounced in Scotland today with the hard 'C') is now bound up inextricably with the commodification of Scottish, Irish, Welsh, Cornish,

Breton, Galician, Asturian and Manx traditional musics that have arrived since the global phenomenon of 'world' music was invented in 1987. Philip Bohlman maps the rise of world music onto the growth of globalisation and the consequent disruptions of the Self in the West, which have opened up a space where 'world music' packages up the Other, enabling the exotic to 'become the everyday as the people without history seize upon world music' (Bohlman 2002: 27) to construct a newly imagined Western Self that relies on a commodified Other. This is also where the power of Celtic music lies; in the discursive and narratological ability to commodify the white, ancient internal Other found on the fringes of Europe as a counterpoint to the dominant capitalist identity. The emergence of Celtic music allows audiences and industry to purchase and make sense of those marginal European identities that did the cultural work of modernity through the mythologising and romanticisation of Gaelic, Breton, Cornish, Welsh, Irish, Scots, Asturian and Manx Others throughout European modernity. Traditional music has served this project well, but is now reclaiming the space from which it was marginalised via its very mediatisation and commodification. Celtic music and musicians have self-consciously managed to create a commodified authenticity that enables an industry to support not only traditional music but cultural tourism, heritage consumption and cultural advocacy across Western Europe and in Anglo-American culture. That is why when we look to Scottish traditional music today and attempt to make sense of it and the discourses that surround it, we require an understanding of how its commercial and global narratives can and should provide the economic basis for a tradition that has emerged as a crucial part of late modern Western culture.

CHAPTER 8

Singing Our Difference

The Multimodal Performance of UK Alterity and Otherness in Scottish Traditional Song

This chapter takes a social semiotic approach to understanding the song performance of Scotland as an internal Other within the union with the United Kingdom. The idea of Scotland and Scottishness as an alterior or marginal identity within this union can be found in many songs, from the medieval Border Ballads to Jacobite and contemporary songs in the traditional canon. This position as an internal minority within a larger political and cultural union has provided the creative agency for many traditional and folk songs since the Union of the Crowns between England and Scotland (1603) and again after the Union of the Parliaments in 1707. Much of this alterior creative agency lies in a sense of Scottish nationalism within a union with a more economically and culturally dominant England. I argue here not for a straightforwardly nationalist reading of Scottish traditional song, but to understand just how this Otherness is performed in the multimodal semiotics of Scottish traditional and folk songs. Previous scholarship has relied almost exclusively upon the texts of traditional songs to examine the socio-cultural sense of nationalism, egalitarianism and leftist politics (see for instance Donaldson 1988; Dossena 2013; Henderson 2004; Howkins 2009; McAulay 2010; McVicar 2010). However, as listeners and audiences attest, much of the power of song lies in the multimodal understanding of text, tune, rhythm, composition and cultural intertextuality that powerfully combine in musical performance. The analytical approach in this paper combines the social semiotic and narratological approaches of Burns (2010), Fludernick (2009) and Van Leeuwen (2004). My approach therefore privileges the intertextual and contextual semiotics set within the larger multimodal rubric of Van Leeuwen's that identifies four key interacting semiotic resources:

- *Rhythm*: the central analytical category that relates to our temporal understanding of multimodal texts.
- *Composition*: how the different modes (image, text, sound, gesture, taste, etc.) are 'articulated in space'.

- *Intertextuality* (or 'information linking'): refers both to the explicit textual conjunctions (e.g. 'next', 'and then', 'previously') which elaborate, extend and explain the various relationships between elements of a text, and also to the relations between image and text.
- *Dialogue*: deals with the narratological exchange in communication, e.g. call and response or initiating move and response, offer, command, refusal, and so on.

(adapted from Van Leeuwen 2004: 179)

It is worth noting that in discussing multimodality, I am taking the view that multimodal texts are those texts that combine different modes in a grammar of communication but that different modes can be perceived within one channel of semiosis or more. In other words, following Machin (2007) and Van Leeuwen (2004) I take the view that multimodality rests upon the interaction and meaning of modes of communication. This follows visual multimodal analyses of posters etc. where different modes can all be perceived through one form of semiosis. This assumes a mode to be a socially agreed means of communication that are culturally recognised as having significant semiotic power in and of themselves within a particular cultural community. O'Halloran takes a stricter, and more phenomenological view of this, distinguishing between multisemiotic and multimodal resources by suggesting that: '[multisemiotic] is used to describe texts that deploy over one semiotic resource, whereas [multimodal] is used for discourse that involves more than one channel of semiosis (i.e. visual, auditory and somatic)' (Liu and O'Halloran 2009: 386). I disagree with this position primarily because I regard audition and vision as foundationally somatic anyway, and I believe that all channels of semiosis are fundamentally understood through cognitive embodiment. Thus making sense of sight, sound, proprioception, taste and touch, are all effectively understood within and through our bodies via embodied cognition. The key distinction in my view is culturally relative; what do given cultures recognise as semiotically significant modes? And when it comes to *Scottish* traditional music, what counts as a mode is culturally determined by insiders.

The history that has been written of Scottish traditional music has been an Anglocentric one. An important consideration in any late modern Western state is the degree to how far the English language can be used to gain a comprehensive perspective on the cultural discourse of the nation. In Scotland, English has been the dominant language for centuries, however Gaelic and Scots have been, and remain, the first language of many Scots. The 2011 census has roughly 1.5 million Scots who speak Scots language as their first language and about 1 per cent of the population who are first-language Gaelic speakers. However, when considering traditional song, one has to understand that in many places the linguistic and cultural references are more mixed. For instance, as early as the 1770s, Thomas Gifford of Busta noted that most Shetlanderers could speak English but many still spoke the more archaic Norn language amongst themselves (Fischer 2003). If we take Gaelic as distinct from Scots and English, this effectively makes for two significant indigenous linguistic cultures within Scotland, ignoring the large immigrant populations of the twentieth century. In Scotland, where the traditional music community is largely divided along linguistic lines, very few individuals have the ability to meaningfully influence the construction of Scottishness and Scottish traditional music across Scots and Gaelic speaking communities. Hamish Henderson was one of the very few people in Scottish culture whose influence did reach out across Gaelic,

Scots and English communities. In part, this was because of his far-reaching reputation for entertaining others with convivial talk and drink (Neat 2009: xiv). However, almost all analytical work done on Scottish traditional music has been pursued in English from an Anglophone perspective, including almost all the work on Gaelic traditional music and song (with some exceptions, particularly work dealing with the relationship between Gaelic language, culture and social music such as Blankenhorn 2013, 2014; Cannon 2000; Lamb 2013; Newton 2009).

This emphasis in monolinguistic analysis is in large part because the scholarly discourse has been produced in English, often by English-educated authors, for an English or even London-focused audience more familiar with classical or art music than any vernacular song. This trend has been prevalent since the scholarly (or antiquarian) interest in Scottish music began in the modern period. For instance, Burney's four-volume work *The General History of Music . . .* (Burney 1776), is a good starting point for understanding the necessary discourses of Scotland-as-Other because it is the first really comprehensive act of ambitious scholarship of music in the United Kingdom that addresses 'national music' as an object of serious enquiry. Within this collection Burney manages to construct a narrative of Scottish traditional music (he uses the more commonplace eighteenth-century term of 'national music') that is essentially colonial, and by a chain of assumptions and rhetorical collocation he manages to produce an 'exotic' Scotland that is primitive, having more in common with the Chinese than the English. Moreover, two of the most important song collections in the late eighteenth and nineteenth centuries, Joseph Ritson's *Scotish Song* [sic] (two vols, 1794) and William Chappell's *Popular Music of the Olden Times* (1855–59), were both works typical in that they were produced by outsiders to the Scottish vernacular song tradition both in terms of their class and their nationality. Both Ritson and Chappell were 'English collectors of Scottish song' (McAulay 2010). Even James Hogg's work on Jacobite song published in his *Jacobite Relics* (1819), which was overwhelmingly a Highland, Gaelic-language genre, is largely a work reliant on Lowland English sources and language (Donaldson 1988: 97). This is partially about the classed division between middle-upper class literati and the vernacular performing Scottish communities, but it is also a story that can be viewed as a form of alterity within an unequal socio-cultural union.

However, despite this, the Scottish national idea really took root in the opening decades of the nineteenth century, as Scotland developed a 'single national consciousness with a collective public symbolism' (Donaldson 1988: 90). The absence of a Gaelic-language history or even short summary book about Scottish traditional music is in my view striking, but as we have seen in Chapter 3, this is partially because over the long duration, Scottish music history has often been approached from without, leaving those inside the tradition to performance. Even Francis Collinson's much quoted (1966) book on Scottish traditional music is, for me, essentially the work of an outsider to the tradition. However, Collinson's work predictably relies upon textual sources for most of his evidence, and is deeply grounded in the understanding of the Western art musician, coming late to traditional music as an interested outsider. Very rarely does Collinson discuss the sonic characteristics of Scottish traditional music, and even more rarely do performers appear. For any multimodal analysis, the starting point must of course be multimodal, that is *performances* of songs, videos or tunes from an emic perspective.

Because of this prevalence of an Anglophone intellectual history of Scottish traditional music it is easy to forget that there are two substantially different, yet culturally authentic, rhythmic modes. These derive directly from the linguistic heritage of

Scotland. There is the Scots and English language repertoire and also Gaelic the canon. Although a distinct language in itself, rhythmically Scots is similar enough to the English language so that the fundamental rhythmical alternation and pulsing can be regarded as one. Consonants tend to be surrounded in language by groups of vowels or other consonants which affords the musical expression infinite varieties of long-short rhythms in speech and so consequently in Scottish traditional music. Gaelic language however is quite different in that it tends to oscillate vowel-consonant-vowel-consonant throughout entire words, phrases and sentences. This gives a quite different feel to the Gaelic traditional song and tunes and often, when combined with some distinct compositional elements such as scale-type and particular intonation, can provide a very distinctively different sound to Scots or English derived Scottish traditional music. These distinctions are culturally legitimate and recognised by musicians and audiences in Scotland, not purely by their identification of Scots or Gaelic language in songs, but also in complex social semiotic judgements about the multimodal effect of this linguistic heritage on their auditory perception. It is not unusual for musicians to identify instrumental music as being 'Hebridean' or having a 'Gaelic' sound. Because Gaelic is the minority culture today in Scotland, these distinctions are generally not made in the other direction, except where there is a distinct recognition of Scots language in song. We are considering English- and Scots-language examples in this chapter but because of the significant differences in the semiotics of English and Gaelic, a *multi*modal reading of Gaelic-language multimodal texts awaits further research. Crucially of course, social semiotic readings, particularly of the relationships between the textual, somatic and sonic require insider analysts, or even better, an ethnography of social semiotics.

Singing the Other

Scots- and English-language traditional songs that directly address the alterity of Scotland within the United Kingdom represent a particular tradition that has been a powerful source of creative inspiration for Scottish singers for generations. Many of these songs can be traced to the Jacobite revolutions of the eighteenth century, and this thread of creativity has carried on through to the present day. However, the earliest songs to deal with unequal power relations within the British Isles directly are found in the Border Ballad tradition (see Moffat 2007; Reed 1973).

The Border Ballads, from the Scottish perspective, form a cohesive canon of repertoire that deals with the disputes, wars, reiving (cattle raiding) and life within the stretch of the Scottish Borders from north Northumberland to East Lothian. These ballads relate to the three centuries directly prior to the Union of the Crowns, and speak to us of a society caught between the two nations either side. Many Border Ballads including some of the best known, such as 'The Raid of the Reidswire' and 'Kinmont Willie', deal with the shifting sands of power in the 'debatable lands' between Scotland and England roughly between the fourteenth and sixteenth centuries, where neither the Scots nor the English had control over the Borderers (see also Chapter 6 on the place of the Scottish Borders). In another sense, they are authentic songs in oral tradition that deal with the lives and disputes between famous Border families, such as the Elliotts, Douglases, Armstrongs, Percys and Grahams. As Reed suggests, much of the Border Ballad repertoire is intimate balladry dealing with the feelings and lives of local families in the Borders, which is not framed in 'national' terms (Reed 1980: 24), because these ballads were composed and passed before the concept of nationalism really took hold in enlightenment Europe.

More direct expressions of national identity have been sung for centuries in the vast corpus of Scottish traditional Scots and Gaelic song. For instance, in the old ballad 'Lang Johnny Moir' (sometimes, 'Lang Johnny More'),[1] A righteous Scottish giant goes to work for the English king and falls in love with his daughter, Lady Jean. The king orders that Johnny Moir be captured and executed for this, and four 'English dogs' use laudanum to subdue the giant Johnny, so that he can be locked up. Whilst incarcerated, Johnny sends word to his family back in Benachie, North East Scotland to come and rescue him. A boy takes a letter to his uncle who is even bigger, and who also brings with him the Scottish giant 'Jock o Noth'; they arrive in London to set him free and smash down the gates at London. They confront the English king who is shocked by their incredible stature and duly lets Johnny go free. The Scottish party rescue Lady Jean, the messenger boy and Johnny Moir himself, and depart for home. In this ballad we witness a narrative that emphasises the honesty, justice and physical prowess of the Scottish citizen over a corrupt, weak and cunning English elite. The narrative sets London as a distant and ambiguously irrelevant source of royal power, positioning the Scots giants as proud, gargantuan warriors.

The tradition of political song in Scotland, has always relied upon the longstanding leftist tradition in Scotland, and particularly since the expansion of the voting franchise in the UK, Scotland has always been politically to the left of England. Some of this has been the result of being the smaller, dominated partner in an unequal union with England. But equally, much of this political tradition stems from the large-scale industrial and unionised working heritage of Scotland. Songs such as 'Thomas Muir of Huntershill', written by Adam McNaughtan, speak directly to this history of radicalism. Thomas Muir was a lawyer in late-eighteenth-century Scotland who was much influenced by Thomas Paine's *Rights of Man*, and was not alone; Robert Burns was also a supporter of the French Revolution and of social egalitarianism. The well-known Scottish song 'Scots Wa Hae' was supposedly written by Burns after witnessing the bound and chained Muir being led into Edinburgh. These songs and others espouse the grand ideals on the left at the time of greater power and franchise to the working classes, egalitarianism and liberty. One song by Burns that directly speaks to these themes is 'The Tree of Liberty'.[2] In this song, Burns bemoans the lack of a 'tree of Liberty' between 'London and the Tweed' (the river Tweed, which traditionally has been seen as a marker of the Border between Scotland and England). To me, Burns' republican and radical socialist politics can be clearly heard in this narrative. He lays out various virtues that accrue to societies that enshrine the values of the French Revolution, liberty, egalitarianism and brotherhood (or perhaps for us today, liberty, equality and community). Burns had a vision that if these values were commonplace then the world would live in greater peace and equality. However, Burns' most famous song dealing with the relationship between Scotland and England within the Union, is undoubtedly 'Parcel O Rogues in a Nation' (see discussion of its political significance in Chapter 4). This is a very popular song even today, and was printed in *The Scots Musical Museum* vol. 2 (1787–1803).

Track 9. 'Parcel O Rogues in a Nation', please see the companion website: www.routledge.com/cw/mckerrell.

One of the best performances of this song comes from the singer Rod Paterson's 1996 album, *Rod Paterson – Sings Burns (Songs From The Bottom Drawer)* (Paterson 1996). Burns' song outlines the traitorous intentions of the Scots aristocracy who sold out Scottish nationhood for 'English gold'. The accusation stands historically correct that the Scottish nobles who received the 'equivalent' (see Chapter 4) effectively signed the Union in 1707 for financial gain. The song ends with the key textual reference, 'we're

Figure 8.1 Plate from *The Scots Musical Museum* showing the song 'Parcel O Rogues'

bought and sold for English gold / Sic a parcel o rogues in a nation'. Within the text of the song, key physical places such as the Solway sands and the river Tweed help to lend authority to the narrator's voice. The Tweed also marks in the song the natural boundary between Scotland and England that has been punctured by the traitorous Scots aristocracy who have been bought 'for English gold'. This helps to construct not only the place-bound authenticity of the narrative, but also presents Scotland and England as historically 'natural' provinces or nations, which the Union has forever undermined. It is a song that satirises the stupidity and greed of the Scottish noblemen, and in this sense, is not an anti-English narrative, but a song of loss of nationhood, pride and disdain.

In the recording, Paterson takes the tune expressively and with gentle acoustic guitar accompaniment, drawing out the sentiment of the song using the full expertise of a remarkable professional singer. It is performed by Paterson in a clear standard Scots accent which does the semiotic work of adding to the authenticity of the first-person narrative in the song. In the instrumental arrangement, the guitar plays a steady 4|4 strum using mostly diatonic chordal accompaniment but with some extended chords which help to support the wandering tonality of the melody moving between major and minor. The instrumental break is provided by the Scottish smallpipes, a marker of Scottish-ness both to insiders and outsiders. Significantly, the stress pattern (or 'agogic stress') remains almost constant throughout the song, with the lead vocal laying the emphasis on beats one and three of each four-crotchet bar. In common with many of the most highly regarded traditional songs, the stressed rhythms marry with the key nouns and adjectives in the text, emphasising their semiotic salience to the listener. The guitar accompani-ment supports this stress pattern but places more emphasis on the second and fourth beat of the bar which allows for some added auditory interest without detracting from the prominence of the textual and vocal emphases. These vocal stresses also coincide with the textual stresses of common ballad metre (lines of four stresses followed by three). This emphatic stress patterning is combined multimodally with the use of melodic contour to emphasise the key affective words of the text, taking the listener down on descending contours to emphasise the semiotic significance of the text. For example, the final line of the chorus, 'sic a parcel of rogues in a nation' is melismatically performed over a B-minor inverted arch, with key words 'rogues' and 'nation' hanging on the key tones of E and B. This enhances their salience to the listener and is just one example of the really important modal interplay of different semiotic resources that can set great songs apart from the rest.

The river Tweed as a significant border between England and Scotland also features in another contemporary performance of Scottish traditional song re-composed by Dick Gaughan, 'Both Sides the Tweed':

> What's the spring-breathing jasmine and rose?
> What's the summer with all its gay train?
> Or the splendour of autumn to those,
> Who've bartered their freedom for gain?
>
> *Chorus*
> Let the love of our land's sacred rights
> To the love of our people succeed
> Let friendship and honour unite
> And flourish on both sides the Tweed.
>
> No sweetness the senses can cheer
> Which corruption and bribery bind
> No brightness that gloom can e'er clear
> For honour's the sum of the mind.
>
> Let virtue distinguish the brave
> Place riches in lowest degree
> Think them poorest who can be a slave
> Them richest who dare to be free.[3]

In Gaughan's performance,[4] like many traditional songs, the real authorial voice and the narrator are one and the same, lending authority to the narrative of loss, egalitarianism and nationalism. The first verse sets out similar sentiments to the feeling after the 1707 Union with England and Scotland suggesting that a few aristocratic Scots had sold the nation for financial bribes. The tune, often thought to be traditional, but composed in fact by Dick Gaughan,[5] supports the text with a modal tune using traditional motivic passages. The contour of the melody supports the meaning of the words by placing the semiotically significant words such as 'love', 'rights', 'unite', 'cheer', 'brave' at the top of the contour, emphasising their positive 'real' qualities within the song, underscoring the authenticity of the principle narrative voice. One key aspect of multimodal analysis in this song is how the harmonic accompaniment on the guitar relates both to the contour of the principal melody and the meaning of the text. A useful means of thinking about this is to introduce the concept of 'tonal gravity' in multimodal analysis.

'Tonal gravity' has been discussed in musicology and was primarily introduced in 1953 by George Russell to explain his novel and holistic theory of music (see revised edition Russell 2001). In this sense, 'tonal gravity' is a foundational principle in Russell's theory that explains how, in equal temperament, the existence of internal relationships between different notes in music based upon the principal relationship of the fifth and how the almost endless possibilities and relationships between melody, rhythm and harmony can be found to be latent within the tonality of music itself.[6] This does not of course (in common with much music theory) get one much further on in terms of the social meaning of tonal gravity. My use of the term is intended to provide the underlying metaphor for a reading of semiotic space in the musical mode and how it maps on to other modes in a given multimodal text. Therefore, 'tonal gravity' can be used to explain how different modes relate to each other metaphorically, and can be used to explain and analyse metaphorical constructions of proximity, salience and verticality. In this case, the tonal centre is A-flat, which automatically brings with it in Western culture a hierarchy of melody and harmony where different notes and chords sit in more or less auditory salience to the tonal centre (or 'tonic' in musicological language).

The key melodic notes in diatonic musics in the West are variable but the key notes are usually 1 (the tonal centre), 5, 2, and 4. The other notes of the diatonic scale are 3, 6, 7 and these usually have less hierarchical importance and therefore less tonal gravity, although there are many songs and tunes where this is not the case. In this song, the tonal centre is A-flat and the song sounds as though it is in A-flat natural minor scale, the tune itself is modal and could be described as an A-flat hexatonic natural minor scale. It employs the pitches A-flat, B-flat, B, D-flat, E-flat, G-flat without using the 6th F-flat of the A-flat natural minor scale. However, again this framework imposes Western art music theoretical assumptions onto traditional music and many traditional tunes are simply complete as pentatonic or hexatonic.[7] In this case, the A-flat is the keynote and G-flat is the next most important in the hierarchy of the song. In relation to a multimodal analytical framework that does not require training in two or more disciplines, what is important for multimodal analysis is the semiotic effects of tonal gravity of the accompaniment in relation to the text and other semiotic resources such as timbre, accent, etc. There is both the tonal gravity of the principal melody or principal melodic voice and that of the harmony.

In this recording by Gaughan, interestingly the key words at the beginnings and endings of the lines of the song almost all fall on the tonal centre of A-flat, or onto G-flat in the case of 'right's at the end of line two of the chorus. Thus the melodic tonal gravity is very strongly focused upon the tonal centre of the song, giving a lot of weight to the first and final words of each phrase. In this way, the song could even be described as 'bitonal', or having a 'double tonic' (see Chapter 9). In the chorus we see this double tonic tonal gravity working together multimodally with the text to allow the semiotic meaning to blossom. In the first line, 'Let the love of our land's sacred rights', the tonality shifts towards the tonal centre of G-flat and the accompaniment brings in fewer fifths and fourths and softer, more emotionally uplifting chords which add to the salience of the text, suggesting a positivity about the sacred rights of the land. This then is immediately contrasted with the tonal gravity shifting back towards the A-flat and a descending contour for the second line, 'To the love of our people succeed'. This more sparse harmonic presence brings a sense of seriousness to the suggestion inherent in the text that the 'natural' land of Scotland should be recognised as a nation, rather than a distinct people subservient within the political union of the United Kingdom. This corresponds to the notion of ideal and real salience, where the more real the semiotic significance of the text, the stronger the tonal gravity of the line or phrase. The same pattern is repeated in the third and fourth lines, where the positive and more ambiguous harmony is coupled with the line, 'Let friendship and honour unite' and in the final line, the air of finality and completion is settled harmonically with the line, 'And flourish on both sides the Tweed'. This brings the listener back to the central message of the song, which is that Scotland and England should be respected as equals, and as distinct nations; not as unequal partners in a union forged for the short-term financial gain of the few.

In a more complete multimodal transcription, we now turn to a recently composed traditional song to present a multimodal semiotic transcription of the song 'Proddy Dogs and Papes' (words and music by Alistair Hulett, sung by Mick West), from the 2004 album *A Poor Man's Labour* by Mick West and his band (West 2004).[8] The song was written to highlight the sectarian problems in Glasgow recalled by the late emigrant Glaswegian and committed socialist singer Alistair Hulett (Howley 1999). The song takes a first person narrative effectively subverting the long and thick mythologisation of Scottish alterior and low Other to England, where the central message of the song is an anti-sectarian satirisation of Scottish internal conflicts which have distracted Scots from their domination by the English within the Union. The song mobilises a number of intertextual references to Scottish national mythologies, which the narrator suggests have distracted Scots themselves from becoming independent from English domination. The narrative here is simple first-person narrator who initiates and continues to provide the information throughout the song as a form of politicised cultural narrative. As in the other examples in this chapter, and in many traditional and folk songs, the authorial voice is collapsed into the narrator and presented as the real author as well. This is common but not universal with folk songs, for instance ballads often use multiple implied authorial voices when presenting direct reported speech from men and women, such as in the ballad 'The Twa Sisters'. So there is no generalisability of authorial, implied or real voices in folk song, each narrative performance has to be treated separately. Although there is potential here for further research to better understand how different cultures employ socially agreed authorial voices in their narratives. The real semiotic work, however, is done with the interaction of musical sound, text and intertextuality in this song. Within the transcription below, I have provided five interpenetrating analytical categories, based upon the work of Theo Van Leeuwen. The first column shows the semiotic moves within the total multimodal performance. This shows how each major section of the song initiates, continues, adds and explains the meaning across all of the modes and semiotic resources used in the song. The second column provides a prescriptive transcription of both the text and the principal melody which provides the framework for the analysis in the other columns and also gives a visual representation of the key relationship between the text and the tune of the song. The other three columns to the right include the analytical categories proposed by Van Leeuwen (2004), composition, rhythm and information linking. I have renamed this last category 'intertextuality' which is essentially a more useful category for highly cultural performances such as song and draws connections to other substantive critical work in the arts and humanities.

In fact, the song is performed a semitone higher, in E-flat major, but I have adopted a practice of transcribing songs into D major which allows for easier comparison on the page. The transposition makes no difference to the concept of tonal gravity given the system of equal temperament where all diatonic keys are founded upon semitones of 100 cents. The central importance of a broad interpretation of rhythm in music is demonstrated by its use as a social semiotic category by Van Leeuwen who says, 'Rhythm is the one thing all time-based semiotic modes have in common, and rhythmic structure is therefore the single most important factor in integrating different time-based modes into a multimodal whole, and therefore in understanding multimodality' (Van Leeuwen 2012).

Track 10. 'Proddy Dogs and Papes', sung by Mick West.

Some Endings

What is clear from this brief examination of the multimodal semiotics of alterior Scottishness in traditional song, is that this sense of alterity manifests itself not only in the straightforwardly first person narrative voices of these songs, but also within the authenticity that emerges from combination of text with melodic contour, emphatic stress patterns, tonal gravity, instrumentation, arrangement and vocal accent. These songs also demonstrate that the creative agency of alterity within the Union has been voiced in some superb performances of traditional song that rely just as much upon the total performance in sound as they do upon the texts and tunes of traditional music. The three examples demonstrate also how that creative agency has resulted in a sense of inter-ethnic satirisation and disdain rather than any anti-English sentiment which is the accusation often levelled (with some truth) at nationalist song in many other traditions.

The Scottish voices in these songs are performing a loss of nationhood and sense of disdain for their fellow Scots who relinquished sovereignty and subversion of the political and cultural change that has come from the Union with England. Importantly, therefore, they do not construct the English-as-strangers which is common to many other border discourses. This is in part due to the fact that given the particular historiography of Scottish traditional music, English audiences for these songs are often also insiders to the Scottish tradition. The multimodality of these songs is inherently socially relational and relies upon the cultural intertextuality of insiders to the tradition. Phrases and place names, and even sounds such as particular pentatonicism or hexatonicism, vocal ornamentation, the sound of the smallpipes or even the strict diatonicism of 'Proddy Dogs and Papes', all work together to perform a sense of familiarity for insiders to the tradition. Some of these semiotic resources, such as the phrase 'parcel of rogues' or the

Multimodal transcription and analysis of 'Proddy Dogs and Papes',[9] as sung by Mick West on the album *A Poor Man's Labour*.

Multimodal semiotic moves	Prescriptive transcription of song text	Composition	Rhythm	Cultural intertextuality
Initiating move First person narrative Establishes physical and ethnic authenticity of narrator via references to Scottish rural places and ethnic ancestry.	*[musical notation]* As a child I was raised on sal-ted oats And *3* tales of the sa-vage past. I *5* learned to love the drif-ting rain, And *7* win-ter's i – cy bla – st. And *9* all day long on the Ho-ly Isle, *11* Far out in Lam-lash Bay, I *13* walked the hills in creaking shoes, Where the *15* bones of the old ones lay.	Introduction to the song sparse using only guitar, voice and sustained chordal colours on keyboard. Tuning is emphatically diatonic which supports multimodal emphasis of the narrator's grounded and authentic voice.	The song consistently uses the common metre, or 'ballad metre' which is overridingly the most common metrical scheme in Anglophone traditional song: Stresses of four and then three lines repeated. Key semiotic signifiers are placed with emphatic on-beat emphasis: e.g. 'child', 'tales', 'past', 'bones' and 'lay' all fall on emphatic first beats. This rhythmic emphasis assists multimodal semiosis through the combination of emphatic beats with key words in the lyrics.	'Salted oats', the use of the term 'tales' and 'savage past' all establish the authorial voice as older and authentically Scottish in relation to today's listeners. The notion of the 'savage past' links this text directly with nineteenth-century romantic Scottish nationalism which drew heavily on Ossianic invention of tradition and the notions of 'the noble savage'. Throughout the song, very strong and real places are used to lend familiarity and authority to the narrator. These include 'Lamlash Bay', the 'Holy Isle', 'Ibrox' (Rangers' football stadium), 'Parkhead' (Celtic football stadium) and 'Glasgow town' – which underscores the message of the song locating internal sectarian conflict around these two football clubs primarily in the West of Scotland. These lend the song further insider authenticity for the narrator. Less specific places are also used, e.g. 'fans on the terraces cheer'.

Chorus **Continuation mythologisation**	 19 And at night the head of Wall-ace bled, On 21 sol-emn flo-ral drapes. And the 23 flower of Scot-land bloo-ms again Am ong pro-ddy d–ogs and papes.	Chorus Tonal gravity shifts auditory salience of first line of chorus to relative minor which emphasises the more uncertain and mythological semiosis of Wallace's head, and then returns to more concrete salience of major tonality combined with rising melodic line to support the positive message of Scotland as a nation 'blooming again'. This use of strong tonal gravity constructs the authenticity of the Scottish self and identifies the weaker tonal gravity collocates with the otherworldly conflict with England via the semiotic significance of Wallace's bleeding head.		The chorus establishes visceral agency of Scottish mythology in order to satirise it elsewhere in the song. William Wallace's ghost-like apparition and use of motif of 'Flower of Scotland' marks signs of mid-twentieth-century kitsch and older forms of banal nationalism. References to 'Proddy' and 'Pape' also establish insider status of narrator through use of vernacular slang words.
Explanation Mythologisation establishing English as Other	 27 I was taught in school how Bri-tann-ia's rule, was 29 forced on the Scots of o – ld. We were 31 bought and sold by a par-cel of rogues. For a hand ful of Eng-lish g – old. Till our	General composition and use of auditory space puts the voice of the narrator at front and centre in terms of salience. This supports the authority of the real author as the same as the narrator and is generally consistent throughout the song. Little dynamic change in volume throughout the song, in common with much of the repertoire in folk and traditional music.	Percussion introduced in verse two to support emphatic positioning of on-beat emphasis.	This verse establishes the English as the dominating Other to the Scots, also uses some key motifs from Scottish culture: e.g. 'parcel of rogues' refers to Burns' song satirising Scots and English aristocracy; 'Britannia's rule' links Scotland with other colonies under aggressive British imperialism; 'handful of English gold' reference to bribery 1707 of the 'equivalent' to Scots aristocracy.

(continued)

Multimodal Semiotic moves	Prescriptive transcription of song text	Composition	Rhythm	Cultural intertextuality
Metaphor blood with racial/ethnic nationalism	33 — fate was sealed on Cu - llo-den field, When the / 35 — blood of the clans run down. Through the / 37 — twis - ted sea of his - to-ry To the / 39 — streets of Glas-gow town.			Use of 'Culloden field', an area close to Inverness, draws listener to the highly mythologised Jacobite revolutions of the eighteenth century, where the final and decisive battle between Scottish (largely Highland) Jacobites and English soldiers in 1745 effectively ended opposition to the Union with England and the Protestant monarchy in Britain. The Jacobites were mainly Catholic royalists who supported Charles Stewart's claim to the Scottish (and by this point English) throne.
Recapitulation (repetition)	19 — And at night the head of Wall-ace bled, On / And the / 21 — sol-emn flo-ral drapes. / flower of Scot-land bloo-ms again Am ong / 23 — pro-ddy d - ogs and papes. / [instrumental bridge]	Harmonic tonal gravity supports shifting message of the chorus (as above). Vocal positioning recedes for first phrase supporting the ideal mythologisation and returns to normal volume for the real and more positive message of the second phrase of the chorus.	The use of repetitive moves, and the metrical regularisation of the song is typical of oral tradition but also helps to formally provide greater salience to the repeated message of the song. In my view, the chorus (as is often the case) becomes via repetition a synechdoche for the message of the entire song.	

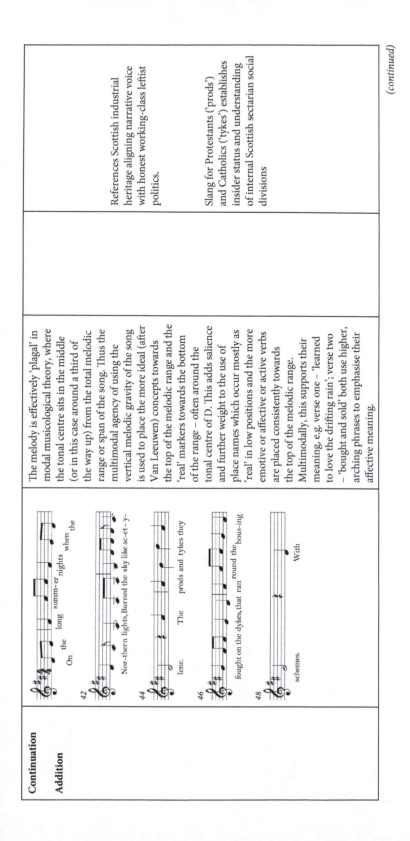

| Continuation Addition | | The melody is effectively 'plagal' in modal musicological theory, where the tonal centre sits in the middle (or in this case around a third of the way up) from the total melodic range or span of the song. Thus the multimodal agency of using the vertical melodic gravity of the song is used to place the more ideal (after Van Leeuwen) concepts towards the top of the melodic range and the 'real' markers towards the bottom of the range – often around the tonal centre of D. This adds salience and further weight to the use of place names which occur mostly as 'real' in low positions and the more emotive or affective or active verbs are placed consistently towards the top of the melodic range. Multimodally, this supports their meaning, e.g. verse one – 'learned to love the drifting rain'; verse two – 'bought and sold' both use higher, arching phrases to emphasise their affective meaning. | References Scottish industrial heritage aligning narrative voice with honest working-class leftist politics.

Slang for Protestants ('prods') and Catholics ('tykes') establishes insider status and understanding of internal Scottish sectarian social divisions |

(continued)

Multimodal semiotic moves	Prescriptive transcription of song text	Composition	Rhythm	Cultural intertextuality
	49 sticks and stoneswe broke our bones. For the	This verse carries the key message of the song (see intertextuality) of England as a dominating Other.	The use of the ballad metre is skilfully negotiated so that the key words in the song fall upon the first and third beats of each line, using the fourth beat often for the anacrusis (both rhythmical and semiotically) to the key words at the start of the following line, e.g. in this verse, 'sake', 'good old', 'cause', 'bound', 'chained', etc. all fall on one or three.	These final lines establish the key narrative agency in the song that attempts to subvert the perceived English domination of the Scots through encouraging internal sectarian division. Parallels with Northern Irish settlement based upon religious majority populations within the United Kingdom.
Explanation	51 sake of the good old cause. That has	Line three shows how the melodic contour supports the salience of the text, as 'kept our country' is rising to the 'ideal' position and 'bound and chained' brings the listener back to the real, and in this case, negative message, emphatically supported by the return to the strongest tonal gravity of the tonic in the last line.		
	53 kept our coun - try bound and chained, and			
Emphasis of English as dominating Other	55 un - der Eng - lish laws.			
	19 And at night the head of Wall-ace bled, On			
Recapitulation	21 sol-emn flo-ral drapes. And the			
	flower of Scot-land bloo-ms again Am ong			
	23 pro-ddy d - ogs and papes.			

Continuation condemnation and satirisation of the collective 'us'	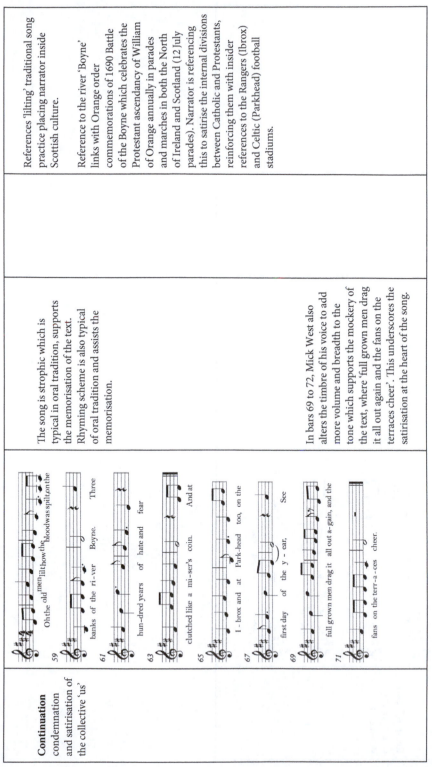	The song is strophic which is typical in oral tradition, supports the memorisation of the text. Rhyming scheme is also typical of oral tradition and assists the memorisation.	References 'lilting' traditional song practice placing narrator inside Scottish culture.
			Reference to the river 'Boyne' links with Orange order commemorations of 1690 Battle of the Boyne which celebrates the Protestant ascendancy of William of Orange annually in parades and marches in both the North of Ireland and Scotland (12 July parades). Narrator is referencing this to satirise the internal divisions between Catholic and Protestants, reinforcing them with insider references to the Rangers (Ibrox) and Celtic (Parkhead) football stadiums.
		In bars 69 to 72, Mick West also alters the timbre of his voice to add more volume and breadth to the tone which supports the mockery of the text, where 'full grown men drag it all out again and the fans on the terraces cheer'. This underscores the satirisation at the heart of the song.	

(continued)

(continued)

Multimodal semiotic moves	Prescriptive transcription of song text	Composition	Rhythm	Cultural intertextuality
Recapitulation (acts as closing statement)	 And at night the head of Wall-ace bled, On sol-emn flo-ral drapes. And the flower of Scot-land bloo-ms again Am ong pro-ddy d-ogs and papes. [instrumental coda]			

use of insider slang such as 'proddy' and 'pape' are aimed at insider semiosis, to establish the authenticity of the narrative voice. Yet some of these semiotic resources, such as the Scots accent and language, the sound of the Scottish smallpipes and the use of melodic contour to place 'ideal' concepts at the top of the melodic range and 'real' ones at the bottom end, are common to listeners beyond Scottish traditional song and carry authentic semiotic significance that speaks to a broader constituency.

Crucially, however, it is clear that the performance of Scottish traditional song brings out much of the multimodal semiotics of music, allowing us to perceive the detailed and rich intersecting relationships between text, sound and image that make listening to music often an extremely powerful and affective experience. The analysis of text and tune in performance brings out what it means to make and hear music. There is much more to be done to establish a social semiotics of music and to develop the methods and analytical techniques appropriate to each individual musical mode, and this requires careful insider analysis and/or ethnography with insiders to understand how musical sound, text, accent, contour, stress, tonal gravity and other semiotic resources all act to produce meaning and belonging within socially cohesive musical texts.

Notes

1 A good version including fifty verses is available in Lyle (1994: 188–95).
2 I am grateful to Anne Neilson and David Francis for sharing their insights around this theme.
3 Words from Dick Gaughan's website, www.dickgaughan.co.uk/songs/texts/tweed.html [accessed 20 August 2014].
4 The performance that has been analysed here is the recording of 'Both Sides the Tweed', from Gaughan (2008). Lyrics: Traditional.
5 Gaughan has adapted the text from an older song but in relation to the tune, comments: 'The tune has been the subject of some speculation and argument. So far as I am aware, I actually composed it and am highly flattered by the presumption that it is traditional, with people claiming to have known it for several decades, if not centuries . . . . For one writing songs in a "traditional" genre, this is the highest compliment imaginable. Like all tunes composed within any aesthetic, it is inevitable that it has similarities to and contains phrases and quotes from earlier tunes.' Quoted from his notes on the song at www.dickgaughan.co.uk/songs/texts/tweed.html [accessed 20 August 2014].
6 For a good brief overview see Monson (1998).
7 See work on 'mode' in ethnomusicology including (Becker and Becker 1982; Nettl 2005; Powers et al. 2008; and my own work on this topic McKerrell 2009).
8 The full lyrics of this song are included by kind permission of the Alistair Hulett Memorial Trust, for further information please see: http://www.alistairhulett.com/alistair-hulett-memorial-trust/.
9 Version recorded on *A Poor Man's Labour* (West 2005).

Theorising Scottish Musical Structure

The Notes of Tradition

As Gelbart (2007) explains, folk modality, or the study of Scottish traditional music with particular musical characteristics, began in 1760 with Charles Burney, who wrote and compiled a monumental four-volume history of music published between 1776 and 1789 (Burney 1776). However, at almost the same time, there emerged a substantial work of early traditional music theory in the writings of the eighteenth-century autodidact, Joseph MacDonald. Burney and MacDonald constitute the beginnings of analytical theory in Scottish traditional music, and they were very different individuals, with very different approaches to understanding the traditional music of Scotland.

In a real sense, Burney and MacDonald stand for the two dichotomous approaches to understanding Scottish traditional music in the modern period. Burney, working largely on paper and drawing upon wide-ranging Western notions theorised Scottishness in music largely from an outsider's perspective. Joseph MacDonald was a player of pipes himself, and was writing from the inside of the tradition, attempting to systematise emic knowledge for others within and also without the Gaelic musical traditions of the late eighteenth century. Of these two perspectives, the outsider's, Western perspective of Scottish traditional music as an internal musical Other was largely to be the more successful analytical tradition up until the folk revival of the mid-twentieth century. From that point onwards, politically motivated insiders and scholarly-trained folklorists and ethnomusicologists began to reposition Scottish traditional music, and its vocabularies and regional traditions, within a more plural and institutionalised context. The shift towards recognising the intrinsic value of traditional musicians' own language, concepts and systems began with the revival movement and the presentation of the Scottish travelling community to Scots themselves and, eventually, to international audiences in the 1970s. This movement met with sonic and musical cultural changes too, brought about by those very revivalists committed to rediscovering Scotland's indigenous and authentic musical heritage.

The revival started the experimental move towards the adoption of more mass-mediated musical standards in intonation, harmonic arrangement, accompaniment, arrangement, instrumentation and structures which has continued to the present day.

In terms of musical analysis, therefore, our understanding has largely depended upon the socio-cultural and political motivations of the analysts themselves and each generation has brought with it, the prevailing musical fashions and ideas of its time. Today, the insider's spirit of Joseph MacDonald can be witnessed in many of the more recent attempts to systematise, and understanding Scottish traditional music and ideas drawn from across musicology, folklore, anthropology, ethnomusicology, linguistics and semiotics are enabling us to see Scottish traditional music from the inside. The evolutionary, preservationist, comparativist and nationalistic instincts of the nineteenth century have given way to more egalitarian, testimonial and relativistic instincts of today. However, this broad shift in thinking, which at its heart reflects the broader scholarly shift from universalism to relativism brings new challenges to the uses of scholarship, and the sorts of analytical questions that are reasonable, and useful, to ask. In this chapter we will examine some of the key analytical frameworks and concepts that have dominated the discourse surrounding the Scottishness of Scottish traditional music, and some of the models that are now possible in increasingly mass-mediated and commercial social contexts, which can help us to understand Scotland musically.

The Pentatonic Problem

One of the most egregious fallacies with highly problematic, yet semantically complex provenance, is the recurrent link made between Scottish music and Chinese music in various analytical texts since the late eighteenth century, which forms the basis for much of the modern reduction of Scottish traditional music to pentatonic, 'ancient' music. Jean-Jacques Rousseau published an 'air Chinois' (Chinese air) in his musical dictionary of 1768, which has been the basis for much confusion and uncritical reproduction of poor theoretical writing on Scottish traditional music over the last 200 years. The English scholar Charles Burney was the first to make the connection between modal scales and Scottish traditional music, linking Rousseau's 'musical ideas of nature to Scotland' (Gelbart 2007: 73).

Burney claimed the connection between Scottish and Chinese music, based upon the similarity of scale-type and a predominance of pentatonic scales in both. There are so many problems with this simplistic approach including: the orientalist essentialising of 'Chinese music' to label a massively diverse and plural range of music cultures; the significant problems of relying upon scale-type as a useful form of analytical rubric; and the lack of any substantial historical context that would support cross-fertilisation between Chinese–Scottish traditional or national musics, etc. These issues have been variously raised and re-examined in Born and Hesmondhalgh (2000), Clayton and Zon (2007), Gelbart (2007), and Harrison (1985), however, the link between scale type and ethnicity still remains in much writing on Scottish and other traditional musics around the world. The basic truth behind these claims is of course that some Chinese and Scottish musical traditions *do* use pentatonic tunes, but to highlight that as an essential characteristic of both cultures, and then to privilege the description of Scottish traditional music as pentatonic, is so reductive as to be almost meaningless. It is the musicological equivalent of observing that many Scottish houses are built from stone.

Charles Burney takes the anhemitonic (i.e. no semitones) pentatonic scale that does exist in much Scottish traditional music and uses it to argue for a strong resemblance between Chinese and Scottish music, and Ancient Greek music that is drawn from their primitive connection to nature that gave rise to these simple scales 'during the infancy of civilisation and arts among them' (Burney in Gelbart 2007: 127). This work by Burney became foundational and often repeated by authors such as William Crotch and others in the nineteenth century, who used his *General History* to suggest that Chinese and Scottish music had a common origin in Ancient Greek modality. We can see how this influenced others such as Ritson (Gelbart 2007: 132) and the semantic construction of a link between simple, pentatonicism and 'natural' music. The most widely used pentatonic scale in nineteenth-century writing, and one that is commonly found in Scottish traditional music is the 1-2-3-5-6 scale type as is found in tunes such as 'John MacColl's March to Kilbowie Cottage' or 'John Keith Laing', the latter composed by the great Scottish dance-band leader Addie Harper, from Wick. The tune was written for the son of Bryce Laing, the producer at Craighall Recording Studio in Edinburgh, where the Wick Scottish Dance Band recorded many albums for EMI:[1]

This scale type is very commonly used in Scottish traditional music in various keys, but often found with a tonic of A due to the prevalence of bagpipe tunes in the total canon

John Keith Lang

(reel)   (comp. Addie Harper)

Figure 9.1 'John Keith Lang', composed by Addie Harper, reproduced here by kind permission of Alastair MacDonald of Harper music

of dance music repertoire. It was used by Alexander Campbell in *Albyn's Anthology*, to link pentatonicism to nature, and subsequently by George Thomson in his 'Dissertation Concerning the National Melodies of Scotland' of 1822 (see McAulay 2013; and also Gelbart 2007: 132). Anne Gilchrist also relies on this scale type in her evolutionary thesis on Gaelic song scales and their 'development' towards filling in the 'gaps' (Gilchrist 1911). This evolutionism was widespread in the emergent discipline of 'folklore' in the late nineteenth century following the widespread adoption of Darwin's concept of evolution in his *On the Origin of Species*, first published in 1859. Folklore itself was founded upon a number of antiquarians' personal interests, which largely 'concentrated on the historicity and consequent legitimation of aspects of contemporary culture' (Boyes 2010: 5). This translation of scientific ideas about biological evolution into music and culture offered a comprehensive theory for legitimating and explaining culture in the nineteenth century but was fundamentally problematic because of the inherent universalism that it embedded within cultural models of transmission and performance. There were also problems in its application to music theories of traditional music.

In the biological model of evolution, for instance, parents vertically transmit their characteristics to their offspring, and these include random genetic variations. The environment then determines which random genetic variations are most advantageous through natural selection. Natural selection then drives the continuous evolution of different species through the selection of the most advantageous variations. The cultural evolutionism of the late nineteenth and early twentieth centuries mistakenly applied this idea of natural selection to traditional tunes, songs and stories by suggesting these items such as songs are passed on orally to down the generations, whereupon subtle changes occur in form, text and style of performance, causing hundreds of variations of the same song. Furthermore, the members of the English Folk Song Society suggested that the evidence of cultural 'survivals' (those items of folklore that have survived into contemporary practice but that have lost their original functional meaning) demonstrated the proof that culture evolves from primitive to the developed West. Many of these collectors who were influential in the first English folk revival supported the idea inherited from the nineteenth-century antiquarians of *gesunkenes Kulturgut*, which says that traditional music originates with the upper classes and professional musicians, and is distorted as it 'descends' or 'sinks' into the urbanised, industrialised working classes.

Folk music, therefore, had to be rural and rustic in order to reinforce the socio-economic hegemony in Edwardian Britain (Boyes 2010: 69). Cultural evolutionism was in part based upon the assumption that all cultures were progressing along a linear evolution towards Western culture and society as represented as the highest form of socio-cultural evolution. Inherent also in the theory is the idea that studying variations and characteristics of songs can reveal how far along the evolutionary cycle a culture is. Today, we know that this view of culture is not only false because of its linearity and universalism and Western ethno-centricism, but also racist and divisive because of the hierarchical view of culture and people that is inherent in this view. We know that oral tradition does not operate in a linear fashion; tunes and songs are newly composed all the time. New material does depend on older material, but not in any evolutionary manner. However, older material is present in newer musical material through the motivic re-use of canonical rhythms, melodic patterns and motifs, and it is in this sense that musical tradition can be understood to perform the past in the present. This does not imply any linear or developmental evolution, but does depend upon social practice, so that people who play music and sing together tend to re-use melodic material that is familiar to them, and that is how the concept of geographical styles have emerged in traditional music. The key issue today is that with the spread of massive improvements in technology and communications, these historical geographical styles of performance practice are being 'deterritorialised' and thus musical styles are becoming dependent upon communities of practice rather than geographically-defined communities.

Scales and Modes

It was one of the founding figures of American independence, Benjamin Franklin, having taken an interest in Scottish music and written about it to his friend Lord Kames, who suggested that the importance of 'emphatical notes' in Scottish tunes lay in their consonant 'affect'. He suggested that because the older minstrels had played on harps, so a form of harmony would have come from the resonating strings within a tune, thereby making consonance between key emphatic notes likely to produce consonant triads within the structure of the key pitches of tunes (Gelbart 2007: 116). Franklin was probably correct in the sense that ringing strings do produce consonance on harps, fiddles, cellos and now guitars and bouzoukis, etc. Most of these instruments are fretted and today, with the exception of bagpipes and some fiddlers, Scottish traditional music is equally tempered music. That is to say, over generations, musicians and audiences have grown accustomed to the sound of tunes and harmonies that use 100 cents between each note in order to assist with modulation between different key signatures, and even pitch sets that are pentatonic, hexatonic and heptatonic all tend to use the notes of the equally tempered scale.

But one of the key problems with the Burney-esque approach to Scottish traditional music has been its readiness to apply Western art music theory to what is essentially a tradition developed orally beyond the sonic reach of equal temperament (see for example McKerrell 2011c). Any cursory listening to archival recordings of Scottish traditional music reveals that older singers and instrumentalists quite often favoured their own local or personal temperaments which can depart significantly from the equally tempered diatonic scale. However, the intonation used in Scottish traditional music is one important aspect of the analytical resources afforded today. Diatonicism brings with it systemic assumptions and tacit knowledge that in much Scottish traditional music do not fit the idiom and can in some instances do a disservice to this type of traditional music. For instance, the modern major diatonic scale with its fixed intonation of 100 cents between each semitone brings with it hierarchical assumptions about the relative importance of each note of the scale. The tonic (I) is assumed to be the most important note, followed often by the fifth (dominant V), fourth (IV), third (iii mediant) and seventh (vii leading) scale degrees, all assume degrees of importance often with the second (ii supertonic) and sixth (vi submediant) scale degrees assuming a lesser importance in diatonic traditions. However, even the most basic knowledge of Scottish traditional music shows that these sorts of tacit hierarchies of scale degrees often are inverted or do not apply in Scottish traditional music, particularly when so much of it is genuinely pentatonic or hexatonic.

In the evolutionist nineteenth century and for much of the twentieth century the pentatonicism or hexatonicism of Scottish traditional music was viewed as a departure from the hegemonic heptatonic Western diatonic tradition. Scottish traditional music (and others besides) were inferior, and 'on their way' towards fuller development and the diatonic standards. Gilchrist (1911) and Jacques (Jacques and Fuller-Maitland 1899) were the founders of this evolutionary view of scale-type in Anglo-American scholarship. In her 1911 paper Gilchrist suggests this explicitly:

> It is in the later bridging of the gaps by filling in the missing notes that the Scottish and Irish modes appear to me to become differentiated . . . [typical of] the pentatonic scale on its way towards a seven-note system.
>
> (Gilchrist 1911: 151–3)

And it was Anne Gilchrist (1863–1954) also who was the most ardent supporter of this cultural evolutionism in Scottish traditional music. She published more than forty articles in the *Journal of the Folk-Song Society* between 1906 and 1950 and was one of the leading authorities on traditional music in England and Scotland in her day. She put forward the view of evolutionism, both in terms of scale development and ballad variant comparisons. Through the comparison of various sources of 'Lambkin and Longkin', Gilchrist suggests that the ballad has been evolving through, 'a process of elimination, selection and development' with different singers who were involved in an evolutionary process through time of eradication of the detail and motives of the tale. She suggests that these singers have been becoming 'feebler' presumably as a consequence of the massive urbanisation and industrialisation of the late eighteenth and nineteenth centuries, and so have deteriorated the original survival, ending with a corrupt version of an earlier, pure version (Gilchrist 1932).

Her language of 'spreading' and 'branching off' of ballads is overtly evolutionary. She also claims the triple time (3|4) is a common sign of authentic oldness, and claims the pentatonicism of the scale as further evidence of its authenticity. In another paper on her evolutionary argument for modal scale types her othering of 'the folk' is clear when she says one version of the tune is 'folk' in character and its unusual cadences are curiously reminiscent of the Faroese ballad-air 'Asmundur Adalsson' (Gilchrist 1932: 16). She is, throughout much of her writing, making many assertions about both the national characteristics of various traditional musics and simultaneously constructing a hierarchical and classed notion of musical authenticity where illiterate, uneducated, rural and sometimes non-English community music stands in opposition to literate, educated, wealthy, urban, white English community. This view of musical structure and evolution assumes that 'the folk' are a sort of internal 'low Other' to the literate, educated English middle and upper classes. In this way, through the misapplication of evolutionism to culture, structural musical characteristics were brought in to make an argument about social class and to provide 'evidence' for the superiority of the hegemonic white, English elites of the time.

This approach to scale type as a key characteristic of traditional Scottish music set the standard for years to come with many key writers, such as Collinson, basing their view of the scales and classification of Scottish traditional music upon the concept of 'gapped scales', with the implicit assumption that they were deviating from the art music's example of sophisticated and fulsome diatonic heptatonic development. Collinson views pentatonic scales as 'missing' two notes, like a primitive form of a major/minor scale, and he bases his hexatonic scales on these pentatonic scales by 'filling-in any intermediate note in either of the two gaps' (Collinson 1966: 10). As performers of Scottish and other traditional musics can attest to, playing traditional pentatonic tunes such as 'The Conundrum' or 'Mrs MacLeod of Rasaay' is hugely enjoyable, and they provide an aesthetic sense of completeness in and of themselves.

The classification of scale type by church mode, introduced in the Edwardian period, has become prevalent, with some people who still use the church mode theory as a classificatory rubric for traditional musics from around the world. For example, Collinson (1966) explores this flaw by applying church mode theory to traditional music and pointing out that the classification by church mode (for example Mixolydian, Aeolian, Locrian, etc.) does not account for the melody as a whole. He shows this with his example of 'The Souters of Selkirk' where he classifies the melody as Locrian but says that the majority of the melody is actually in C major. Therefore the final cadence feels as though it finishes on the seventh degree of the scale. This is only one example of the misapplication of Western diatonic music theory to traditional Scottish music, where a simple cyclical tune demonstrates the type of contradictions that arise when traditional music is classified by church mode. The 'Locrian' classification does not have any real relevance to the conceptualisation of the tune by musicians, as there are many cyclical tunes in Scottish music that are designed to be repeated or joined to other tunes, i.e. many of these tunes do not finish on the implied 'tonic'. Musicians and audiences tend not to classify tunes and songs by their scale type, but tend to learn and classify tunes by their genre; march, strathspey, reel, jig, piobaireachd, air, etc. Church mode theory and classification by scale type may be a useful short hand for some musicians, but it reveals little or nothing at all about the semiotic significance of a tune or a song. Knowing for instance that a tune is in the Aeolian mode starting on C does not offer any answers to why it is regularly performed as the first wedding dance, or why a particular tune can consistently evoke melancholy in a listener to the point of tears.[2]

The Double Tonic

Another of the oft-cited characteristics of Scottish traditional music is the 'double tonic' structure. This is where a tune or song melody has two obvious tonics around which phrases alternate. This is a very real phenomenon which is widespread in Scottish traditional instrumental music. Often, the tonal gravity shifts between the primary tonal centre and a secondary one usually one step away. The eighteenth-century Scottish fiddler and collector Finlay Dun (following Sassure and Thomson) was really the first to identify the double tonic as an 'essential property of Scottish music' (Dun in Gelbart 2007: 142). This is sometimes discussed as 'bitonality' and is common in bagpipe music primarily because of the very strong tonal gravity of the drones which structure much of the music (for discussion of this structure in bagpipe music see Buisman 1992: 2, 1995; Cannon 1972). A classic example of an authentic Scottish song and tune that employs the double tonic is the old Gaelic song 'Far am bi mi fhìn is ann a bhios mo dhòchas' (trans. 'what I hope for is wherever I am'), known usually in English as 'The Drunken Piper'. The song is a *puirt-à-beul* that actually mentions dancing at the piper's house.[3] It is often played by beginner pipers and other musicians because it contains very typical motivic content common to much Scottish traditional music. The tune uses an emphatic double tonic centred around the tones A and G (see Figure 9.2).

Double tonic, or 'bi-tonal', tunes and songs are common in Scottish music, particularly in bagpipe music. One reason for this may be found in the relationship of the drones to the melody. The drone of the bagpipe acts almost like a magnetic force, that has a generative melodic force where the forward motion of the tune can be understood sonically in its

The Drunken Piper

(trad. arr. S. McKerrell)

Figure 9.2 Musical example of 'The Drunken Piper'

changing relationship of consonance and dissonance against the drones. On the bagpipes, the three drones are all tuned to A, and the fundamental of the chanter is also called A. This note is of course higher pitched than the diatonic 'A' at 440Hz, as the pipes are a transposing instrument (McKerrell 2011c). However, the double tonic allows for a musical structure that produces forward motion and melodic impetus in traditional music because the phrases of a part or a tune move from consonance to dissonance and (usually) resolve back to consonance in the final phrase. So that, in for example, 'The Drunken Piper', where each phrase lasts for two bars, the tune moves from phrase A (consonant centred upon the note 'A') to phrase B (more dissonant centred upon the note 'G') back to phrase A (consonant focused upon 'A') and resolves by quickly moving through a more dissonant passage in bar 7 and finally resolving in bar 8 back to the note 'A', which is in total consonance with the drones. This is an explanation for the genesis of the double tonic structure in Scottish music, and other pairings of tonics is commonly found in double tonic tunes using D and E, (e.g. 'Mrs MacPherson of Inveran', 'Babados Bells', 'Jig of Slurs' [first two parts]) or the double tonics of B against A in tunes such as 'Donald MacLellan of Rothsay', 'MacLeod of Mull' or the ever popular 'Mist Covered Mountains' (see Figure 9.3).

These sorts of tunes are of course structured differently to diatonic tunes and straightforward 'authentic'[4] pentatonic or hexatonic modal tunes, where melodic impetus is provided largely through contour and rhythm, e.g. 'Auld Lang Syne', 'High Road to Linton' (for a more detailed discussion see McKerrell 2009). In terms of performance too, it is a common misunderstanding of double tonic structures that can lead novice accompanists to use standard diatonic chordal accompaniment patterns inappropriately in double tonic tunes that revolve essentially around only two tonal centres.

Another obvious sonic characteristic of Scottish traditional music is the flattened seventh. In many tunes and songs, Scottish traditional musicians opt for the flattened seventh note of the scale, which for contemporary ears used to the semitone from the leading note to the tonic, constructs a sense of Otherness. Much like in the early discussion

The Mist Covered Mountains

(Also known as, Chì mi na mòrbheanna)

(John Cameron, arr. McKerrell)

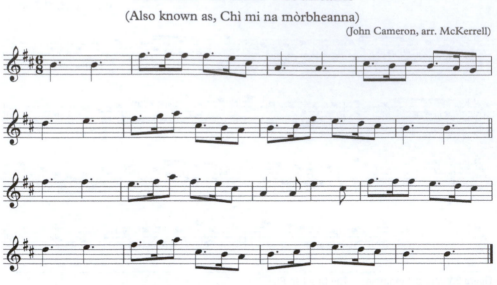

Figure 9.3 Musical example of 'The Mist Covered Mountains'

of so-called 'gapped scales', the flattened seventh has almost always been attributed to the limitations of Scottish instruments, and in particular the bagpipes. For example, even as far back as the early eighteenth century the writer Dauney was linking the 'missing' scale-degree to the construction of the bagpipes in his 1838 book *Ancient Scotish Melodies from a Manuscript of the Reign of King James VI*, based upon the Skene MS from the seventeenth century (Gelbart 2007: 140). It is true that the bagpipe plays a whole tone note below the tonic as its seventh note in a limited 9-note scale. Pipers call this note 'high G', where 'high A' and 'low A' act as the tonic or fundamental tone of the instrument and much of the repertoire. What is incorrect, and has never really been explored due to the lack of engagement with performance practice by many theoreticians of Scottish traditional music, is that the bagpipe cannot produce a 'sharp seventh', in other words, the use of the flattened seventh in bagpipe music is not a conscious choice over a sharp seventh but a product of the indigenous organological development of the instrument. Furthermore, the basis for discussing the intonation of the bagpipes has again relied unquestioningly upon Western art music theory and diatonicism, up until some detailed and important work by Alexander MacKenzie presented at The Piobaireachd Society Conferences (MacKenzie 1978, 1995).

MacKenzie showed in fact, that the bagpipe uses an intonational system of greatest consonance, which most closely relates to just intonation in the tuning of the chanter where in general, each note of the chanter is tuned by attempting to find the most consonant frequency ratio against the drone fundamental of A, which is today usually pitched between 470 to 480Hz (for more detailed analysis of this area see McKerrell 2011c). Again, what this demonstrates, whether in relation to intonation, scale type, oral transmission or classificatory systems, is that in general applying the precepts of classical music or Western diatonicism results in a flawed understanding of Scottish traditional

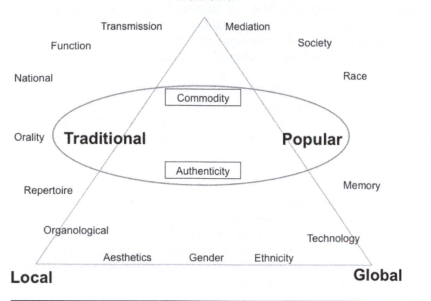

National

Transmission   Mediation

Function   Society

National   Race

Commodity

Orality   **Traditional**   **Popular**

Authenticity

Repertoire   Memory

Organological

                                            Technology

Aesthetics   Gender   Ethnicity

Local   Global

Figure 9.4 Diagram showing the key analytical concepts in understanding Scottish traditional music as social life

music which has only really been corrected since the 1960s. Since that time and under the influence of ethnomusicology and ethnology of Scottish traditional music, a wider and more authentic human framework for understanding how traditional music constructs social semiotics has emerged. This takes into account not only the spatial dimensions of the local, national and global, but the spatial relationships between traditional music and its porosity with popular music. Figure 9.4 attempts to capture some of the key concepts that have emerged in the analytical understanding of Scottish traditional music and its various dimensions.

Tune family and mode in Scottish traditional music

In more recent times since the 1960s, the most prominent analytical framework for understanding the metaphorical and semiotic relationships between musical structures and social structures has come from ethnomusicology. Americans made the greatest contributions to the theoretical study of Anglo-American traditional music in the immediate post-war period. The two principal figures in this advancement of knowledge were Samuel Bayard and Bertrand Bronson. Other figures such as Charles Seeger and Alan Lomax all contributed to the theoretical and analytical understanding of Scottish traditional music, usually within a broader Anglo-American context of ballad studies. The two key models for understanding orally-transmitted traditional songs and tunes that have emerged are tune family analysis and the ethnomusicological concept of mode.

The ethnomusicological concept of mode offers an analytical framework whose fundamental principles are drawn from inside the tradition under study, but that relate those principles to oral musical traditions from other cultures around the world. Many orally-transmitted, or even orally-derived music cultures around the world rely upon small musical motifs or ideas that can be manifested as a few notes, a rhythmical pattern, a phrase or sentence of song text which are always performed in the same way across the canonical repertoire. Judith Becker puts it better when she says,

> Like languages, musical systems are learned subliminally and reproduced without effort. The complex structure underlying both language systems and music systems is apparent only to the analyst . . . . In Burma, it is the modal system which, while seeming to put great restraints upon the artist, actually frees him to practice his art.
>
> (Becker 1969: 278)

The central point is that motivic content actually forms the basis for the shared sense of 'tradition' and melodic 'authenticity'. Learning to play Scottish traditional music, like many other types of traditional music, involves learning a large repertoire of tunes. The very act of learning these tunes provides us with an understanding of the melodic motifs and other modal characteristics of the repertoire. Once one has learned enough music to be confident of having an understanding of a sense of core and peripheral canonical repertoire, or to know what is generally considered to be 'traditional', then that is a sign that the motivic content has been acquired through a sort of musical osmosis and that melodic aesthetics can be negotiated by comparing new material to the internal motivic content of your core repertoire. This is why mode as an ethnomusicological concept is so important to traditional music; because it offers a comprehensive, yet culturally relative theorisation of musical structure and its semiotic salience to the insiders to the tradition.

Some of the key Scottish motifs are fairly obvious to those of us accustomed to listening to Scottish traditional music. Within ballads there are many textual stock phrases which transcend the national but are cohesive within the Anglo-American ballad repertoire, such as 'lilly white hand', 'down by the green woodside', 'blood red hand', etc.: where the colours and objects contribute to a social semiotics kept alive in oral tradition down to the present day. Instrumentally, it is more difficult to establish the motivic content and modal characteristics but various attempts have been made, often in support of quite reductive and categorising analyses.

In his 'Prolegomena to the study of tune families', Samuel Bayard marks out the analytical territory of his tune family theory. Tune family analysis is a reductive technique used in orally-transmitted traditions to understand the core musical elements that lie within the generative pattern of the tune. Bayard's definition is as follows:

> A tune family is a group of melodies showing basic interrelation by means of constant melodic correspondence, and presumably owing their mutual likeness to descent from a single air that has assumed multiple forms through processes of variation, imitation, and assimilation.
>
> (Bayard 1950: 33)

As can be seen, Bayard's definition contains within it both the idea of melodic correspondence between different tunes and also the very Sharpian notion of evolutionary development. Although Cecil Sharp's classic definition of folk song includes the use of his evolutionary concepts of continuity, variation and selection (Sharp 1907), Bayard suggests that tune family analysis is a way of essentialising the essence of folk music to get at the fundamental elements and that analysis of large numbers of tunes would reveal their characteristics. A kind of corpus analysis of traditional tunes.

Bayard looked internally within tunes at corresponding melodic lines, rhythmic stress patterns, tonal range, rhythm, melodic motifs (formulae) and cadential points. Although he is careful not to say definitively that national characteristics of tunes correspond to national origins, he does base much of his argument upon a cultural evolutionism tied in to a discourse of ethnic nationalism. His model explains the relatedness of tunes through the close correspondence of their structural features including formulae, and assumes a common ancestor in a single tune is key to his theorising. Bayard goes on to suggest therefore that there may be no more than around thirty-five or so tune families in the British folk music tradition (Bayard 1950: 13). He eventually went on to identify fifty-five tune families, but only outlined seven of them, of which only '"Lord Randal" has been comprehensively illustrated' (McLucas n.d.). This reduction of many tens of thousands of tunes to a small sample of tune families of course seems incredible to anyone with even a passing familiarity with Scottish, English, Welsh and Irish traditional music. And for any musician looking at tunes which Bayard suggests are related would sometimes be hard pushed to observe the structural similarities within the surface structure of the tunes. However, the ultimate aim of this type of analysis was to explain just how the rich diversity of traditional music in practice could be understood in a totalising system which incorporated the evolutionism of earlier writers.

I would suggest that Bayard's work was a valuable precursor to the later analytical work in ethnomusicology, however, it was problematically founded upon the false notion that tradition, and its constant diversity, can be understood within a single totalising system. Time and again, this enlightenment insistence on one system to explain the totality of a culture has been seen in the scholarship of not only traditional music, but in other music, literature and art. Culture is not like that, it is messy, plural and often contradictory. Traditional music is a human activity and is consequently enjoyed by many people who renegotiate and reinvent the tunes and songs of earlier generations. There is no linear historical development that can be traced in the structure of tunes, but there are of course shared characteristics and patterns that can emerge when one examines a cohesive canonical repertoire. In this regard, the key elements of Bayard's work were taken up in a more meaningful and sophisticated manner in the work of James Cowdery (Cowdery 1984, 1990). Cowdery, although dealing with Irish traditional music, demonstrates the usefulness of tune family analysis to show how it can be used to understand the individual variations of an individual or group. Essentially Cowdery provides a model through tune family analysis of how to theorise an individual's aesthetics comparatively within a cohesive cultural canon. To do this, he introduces the concept of the 'tune model' which he defines as:

> a generating pattern in the mind of the individual and, by extension, of the group. Any given rendition is one of an infinite number of possible manifestations of the tune model, which can be studied on the individual level (comparing renditions by one person) or various group levels. On any level, a tune model is a living potential which may unfold slightly differently in different situations, but which will always be recognizable as itself, just as a plant retains its identity whether it grows in sun or shade, soil or sand.
>
> (Cowdery 1990: 44)

Therefore, the idea that there is a tune model upon which the player re-composes the tune allows for a fairly explicit model of how individual creativity can be analytically understood within the confines of tradition. This is an important analytical method which has been applied to Scottish traditional music by the late Anne Dhu MacLucas (née Shapiro) in her work on tune families and contour in Scottish traditional song (Shapiro 1975, 1985). Her work is important because she recognised that scale type as an analytical category is so reductive as to be largely meaningless and that any useful analysis of orally-transmitted traditional music must rely upon melodic motifs (or 'formulae') which are much closer to what traditional musicians themselves actually conceive of and perform:

> Modal nomenclature is largely irrelevant to scholarly research on folk-tunes ... modality is the most variable element of a tune's identity ... The most useful concept is melodic formulae ... the discovery of a few tonal shapes basic to Anglo-American song could then be termed the 'modes' of our oral tradition. These would not really correspond to the modes of Sharp/Bronson because their outlines would be more relevant to actual folk-tunes, than a series of notes arranged in a scale.
>
> (Shapiro 1975: appendix 2)

My own scholarship on mode has focused primarily on the bagpipe repertoire and examines the canonical repertoire of 2|4 competition bagpipe marches to better understand the motivic content and the deep and surface structures that emerge in traditional music. One of the principal findings of my earlier research was that certain key motifs in Scottish bagpipe marches are reproduced in structurally similar positions with very specific rhythm and pitches, so that certain modes have characteristic motifs. Furthermore, there is a class of motifs that is shared across different modes and used as the melodic 'building blocks' of oral tradition. It is these motivic 'building blocks' that give coherence and a sense of melodic tradition to many traditional musics around the world. In this sense, 'tradition' is an aesthetic quality of the experience of music, rather than being understood as a practice. To get a better understanding of what this might mean in a tune, we will examine the motivic content of the tune 'The Braes of Brecklet', a well-known bagpipe march composed by Willie Lawrie.

Willie Lawrie (1881–1916) was a noted composer and piper who wrote some of the most popular bagpipe tunes, such as 'John MacDonald of Glencoe', 'Captain Carswell', 'Inverary Castle', etc., still regularly performed today. The tune itself has four parts, each 8 bars long. It is a pentatonic tune in A using the pitch set A, B, C, E, F (D, G); where D

The Braes of Brecklet (first part)   Willie Lawrie

Figure 9.5 The first part of 'The Braes of Brecklet'

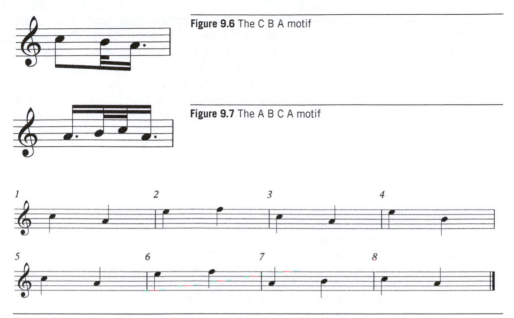

Figure 9.6 The C B A motif

Figure 9.7 The A B C A motif

Figure 9.8 The structural tones of the first part of 'The Braes of Brecklet'

and G are simply used as insignificant passing notes. The first part of the tune is reproduced here with bagpipe ornamentation which holds no rhythmical value in bagpipe music and as such is not counted against the time signature (Figure 9.5).[5]

In this tune some of the key motifs of bagpipe marches can be seen in key positions in the tune. Motifs such as the falling C B A motif (Figure 9.6).

Or the rising and falling A B C A motif which appears in bar 7 (Figure 9.7).

This motif also occurs from G with identical rhythm in many pipe marches, and so one can speak of a 'rhythm-contour' motif as well as simply a specific motif that can be flexibly re-used in composition. These motifs are crucial to the aesthetic sense of traditionality in the tune, and lend it a sense of conformity with the past. In traditional music, contrary to classical music, this is usually considered to be a positive characteristic of a tune. If we examine the underlying structure of the tune, in this instance by simply extracting the most significant tone in each crotchet beat of the first part of 'The Braes of Brecklet', we find the following structure (see Figure 9.8).

As can be seen in the skeletal structure, bars 7 and 8 reproduce the same A B C A rising and falling motif that is used in the surface of the tune at the start of bar 7. These sorts of motivic structures are embedded in much Scottish traditional music, and are essentially part of what lends it a 'traditional' aesthetic, yet are rarely verbalised by musicians. Learning these patterns and motivic content are essential aspects of becoming a traditional musician in Scotland, just as they are in many other oral and modal traditions throughout the world, such as in Karnatic classical music, or in the Turkish *maqam* (for further reading see McKerrell 2009; Powers et al. 2008).

Beyond that work on tune families and mode, most scholarly publication on Scottish traditional music has continued to focus on the historical and ethnological dimensions of Scottish traditions. Further musicologically analytical and taxonomical work that relates to musical surface structures includes important work on the Shetland tradition

(Cooke 1986), Scottish fiddle music (Alburger 1983; Campbell 2008; Gore 1994; Russell and Alburger 2006), piping (Cannon 1988, 1995; Dickson 2009), the development of *cèol beag* in piping (Forrest 2009), strathspeys (Lamb 2013, 2014), mode (McKerrell 2009) and double tonics (Gelbart 2013). There has also been a valuable emergence of music education literature dealing with Scottish traditional music and the benefits and issues of embedding its cultural practice into education (Byrne 2011; Cope 2005; Creech et al. 2008; Miller 2007; Sheridan et al. 2011; Sheridan and Byrne 2008; Symon 2003).

Notes

1 See www.addieharper.com.
2 For further discussion of the problems of church mode theory and its rejection in ethnomusicology see McKerrell (2009).
3 Full lyrics and a translation can be found on the Education Scotland website, www.educationscotland.gov.uk/scotlandssongs/primary/faranbimifhin.asp.
4 'Authentic' in this context means a modal scale type where the tonic lies at the bottom of the melodic range used in the tune. Tunes and songs where the tonic lies in the middle of the melodic range are usually labelled 'plagal' scale types in modal theory.
5 Bagpipe music is always written without any key signature but should be read as though with two sharps, F and C, to make musical sense for the lay reader.

References

Alburger, Mary Anne. 1983. *Scottish Fiddlers and Their Music* (London: V. Gollancz).

Alferov, Sergey. n.d. 'Scottish Dancing and Patterns of Gender Identity', www.inter-disciplinary.net/at-the-interface/wp-content/uploads/2012/01/Sergey-Alferov.-Scottish-Dancing-Gender-1.pdf [accessed 10 August 2014].

Anonymous. 1968. *The Rebels Ceilidh Song Book*.

——. n.d. *The Traditional Arts of Scotland: Report of the Traditional and Folk Arts Working Party* (Edinburgh: The Scottish Arts Council), p. 1984.

Appadurai, Arjun. 1996. *Modernity Al Large: Cultural Dimensions of Globalization* (Minneapolis, MN: University of Minnesota Press) [accessed 17 April 2014].

Atkins, G. H. 2010. *German Literature Through Nazi Eyes (RLE Responding to Fascism)* (Taylor & Francis).

Auslander, Philip. 2008. *Liveness: Performance in a Mediatized Culture*, 2nd edn (Abingdon, Oxon: Taylor & Francis).

Banet-Weiser, Sarah. 2012. *Authentic™: The Politics of Ambivalence in a Brand Culture* (New York: NYU Press).

Barker, John Wesley. 2004. 'The Telfer Manuscript: Ballad and Song Collecting in the Northumbrian Borders', in Ian Russell and David Atkinson (eds), *Folk Song Tradition, Revival, and Re-Creation* (Aberdeen: Elphinstone Institute, University of Aberdeen), pp. 163–74.

Barthes, Roland. 1993. *Mythologies* (new edition, London: Vintage).

Bassin, Ethel. 1977. *The Old Songs of Skye: Frances Tolmie and Her Circle* (Routledge/Thoemms Press).

Bayard, Samuel P. 1950. 'Prolegomena to a Study of the Principal Melodic Families of British-American Folk Song', *Journal of American Folklore*, 63: 1–44.

BBC. 2013. *BBC Scotland Management Review 2012/13* (London: British Broadcasting Corporation).

Becker, Judith. 1969. 'The Anatomy of a Mode', *Ethnomusicology*: 267–79 [accessed 21 August 2014].

Becker, Judith, and Alton Becker. 1982. 'A Grammar of the Musical Genre Srepegan', *Asian Music*: 30–73 [accessed 21 August 2014].

Bennett, Margaret. 1992. *Scottish Customs: From the Cradle to the Grave* (Edinburgh: Polygon).

——. 1994. 'Step-Dancing: Why We Must Learn from Past Mistakes', *West Highland Free Press*, n.p.

Bennett, Tony, Mike Savage, Elizabeth Bortolaia Silva, Alan Warde, Modesto Gayo-Cal, and others. 2009. *Culture, Class, Distinction* (Abingdon, Oxon: Routledge).

Blacking, John. 1973. *How Musical is Man?* (Seattle, WA: University of Washington Press) [accessed 25 September 2014].

Blankenhorn, Virginia. 2013. 'Verse Structure and Performance in Scottish Gaelic Vernacular Poetry', *Rannsachadh Na Gàidhlig 6: Papers Read at Rannsachadh Na Gàidhlig 6 Held at the University of Aberdeen 23–26 August 2010*, 53–92 [accessed 20 November 2013].

——. 2014. '"Griogal Cridhe" Aspects of Transmission in the Lament for Griogair Ruadh Mac Griogair of Glen Strae', *Scottish Studies (Craobh Nan Ubhal: A Festschrift for John MacInnes)*, 37.

Bohlman, Philip V. 2002. 'World Music at the "End of History"', *Ethnomusicology*, 46: 1–32, http://dx.doi.org/10.2307/852806.

Bohlman, Philip Vilas. 2011. *Focus: Music, Nationalism, and the Making of the New Europe* (New York: Routledge).

Bold, Valentina. 2001. '"Rude Bard of the North": James Macpherson and the Folklore of Democracy', *Journal of American Folklore*, 114: 464–77, http://dx.doi.org/10.2307/542051.

——. 2006. '"Lords O' State" and "Lusty Banqueting": Public Representations of Scotland 1999–2003', in Caroline McCracken-Flescher (ed.), *Culture, Nation, and the New Scottish Parliament* (Lewisberg, PA: Bucknell University Press), pp. 199–214, http://eprints.gla.ac.uk/63652/ [accessed 30 September 2014].

Born, Georgina, and David Hesmondhalgh. 2000. *Western Music and its Others: Difference, Representation, and Appropriation in Music* (Berkeley, CA: University of California Press).

Bourdieu, Pierre. 1984. *Distinction: A Social Critique of the Judgement of Taste* (Cambridge, MA: Harvard University Press).

Boyes, Georgina. 2010. *The Imagined Village: Culture, Ideology, and the English Folk Revival* (Leeds: No Masters Co-operative).

Brown, Barnaby. 2006. 'Retrieving Gaeldom's Forerunner of the Pipes', *Piping Today*, pp. 30–33.

Buisman, Frans. 1992. 'The System of Modes in Ceòl Mór: Some of Its Applications and Consequences', *Proceedings of the Piobaireachd Society Conference* (Piobaireachd Society).

——. 1995. 'Melodic Relationships in Pibroch', *British Journal of Ethnomusicology*, 4: 17–39 [accessed 8 October 2014].

Burney, Charles. 1776. *A General History of Music: From the Earliest Ages to the Present Period*, 4 vols (Cambridge: Cambridge University Press).

Burns, Lori. 2010. 'Vocal Authority and Listener Engagement: Musical and Narrative Expressive Strategies in Alternative Female Rock Artists (1993–95)', in Mark Stuart Spicer and John Rudolph Covach (eds), *Sounding Out Pop: Analytical Essays in Popular Music* (Chicago, IL: University of Michigan Press), pp. 154–92.

Byrne, C. 2011. '"Scottish Traditional Music: Identity and the 'Carrying Stream'",' in Lucy Green (ed.), *Learning, Teaching and Musical Identity: Voices across Cultures* (Bloomington, IN: Indiana University Press), pp. 239–51.

Byrne, Michel. 2010. 'A Window on the Late Eighteenth-Century Scottish Highlands: The Songs of Mairearad Ghriogarach', *Proceedings of the Harvard Celtic Colloquium*, 30: 39–60, http://dx.doi.org/10.2307/41219651.

Cameron, Alex (ed.). n.d. *Poetry of the Scottish Borders* (Edinburgh: Albyn Press Ltd).

Campbell, Katherine, Ewan McVicar, Iseabail T. MacDonald, and Mary Ann Kennedy. 2014. 'Scotland's Songs', *Scotland's Songs (online Resource)* (Education Scotland, Foghlam Alba), www.educationscotland.gov.uk/scotlandssongs/creditsthanks/index.asp.

Cannon, Roderick D. 1972. 'English Bagpipe Music', *Folk Music Journal*: 176–219 [accessed 8 October 2014].

——. 1988. *The Highland Bagpipe and Its Music* (Edinburgh: John Donald).

——. 2000. 'Gaelic Names of Pibrochs: A Classification', *Scottish Studies*, 34: 20–59 [accessed 9 August 2013].

Cheape, Hugh. 2008. *Bagpipes: A National Collection of a National Instrument* (Edinburgh: National Museums of Scotland).

Clayton, Martin. 2013. 'Entrainment, Ethnography and Musical Interaction', in Clayton, Martin, Byron Dueck and Laura Leante (eds), *Experience and Meaning in Music Performance* (Oxford: Oxford University Press), pp. 17–39.

Clayton, Martin, and Bennett Zon. 2007. *Music and Orientalism in the British Empire, 1780s–1940s: Portrayal of the East* (Aldershot: Ashgate).

Clements, Joanna. 2009. 'Music in Scotland before the Mid-Ninth Century: An Interdisciplinary Approach' (unpublished MMus thesis, University of Glasgow), http://theses.gla.ac.uk/2368/.

Cloonan, Martin. 2007. 'Lessons from Down Under?: Popular Music Policy and Decentralised Government in Scotland and Australia', *Scottish Music Review*, 1, www.scottishmusicreview.org/index.php/SMR/article/viewArticle/8 [accessed 9 August 2013].

Cohen, Robin. 2000. 'Review: The Incredible Vagueness of Being British/English', *International Affairs* (Royal Institute of International Affairs 1944–), 76: 575–82.

Collinson, Francis. 1966. *The Traditional and National Music of Scotland* (London: Routledge and Kegan Paul), www.getcited.org/pub/101219905 [accessed 4 September 2013].

Conn, Stephanie. 2012. 'Fitting between Present and Past: Memory and Social Interaction in Cape Breton Gaelic Singing', *Ethnomusicology Forum*, 21: 354–73, http://dx.doi.org/10.1080/17411912.2012.702582.

Conquergood, Dwight. 1991. 'Rethinking Ethnography: Towards a Critical Cultural Politics', *Communication Monographs*, 58: 179–94, http://dx.doi.org/10.1080/03637759109376222.

Cook, Nicholas. 2001. 'Theorizing Musical Meaning', *Music Theory Spectrum*, 23: 170–95.

——. 2012. 'Anatomy of the Encounter: Intercultural Analysis as Relational Musicology', *Critical Musicological Reflections: Essays in Honour of Derek B. Scott*: 193–208 [accessed 25 September 2014].

Cooke, P. 1986. *The Fiddle Tradition of the Shetland Isles* (Cambridge: Cambridge University Press).

Cope, Peter. 2002. 'Informal Learning of Musical Instruments: The Importance of Social Context', *Music Education Research*, 4: 93–104, http://dx.doi.org/10.1080/14613800220119796.

——. 2005. 'Adult Learning in Traditional Music', *British Journal of Music Education*, 22: 125–40 [accessed 9 October 2014].

Couldry, Nick, and Andreas Hepp. 2013. 'Conceptualizing Mediatization: Contexts, Traditions, Arguments', *Communication Theory*, 23: 191–202, http://dx.doi.org/10.1111/comt.12019.

Cowan, Edward J. 1991. *The People's Past* (Edinburgh: Polygon).

Cowdery, James R. 1984. 'A Fresh Look at the Concept of Tune Family', *Ethnomusicology*: 495–504 [accessed 9 October 2014].

——. 1990. *The Melodic Tradition of Ireland* (Kent, OH: Kent State University Press).

Creech, Andrea, Ioulia Papageorgi, Celia Duffy, Frances Morton, Elizabeth Hadden, and others. 2008. 'Investigating Musical Performance: Commonality and Diversity among Classical and Non-Classical Musicians', *Music Education Research*, 10: 215–34 [accessed 9 October 2014].

Dean-Myatt, William. 2009. 'Scottish Vernacular Discography, 1888–1960', www.nls.uk/catalogues/scottish-discography.

DeNora, Tia. 2000. *Music in Everyday Life* (Cambridge: Cambridge University Press).

Devine, T. M. 1999. *The Scottish Nation, 1700–2000* (London: Allen Lane, The Penguin Press).

Dickson, Joshua. 2009. '"Tullochgorm" Transformed: A Case Study in Revivalism and the Highland Pipe', *The Highland Bagpipe: Music, History, Traditon* (Farnham: Ashgate), pp. 191–219.

Dixon, Keith. 1993. 'Making Sense of Ourselves, Nation and Community in Modern Scottish Writing', *Forum for Modern Language Studies*, 29: 359–68.

Doherty, Elizabeth Anne. 1996. 'The Paradox of the Periphery: Evolution of the Cape Breton Fiddle Tradition C1928–1995' (Limerick: University of Limerick).

Donaldson, William. 1988. *The Jacobite Song: Political Myth and National Identity* (Aberdeen: Aberdeen University Press).

Dossena, Marina. 2013. '"And Scotland Will March Again". The Language of Political Song in 19th- and 20th-Century Scotland', in J. Cruikshank and R. M. Millar (eds), *After the Storm: Papers from the Forum for Research on the Languages of Scotland and Ulster Triennial Meeting, Aberdeen 2012* (Aberdeen: Forum for Research on the Languages of Scotland and Ireland), pp. 141–65, www.abdn.ac.uk/pfrlsu/uploads/files/Dossena.%20__And%20Scotland%20will%20march%20again__.pdf [accessed 27 August 2014].

Dougal, Josephine. 2011. 'Popular Scottish Song Traditions at Home (and Away)', *Folklore*, 122: 283–307, http://dx.doi.org/10.1080/0015587X.2011.608265.

Duesenberry, Margaret Patricia. 2000. 'Fiddle Tunes on Air: A Study of Gatekeeping and Traditional Music at the BBC in Scotland, 1923–1957' (unpublished PhD Thesis, Berkeley: UCLA).

Durie, Alastair. 2005. 'How the History of Scotland Creates a Sense of Place', *Place Branding*, 2: 43–52.

Farmer, Henry George. 1929. 'Music in Mediæval Scotland', *Proceedings of the Musical Association*, 56: 69–90.

——. 1947. *A History of Music in Scotland* (London: Da Capo Press).

Feintuch, Burt. 2004. 'The Conditions for Cape Breton Fiddle Music: The Social and Economic Setting of a Regional Soundscape', *Ethnomusicology*, 48: 73–104.

Feld, Steven. 1981. '"Flow like a Waterfall": The Metaphors of Kaluli Musical Theory', *Yearbook for Traditional Music*, 13: 22–47, http://dx.doi.org/10.2307/768356.

——. 2012. *Sound and Sentiment: Birds, Weeping, Poetics, and Song in Kaluli Expression, with a New Introduction by the Author* (Durham, NC: Duke University Press) [accessed 1 October 2014].

Feld, Steven, and Aaron A. Fox. 1994. 'Music and Language', *Annual Review of Anthropology*, 23: 25–53.

Fischer, Frances J. 2003. 'Scotland's Nordic Ballads', *The Flowering Thorn, International Ballad Studies* (Logan, UT: Utah State University Press), pp. 307–17.

Fisher, Archie. 2008. *Windward Away* (Cockenzie: Red House Records, Licensed to Greentrax Recordings Ltd).

Fludernik, Monika. 2009. *An Introduction to Narratology* (London and New York: Routledge).

Forrest, Decker. 2009. 'Ceòl Beag: The Development and Performance Practice of the "Small Music" of the Highland Bagpipe (c.1820–1966)' (unpublished PhD thesis, Royal Scottish Academy of Music and Drama & University of St Andrews).

Francis, David. 1999. *Traditional Music in Scotland: Education, Information, Advocacy* (Scottish Arts Council).

——. 2010. *Traditional Arts Working Group Report – January 2010* (Edinburgh: Scottish Government).

Gaughan, Dick. 2008. *Gaughan Live! At the Trades Club* (Cockenzie: Greentrax CDTRAX322).

Gelbart, Matthew. 2007. *The Invention of 'Folk Music' and 'Art Music' Emerging Categories from Ossian to Wagner* (Cambridge and New York: Cambridge University Press), http://hdl.handle.net/2027/heb.07639.

——. 2013. 'Once More to Mendelssohn's Scotland: The Laws of Music, the Double Tonic, and the Sublimation of Modality', *Nineteenth Century Music*, 37: 3–36 [accessed 22 November 2013].

Gibson, John G. 1998. *Traditional Gaelic Bagpiping, 1745–1945* (Montreal: McGill-Queen's University Press MQUP).

Gibson, Ronnie. 2013. 'Tullochgorm – Scottish Fiddle Music', *Tullochgorm*, http://scottishfiddlemusic.com/tag/tullochgorm/ [accessed 10 February 2015].

Gilbert, Suzanne. 2006. 'Hogg, Traditional Culture, & The Mountain Bard', *Paper Presented at a Symposium on the Songs of James Hogg*, University of Stirling, www.jameshogg.stir.ac.uk/showrecord.php.

Gilchrist, Annie G. 1911. 'Note on the Modal System of Gaelic Tunes', *Journal of the Folk-Song Society*, December: 150–53 [accessed 19 August 2014].

Goldstein, Kenneth S. 1991. 'Notes toward a European-American Folk Aesthetic: Lessons Learned from Singers and Storytellers I Have Known', *Journal of American Folklore*, 104: 164–78.

Gray, John N. 2000. *At Home in the Hills: Sense of Place in the Scottish Borders* (Oxford & New York: Berghahn Books).

——. 2003. 'Iconic Images: Landscape and History in the Local Poetry of the Scottish Borders', in Pamela J. Stewart and Andrew Strathern (eds), *Landscape, Memory and History: Anthropological Perspectives* (London & Virginia: Pluto Press), pp. 16–46.

Green, T. A. 1997. *Folklore: An Encyclopedia of Beliefs, Customs, Tales, Music, and Art* (ABC-CLIO).

Grills, Scott. 2009. 'Situating Public Performances: Folk Singers and Song Introductions', *Studies in Symbolic Interaction*, 33: 19–34, http://dx.doi.org/10.1108/S0163-2396(2009)0000033004.

Hand, Chris. 2011. 'Do Arts Audiences Act like Consumers?', *Managing Leisure*, 16: 88–97, http://dx.doi.org/10.1080/13606719.2011.559088.

Harris, Jason Marc. 2008. *Folklore and the Fantastic in Nineteenth-Century British Fiction* (Farnham: Ashgate).

Harrison, Frank L. 1985. 'Observation, Elucidation, Utilization: Western Attitudes to Eastern Musics, Ca. 1600-Ca. 1830', in Malcolm H. Brown and Roland J. Wiley (eds), *Slavonic and Western Music. Essays for Gerarld Abraham* (Ann Arbor: UMI Research Press), pp. 5–31.

Harvie, Christopher. 1998. *No Gods and Precious Few Heroes: Twentieth-Century Scotland* (Edinburgh: Edinburgh University Press).

Harvie, Christopher. 2002. *Scotland: A Short History* (New York: Oxford University Press).

Heaney, Seamus. 2003. 'The Shining Streams: A Tribute to MacDiarmid', *The Dark Horse*, 11: 8–18.

Henderson, Hamish. 1964. 'Scots Folk-Song Today', *Folklore*, 75: 48–58.

——. 2004. *Alias MacAlias, Writings on Song, Folk and Litrature* (Edinburgh: Birlinn).

Henderson, Kathy, Frankie Armstrong, and Sandra Kerr (eds). 1982. *My Song is My Own, 100 Women's Songs* (London & Virginia: Pluto Press).

Hesmondhalgh, David. 2013. *Why Music Matters* (Chichester: Wiley Blackwell).

Hibberd, Lynne. 2009. 'Review of Scottish Arts Council Report, Taking Part in Scotland 2008', *Cultural Trends*, 18: 333–36, http://dx.doi.org/10.1080/09548960903268154.

Hillers, Barbara. 2006. 'Dialogue or Monologue? Lullabies in Scottish Gaelic Tradition', in Michael Byrne, T. O. Clancy and S. Kidd (eds), *Litreachas & Eachdraidh: Rannsachadh Na Gàidhlig 2 / Literature & History: Papers from the Second Conference of Scottish Gaelic Studies, Glasgow 2002* (Glasgow: Privately Published).

Hobsbawm, E. and T. O. Ranger. 1992. *The Invention of Tradition* (Cambridge: Cambridge University Press).

Hogg, James (ed.). 1819a. *The Jacobite Relics of Scotland; Being The Songs, Airs, and Legends, of the Adherents to the House of Stuart*, 2 vols (Edinburgh: Privately Published).

——. 1819b. *The Queen's Wake: A Legendary Poem* (Edinburgh: William Blackwood and John Murray).

Howkins, Alun. 2009. 'The Left and Folk Song', *History Workshop Journal*, 68: 273–79, http://dx.doi.org/10.1093/hwj/dbp019.

Howley, Mel. 1999. 'Alistair Hulett', *The Living Tradition*, www.livingtradition.co.uk/articles/alistairhulett.

Inverness Courier. 2015. 'Celtic Connections Tops £1 Million Ticket Sales Once Again', *Inverness Courier* (Inverness), (online edition), section Music, p. n.p. [accessed 3 February 2015].

Irving, Gordon. 1968. *Great Scot: The Life Story of Sir Harry Lauder, Legendary Laird of the Music Hall* (London: Leslie Frewin)

Jacques, E. F., and J. A. Fuller-Maitland. 1899. 'Modal Survivals in Folk-Song', *Journal of the Folk-Song Society*, 1: 4–15 [accessed 19 August 2014].

Johnson, David. 1972. *Music and Society in Lowland Scotland in the Eighteenth Century*, 2nd ed. 2003 (Edinburgh: Mercat Press).

Johnson, James. 1787. *The Scots Musical Museum*, 6 vols (Edinburgh: Privately Published J. Johnson).

Kaul, Adam R. 2007. 'The Limits of Commodification in Traditional Irish Music Sessions', *Journal of the Royal Anthropological Institute*, 13: 703–19, http://dx.doi.org/10.2307/4623018.

Kearney, Daithí. 2007. 'Crossing the River: Exploring the Geography of Irish Traditional Music', *Journal of the Society for Musicology in Ireland*, 3: 127–39.

Lamb, William. 2013. 'Reeling in the Strathspey: The Origins of Scotland's National Music', *Scottish Studies*, 36: 66–102.

——. 2014. 'Grafting Culture: On the Development and Diffusion of the Strathspey in Scottish Music', *Scottish Studies*, 37: 94–104.

Lamont, Claire, and Michael Rossington (eds). 2007. *Romanticism's Debatable Lands* (Basingstoke: Macmillan).

Leyshon, Andrew, David Matless, and George Revill. 1995. 'The Place of Music', *Transactions of the Institute of British Geographers, New Series*, 20: 423–33.

——. 1998. *The Place of Music* (New York, NY: Guilford Press).

Liu, Yu, and Kay L. O'Halloran. 2009. 'Intersemiotic Texture: Analyzing Cohesive Devices between Language and Images', *Social Semiotics*, 19: 367–88, http://dx.doi.org/10.1080/10350330903361059.

Lucas, Caroline. 2013. 'The Imagined Folk of England: Whiteness, Folk Music and Fascism', *Critical Race and Whiteness Studies*, 9, www.acrawsa.org.au/ejournal[https://www.academia.edu/5127020/The_Imagined_Folk_of_England_Whiteness_Folk_Music_and_Fascism] [accessed 18 November 2013].

Lyall, Scott. 2006. *Hugh MacDiarmid's Poetry and Politics of Place, Imagining a Scottish Republic* (Edinburgh: Edinburgh University Press).

Lyle, Emily (ed.). 1994. *Scottish Ballads* (Edinburgh: Canongate Classics).

MacAndrew, Hector. 2009. *Legend Of The Scots Fiddle* (Greentrax CDTRAX335).

Machin, David. 2007. *Introduction to Multimodal Analysis* (London: Hodder Arnold).

Machin, David, and John E. Richardson. 2012. 'Discourses of Unity and Purpose in the Sounds of Fascist Music: A Multimodal Approach', *Critical Discourse Studies*, 9: 329–45, http://dx.doi.org/10.1080/17405904.2012.713203.

MacInnes, Iain I. 1989. 'The Highland Bagpipe: The Impact of the Highland Societies of London and Scotland, 1781–1844' (Edinburgh: MLitt thesis, University of Edinburgh).

Mack, Douglas S. 1993. 'James Hogg and The Ettrick Shepherd', *Library Review*, 22: 307–9.

MacKenzie, Alexander C. 1978. 'Comparison of Bagpipes by Harmonic Measurement', *Proceedings of the Piobaireachd Society Conference, April 1978* (Glasgow: College of Piping).

——. 1995. 'Some Recent Measurements on the Scale of the Great Highland Bagpipe', *Proceedings of the Piobaireachd Society Conference, April 1995* (Glasgow: College of Piping).

MacKenzie, John M. 1998. 'Empire and National Identifies: The Case of Scotland', *Transactions of the Royal Historical Society*, 8: 215–32 [accessed 28 October 2013].

MacRae, Lucy. 2014. 'Local Explanations: Editing a Sense of Place in Walter Scott's "Minstrelsy of the Scottish Border"', *FORUM: University of Edinburgh Postgraduate Journal of Culture and the Arts* www.academia.edu/6108006/Local_Explanations_Editing_a_Sense_of_Place_in_Walter_Scotts_Minstrelsy_of_the_Scottish_Border_ [accessed 18 February 2014].

Matarasso, François. 1996. *Northern Lights: The Social Impact of the Feisean (Gaelic Festivals)* (Stroud, Glos: Comedia).

McAulay, Karen. 2013. *Our Ancient National Airs: Scottish Song Collecting from the Enlightenment to the Romantic Era* (Farnham: Ashgate).

McAulay, Karen E. 2010. 'From "Anti-Scot", to "Anti-Scottish Sentiment": Cultural Nationalism and Scottish Song in the Late Eighteenth to Nineteenth Centuries', *Library & Information History*, 26: 272–88, http://dx.doi.org/10.1179/175834910X12816060984430.

McFadyen, Mairi Joanna. 2012. '"Presencing" Imagined Worlds – Understanding the Maysie: A Contemporary Ethnomusicological Enquiry into the Embodied Ballad Singing Experience' (unpublished PhD thesis, University of Edinburgh), www.era.lib.ed.ac.uk/handle/1842/7948 [accessed 30 October 2014].

McKean, Thomas A. 2001. 'The Fieldwork Legacy of James Macpherson', *Journal of American Folklore*, 114: 447–63.

McKerrell, Simon. 2009. 'The Concept of Mode in Scottish Bagpipe Music', *The Highland Bagpipe: Music, History, Traditon* (Farnham: Ashgate Publishing), pp. 279–300.

——. 2011a. 'Modern Scottish Bands (1970–1990): Cash as Authenticity', *Scottish Music Review*, 2: 1–14.

——. 2011b. 'Review Bagpipes: A National Collection of a National Instrument Cheape Hugh National Museums of Scotland Edinburgh', *Ethnomusicology*, 55: 508–11 [accessed 22 November 2013].

——. 2011c. 'Sound Performing: Sound Aesthetics among Competitive Pipers', *International Review of the Aesthetics and Sociology of Music*: 165–87 [accessed 25 February 2014].

——. 2012a. 'An Ethnography of Hearing: Somaesthetic Hearing in Traditional Music', in B. Flath, A. Pirtchner, E. Pölzl and S. Sackl (eds), *The Body Is the Message* (Graz, Austria: Grazer Universitätsverlag Leykam), pp. 76–89, www.musicmediapublishing.com/fileadmin/band2/Artikel/06%20Simon%20McKerrell.pdf.

——. 2012b. 'Hearing Sectarianism: Understanding Scottish Sectarianism as Song', *Critical Discourse Studies*, 9: 1–12, http://dx.doi.org/10.1080/17405904.2012.713315.

——. 2014. 'Traditional Arts and the State: The Scottish Case', *Cultural Trends*, 23: 1–10, http://dx.doi.org/10.1080/09548963.2014.925281.

McLaughlin, Seán. 2012. 'Locating Authenticities: A Study of the Ideological Construction of Professionalised Folk Music in Scotland' (unpublished PhD thesis, Edinburgh: University of Edinburgh).

McLean, Ralph, Kirsteen McCue, Pia Osberg, and Murray Pittock. 2015. 'Auld Lang Syne', *Editing Robert Burns for the 21st Century*, http://burnsc21.glasgow.ac.uk/online-exhibitions/auld-lang-syne/ [accessed 3 March 2015].

McLucas, Anne Dhu. n.d. 'Tune Families', *Grove Music Online*.

McVicar, Ewan. 2010. *The Eskimo Republic, Scots Political Folk Song in Action, 1951–1999* (Linlithgow: Gallus Publishing).

Melin, Mats. 2005. '"Putting the Dirt Back In": An Investigation of Step Dancing in Scotland' (unpublished MA thesis, University of Limerick), www.academia.edu/634630/_Putting_the_Dirt_Back_In_An_Investigation_of_Step_Dancing_in_Scotland_a_Thesis_Submitted_in_Partial_Fulfilment_of_the_Requirements_for_the_Degree_of_ [accessed 8 August 2013].

Miller, Josephine L. 2007. 'The Learning and Teaching of Traditional Music', *Oral Literature and Performance Culture*, Scottish Life and Society, A Compendium of Scottish Ethnology, 10 (Edinburgh: John Donald), x, pp. 288–304.

Miller, Karl. 1970. *Memoirs of a Modern Scotland* (London: Faber & Faber).

Milosavljevic, Daniel. 2014. 'Piobaireachd in New Zealand: Culture, Authenticity and Localisation' (unpublished PhD thesis, New Zealand: University of Otago), https://ourarchive.otago.ac.nz/handle/10523/4781.

Moffat, Alistair. 2007. *The Reivers: The Story of the Border Reivers* (Edinburgh: Birlinn).

Monson, Ingrid. 1998. 'Oh Freedom: George Russell, John Coltrane, and Modal Jazz', *In the Course of Performance: Studies in the World of Musical Improvisation* (Chicago, IL: University of Chicago Press), pp. 149–68.

Moore, Allan. 1993. *Rock: The Primary Text – Developing a Musicology of Rock*, Ashgate Popular and Folk Music Series (Farnham: Ashgate).

Munro, Ailie. 1996. *The Democratic Muse: Folk Music Revival in Scotland* (Aberdeen: Scottish Cultural Press).

Murray Schafer, Raimond. 1977. *The Tuning of the World* (Vancouver: Destiny Books).

Neat, Timothy. 2009. *Hamish Henderson v.2: Poetry Becomes People* (Edinburgh: Birlinn).

Nettl, Bruno. 2005. *The Study of Ethnomusicology: Thirty-One Issues and Concepts* (Champaign, IL: University of Illinois Press).

Newton, Michael. 2003. '"Vain, Hurtful, Lying, Worldly Tales": Creed, Belief, and Practice in the Life of Argyll Highlanders, in Scotland and America' (North Carolina Scottish Heritage Society), www.academia.edu/5153486/Vain_hurtful_lying_worldly_tales_Creed_belief_and_practice_in_the_life_of_Argyll_Highlanders_in_Scotland_and_America [accessed 20 November 2013].

——. 2009. *Warriors of the Word: The World of the Scottish Highlanders* (Edinburgh: Birlinn).

Niles, John D. 1977. 'Tam Lin: Form and Meaning in a Traditional Ballad', *Modern Language Quarterly*, 38: 336–47.

Paterson, Rod. 1996. *Rod Paterson – Sings Burns (Songs From The Bottom Drawer)* (East Lothian: Greentrax CDTRAX117).

Pittock, Murray. 2013. 'History of Scottish Nationalism' (Scotland: BBC Radio Scotland).

Porter, James. 2001. '"Bring Me the Head of James Macpherson": The Execution of Ossian and the Wellsprings of Folkloristic Discourse', *Journal of American Folklore*, 114: 396–435.

Post-Gazette, Elizabeth Bloom/Pittsburgh. n.d. 'PSO's Scottish Flavor Appealing', *Pittsburgh Post-Gazette*, www.post-gazette.com/ae/music-reviews/2013/10/26/PSO-s-Scottish-flavor-appealing/stories/201310260115 [accessed 26 October 2013].

Powers, Harold S., Frans Wiering, James Porter, James Cowdery, Richard Widdess, and others. 2008. 'Mode', *Grove Music Online*.

Reed, James. 1973. *The Border Ballads* (Edinburgh: Athlone Press).

——. 1980. 'The Border Ballads', *The People's Past* (Edinburgh: Polygon), pp. 17–31.

——. 1991. *Border Ballads, A Selection* (Manchester and Northumberland: Carcanet Press Ltd. with MidNAG).

Risk, Laura. 2013. 'The Chop: The Diffusion of an Instrumental Technique across North Atlantic Fiddling Traditions', *Ethnomusicology*, 57: 428–54 [accessed 9 October 2014].

Russell, George. 2001. *The Lydian Chromatic Concept of Tonal Organization, Volume One: The Art and Science of Tonal Gravity* (Concept Publishing Company).

Russell, Ian, (ed. and intro.), and Mary Anne, (ed. and intro.) Alburger. 2006. *Play it Like it is: Fiddle and Dance Studies from Around the North Atlantic*, Conference Source: North Atlantic Fiddle Convention (2001) (Aberdeen: Aberdeen University).

Sanger, Keith, and Alison Kinnaird. 1992. *Tree of Strings: A History of the Harp in Scotland* (Midlothian: Kinmor Music).

Scott, Walter. 1802. *Minstrelsy of the Scottish Border, Consisting of Historical and Romantic Ballads, Collected in the Southern Counties of Scotland; with a Few of Modern Date, Founded upon Local Tradition, in Two Volumes*, 1st Edition, 2 vols (Kelso: James Ballantyne).

Scottish Government. 2009. *People and Culture in Scotland 2008: Results from the Scottish Household Survey Culture and Sport Module 2007/2008* (Edinburgh: Scottish Government, National Statistics), www.scotland.gov.uk/Publications/2009/11/24085939/0.

——. 2014. *Scotland's People Annual Report: Results from 2013 Scottish Household Survey* (Edinburgh: Scottish Government, National Statistics), www.scotland.gov.uk/Publications/2014/08/7973/downloads#res-1.

Shapiro, Anne Dhu. 1975. 'The Tune-Family Concept in British-American Folk-Song Scholarship' (unpublished PhD thesis, Cambridge, MA: Harvard University).

——. 1985. 'Regional Song Styles: The Scottish Connection', in A. D. Shapiro and P. Benjamin (eds), *Music and Context: Essays for John M. Ward* (Cambridge, MA: Harvard University Press), pp. 404–17.

Sharp, Cecil James. 1907. *English Folk-Song: Some Conclusions* (London: Simpkin).

Sheridan, Mark, Iona MacDonald, and Charles G. Byrne. 2011. 'Gaelic Singing and Oral Tradition', *International Journal of Music Education*, 29: 172–90 [accessed 27 August 2014].

Sheridan, M., and C. Byrne. 2008. 'Ceilidh Culture and Higher Education', *International Journal of Music Education*, 26: 147–59, http://dx.doi.org/10.1177/0255761407088488.

Simpson, Ludi, and Andrew Smith. 2014. *Who Feels Scottish? National Identities and Ethnicity in Scotland*, Dynamics of Diversity: Evidence from the 2011 Census (ESRC Centre on Dynamics of Ethnicity [CoDE]), www.ethnicity.ac.uk.

Slobin, Mark. 1993. *Subcultural Sounds: Micromusics of the West* (Middletown, CT: Wesleyan University Press).

Small, Christopher. 1998. *Musicking: The Meanings of Performing and Listening*, Music/culture (Hanover, NH: University Press of New England).

Smith, Stephanie D. L. 1988. 'A Contextual Study of Singing in the Fisher Family' (unpublished PhD thesis, Edinburgh: University of Edinburgh).

Smith, Susan J. 1993. 'Bounding the Borders: Claiming Space and Making Place in Rural Scotland', *Transactions of the Institute of British Geographers, New Series*, 18: 291–308.

——. 1994. 'Soundscapes', *Area*, 26: 232–40.

Smyth, Adam. 2007. 'Pipework', *Early Music Today*, http://triplepipe.net/media/07EarlyMusicToday.pdf.

Sparling, Heather. 2007. 'Transmission Processes in Cape Breton Gaelic Song Culture', *Folk Music, Traditional Music, Ethnomusicology: Canadian Perspectives, Past and Present*, Edited by Anna Hoefnagels and Gordon E. Smith: 13–26.

——. 2008. 'Categorically Speaking: Towards a Theory of (Musical) Genre in Cape Breton Gaelic Culture', *Ethnomusicology*, 52: 401–25, http://dx.doi.org/10.2307/20174606.

——. 2011. 'Cape Breton Island: Living in the Past? Gaelic Language, Song and Competition', *Island Songs: A Global Repertoire*: 49–63 [accessed 8 August 2013].

Spracklen, Karl. 2013. 'Nazi Punks Folk off: Leisure, Nationalism, Cultural Identity and the Consumption of Metal and Folk Music', *Leisure Studies*, 32: 415–28, http://dx.doi.org/10.1080/02 614367.2012.674152.

Steel, Judy. 1985. *A Shepherd's Delight, A James Hogg Anthology* (Edinburgh: Canongate Publishing).

Stewart, Pamela J., and Andrew Strathern. 2001. *Minorities and Memories: Survivals and Extinctions in Scotland and Western Europe* (Durham, NC: Carolina Academic Press).

—— (eds). 2003. *Landscape, Memory and History: Anthropological Perspectives* (London & Virginia: Pluto Press).

Stewart, Sheila. 2000. *From the Heart of the Tradition* (London: Topic Records TSCD515).

Stock, Jonathan P.J. 2001. 'Toward an Ethnomusicology of the Individual', *World of Music*, 43: 5–19.

Stokes, Martin. 1994. *Ethnicity, Identity and Music: The Musical Construction of Place* (Oxford and Providence: Berg Publishers).

Thomson, George. 1793. *Select Collection of Original Scottish Airs for the Voice: With Introductory and Concluding Symphonies and Accompaniments for the Pianoforte, Violin and Violoncello*, 6 vols (Edinburgh: George Thomson).

Tolmie, Frances. 1997. *One Hundred and Five Songs of Occupation from the Western Isles of Scotland*, 16 (Llanerch Publishers reprint).

Tolmie, Frances, A. G. Gilchrist, Lucy E. Broadwood, and George Henderson. 1911. 'Songs of Labour', *Journal of the Folk-Song Society*, 4: 196–244, http://dx.doi.org/10.2307/4433972.

Trevor-Roper, Hugh. 2008. *The Invention of Scotland* (New Haven, CT: Yale University Press).

Turino, Thomas. 2008. *Music as Social Life: The Politics of Participation* (Chicago, IL: University of Chicago Press).

Unknown. 2008. 'Archie Fisher', *Scottish Traditional Music Hall of Fame*, www.tradmusichall.com/ArchieFisher.htm.

Van Leeuwen, Theo. 2004. *Introducing Social Semiotics: An Introductory Textbook* (Routledge).

——. 2012. 'Multimodality and Rhythm', *The Encyclopedia of Applied Linguistics* (Blackwell Publishing), http://onlinelibrary.wiley.com/doi/10.1002/9781405198431.wbeal0832/abstract [accessed 15 May 2014].

Wenger, Etienne. 1998. *Communities of Practice: Learning, Meaning, and Identity* (Cambridge: Cambridge University Press).

West, Gary. 2012. *Voicing Scotland: Folk, Culture, Nation* (Luath Press Ltd).

West, Mick. 2005. *A Poor Man's Labour* (Claytara Music CLCD042).

Williamson, Kevin. 2009. 'Language and Culture in a Rediscovered Scotland', in Mark Perryman (ed.), *Breaking up Britain: Four Nations after a Union* (London: Lawrence & Wishart), pp. 53–67.

Wimberly, Lowry Charles. 1965. *Folklore in the English and Scottish Ballads* (New York: Dover Publications [1928]).

Index